Innovating for Sustainability

One of the challenges met by green entrepreneurs and product developers who have tried to develop more sustainable products is that efforts to create better products in environmental terms do not always translate into effective business cases. The purpose of this book is to promote a better understanding of the implications of environmental issues in new product development. Through an empirical study in the human-powered vehicle sector, Luca Berchicci examines how and to what extent the environmental ambition of product developers and managers influences the way new products and services are developed. Understanding of this phenomenon is particularly important since managers are encouraged and/or motivated to undertake environmental new product development projects.

From the descriptions and analyses of the two case studies Luca Berchicci suggests that a high level of environmental ambition increases the complexity of the product innovation process. Moreover, a high level of environmental ambition may hamper a product innovation process because it may lead the developers away from the market that their product is to serve. Accordingly, this book attempts to explain and predict how environmental ambition influences new product development processes. This claim represents a theoretical contribution to existing research in both product innovation and green product innovation. Moreover, this volume vouchsafes an original and deep insight into the diverse facets of greening.

This book will be of interest to students and researchers engaged with new product innovation, entrepreneurship and sustainability.

Luca Berchicci is an assistant professor at the Centre for Entrepreneurship, at the Rotterdam School of Management, Erasmus University.

RIOT!

Routledge studies in innovation, organization and technology

Innovating for Sustainability

Green entrepreneurship in
personal mobility

Luca Berchicci

Routledge
Taylor & Francis Group

LONDON AND NEW YORK

First published 2009
by Routledge
2 Park Square, Milton Park, Abingdon, Oxon OX14 4RN

Simultaneously published in the USA and Canada
by Routledge
270 Madison Ave, New York, NY 10016

Routledge is an imprint of the Taylor & Francis Group, an informa business

© 2009 Luca Berchicci

Typeset in Times by Wearset Ltd, Boldon, Tyne and Wear
Printed and bound in Great Britain by MPG Books Ltd, Bodmin

British Library Cataloguing in Publication Data
A catalogue record for this book is available from the British Library

Library of Congress Cataloging in Publication Data
A catalog record for this book has been requested

ISBN10: 0-415-45464-6 (hbk)
ISBN10: 0-203-88956-8 (ebk)

ISBN13: 978-0-415-45464-3 (hbk)
ISBN13: 978-0-203-88956-5 (ebk)

Contents

Figures

Tables

Boxes

1 Introduction

> Environment/Innovation is much like motherhood: everyone thinks it's great, but nobody seems to know how to get pregnant.
>
> (Hall & Clark, 2003a: 343)

1.1 The problem definition

As Hall and Clark suggest, this saying is often heard in the environmental field and it denotes the paradox of developing environmentally driven[1] innovations. The ambition to develop new products and services with potential environmental benefits occasionally clashes with the less than exciting performance of these products. The electric car is a notorious example of environmental technology on which national governments, green activists and green entrepreneurs in general have bet their future stakes. The market, however, has welcomed the electric car lukewarmly.

Here the term green entrepreneur refers to individuals who see environmental issues[2] as market opportunities and are willing to exploit them. Entrepreneurs, as discussed in Chapter 3, are individuals who search for systemic innovation and the exploitation of opportunities to create economic value (Drucker, 1985). The green entrepreneur wants their businesses to be environmentally responsible and "to make a social statement, not just to make money" (Isaak, 2002). The green entrepreneur may be a designer, a product developer, a manager in an established firm or an individual ready to start a company.[3] Therefore, the title refers to the challenging task facing environmental entrepreneurs of matching environmental issues with market demands in new product development projects. Social needs and values for customers may not necessary overlap with one another as the case of electric cars demonstrates. The integration of environmental issues into new product development is the platform of this research.

1.1.1 New product development and environmental new product development

In recent years new product development has become critically important for firms to enable them to compete successfully in new and existing markets

(Calantone, Vickery, & Droge, 1995). New product development is crucial for firms not only as a potential source of competitive advantage, but also as means to diversify, adapt and reinvent the firm itself in a fast-changing market (Brown & Eisenhardt, 1995).

New product development (NPD) is defined here as the transformation of market opportunities (and a set of assumptions about product attributes) into a product that meets the needs of consumers and other internal and external stake-holders[4] (Krishnan & Ulrich, 2001; Pujari, Wright, & Peattie, 2003). These stakeholders include consumers, government and nongovernmental organizations (NGOs), and they require products that are designed with specific attributes like quality and safety standards for humans and the environment, which generally encompass the concept of sustainability. It is important to clarify that this research focuses on two of the three elements of the sustainability concept: the economical and ecological pillars excluding the social dimension (i.e. working condition, protection of cultural properties or occupational health).[5]

The interest in the natural environment has been one of the driving forces in the last decade motivating the redesign of existing products and the creation of new ones to make them more energy-efficient or less material-intensive (e.g. Brezet & Hemel, 1997; Graedel, Allenby, & AT&T, 1995; Hart, 1995; Shrivastava, 1995b). The challenging task for industry, practitioners and scholars supported by policy agendas has been the incorporation of environmental considerations into product development, aligning the natural environment with regulations and market demands. This field of research is defined here as environmental product development (EPD), which includes the redesign of existing products and the development of new ones. The development of environmental products and services includes a normative aspect – the new products should have a lower impact on the natural environment compared to the products that they aim to replace (Markusson, 2001). Therefore EPD differs from NPD in the intentionality to reduce the environmental impact.

Many scholars in the EPD field argue that by going green, corporations may reduce costs, capture emerging market, gain first-mover advantage and improve the corporate image (Hart, 1995, 1997; Porter & Van der Linde, 1995; Roome, 1992; Shrivastava, 1995c). In other words, the environmental imperatives can represent market opportunities rather than business constraints, creating a win-win paradigm (Hunt & Auster, 1990). Moreover, win-win theories suggest that there are systematically unexploited opportunities for increasing private profits while providing reduced environmental damage (Porter et al., 1995). Porter argues that the current market inefficiency may be overcome by just picking up the environmental challenge.[6] Perceiving environmental issues as market opportunities may open up an additional range of opportunities, thus providing numerous niches for enterprising individuals and firms to successfully identify and exploit.

Accordingly, this research study focuses on environmental *new* product development (ENPD), which excludes the redesign of existing products (as discussed in Chapter 4). Here ENPD is defined as new product development where

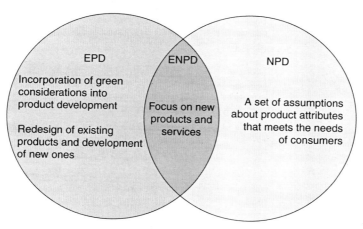

Figure 1.1 The intersection between EPD and NPD is the focus of this research study: ENPD.

the goal is to design, develop and implement *new* products or services that can successfully replace existing products that are more harmful to the natural environment (Figure 1.1). Moreover, ENPD is driven by market opportunities, rather than regulatory pressure, where environmental products and services are increasingly proposed as strategic options for increasing profits and solving environmental problems (Shrivastava, 1995b).

1.1.2 The gap: the environmental ambition in NPD

Although many authors support the win-win logic of being "green and competitive" (Hart & Ahuja, 1996; Porter et al., 1995; Schaltegger & Synnestvedt, 2002), the effort to create better products in environmental terms does not always translate into a commercial or viable business case resulting in new and/or expanding markets (Hall et al., 2003a).

One of the possible explanations may be found in the intrinsic uncertainty of the product innovation process which is extensively discussed in Chapter 2. The innovation process, and specifically the way new products are designed, developed and implemented, is *an uncertain journey in the unknown* (Arrow, 2000). Drawbacks, changes and twists are the very characteristics of the innovation process in which just a small number of products are implemented as expected.

Furthermore, the more radical the innovation process, the more uncertain the journey. Overlooking this uncertainty may jeopardize regular as well as environmental product development. This is especially important since scholars, practitioners and policy makers in the environmental field assume that, only by shifting from incremental innovation to a more radical innovation, can the win-win paradigm be achieved (e.g. Ashford, 2000; Brezet *et al.*, 2000; Charter & Tischner, 2001; Fussler & James, 1996; Hart & Milstein, 1999; Weaver, Jansen, Grootveld, Spiegel, & Vergragt, 2000; Weiszäcker, Lovins, & Lovins, 1997; Weterings & Opschoor, 1992). Despite the importance of the innovation process, it would appear that ENPD research has few links with regular new product development literature (as suggested by Baumann, Boons, & Bragd, 2002).

In light of this, this research study attempts to improve our understanding of existing product development and innovation theories and to demonstrate how existing theoretical models in NPD literature may help address questions raised within the environmental field. This research study also attempts to address the request by some scholars to integrate and link existing theories with the greening process (Starik & Marcus, 2000).

A second explanation may be related to the nature of environmental issues (see Chapter 4). "Greening" is an ill-defined concept (Chen, 2001) and the degree of greening is perceived differently by consumers, producers and governments (Kleiner, 1991). Although many studies have contributed significantly to our understanding of how firms can develop and implement green products (e.g. Brezet et al., 1997; Lenox & Ehrenfeld, 1997; Pujari & Wright, 1996), they tend to be rather conceptual, normative and prescriptive. Such studies have less emphasis on exploring or explaining the implications of incorporating environmental issues into product development (as suggested by Baumann et al., 2002; Lenox et al., 1997). This research study suggests combining the prescriptive and normative approaches, along with the exploratory and explanatory approaches, to address the implications of designing and developing new environmentally ambitious products and services.

Finally, another explanation can be found in a combination of the two above-mentioned explanations, that is the relationship between environmental issues and the product innovation process. Although concerns for the natural environment may lead to the discovery of new opportunities for innovation (Hunt et al., 1990; Sharma, 2000), we do not know exactly how the environmental concern may influence the exploitation of new opportunities, such as the development of new products and services. Concern for the natural environment is pervasive among both consumers and business organizations and it is therefore an important phenomenon that demands more scholarly attention (Banerjee, 2001; Bansal, 2003; Starik et al., 2000).

In organization and the natural environment studies, many scholars suggest that the recognition and integration of environmental concerns into a firm's decision-making process is becoming an increasingly accepted way to address environmental issues in business (e.g. Banerjee, 2002; Banerjee, Iyer, & Kashyap, 2003; Hoffman, 2001; Menon & Menon, 1997). Prior research has investigated managers' responses to environmental issues, identifying antecedents (Banerjee et al., 2003; Flannery & May, 2000; Menon et al., 1997), scale and scope of the responses (e.g. Andersson & Bateman, 2000; Bansal, 2003; Banerjee, 2001; Drumwright, 1994).

For example, Bansal (2003) found that individual concerns and organizational values are necessary conditions to explain organizational responses to environmental issues. Flannery and May (2000) found that U.S. metal-finishing companies' environmental attitudes, norms and ethical climates were all positively associated with their managers' environmental intentions, but that personal moral obligation, self-efficacy and financial cost were negatively associated with those intentions. They concluded that managers continued to frame environmental issues in legal rather than moral terms. Sharma (2000) found that the extent to which some of the firms in the Canadian oil and gas industry went further in incorporating environmental concerns into decision making was heavily dependent on the degree to which their managers perceived these issues as opportunities and not threats. Others have explored the conditions under which environmental issues and sustainable business practices are introduced in the very beginning of new business ventures (e.g. Larson, 2000; Schaltegger, 2002; Walley & Taylor, 2002). For example, Schick et al. (2002) found that the entrepreneur's belief is one of the most important factors governing their response to environmental issues when comparing conventional start-ups with ecologically oriented ones.

These scholars explain *what* guides managers' and other employees' sustainability-oriented decisions and behaviors, although it seems that few studies are concerned with the question of *how* the environmental concern of managers and product developers influence their decisions in organizational activities. An example is Baumgartner, Faber and Proops (2002), who developed a conceptual analysis based on capital theory investigating the influence of the environmental concern on long-term decisions. They concluded that the integration of environmental issues increases the complexity of economic valuation when making an investment decision. The complexity refers to the greater number of uncertainties involved in the combination of environmental and economic concerns that may be driving the difficulties of forming accurate expected returns from investments.

Furthermore, it seems that previous research has analyzed how managers respond to environmental issues in relation to managerial practices and strategic management. Few studies have, however, addressed the influence of environmental concern on decisions dealing with new product development activities. Understanding this phenomenon is particularly important since managers are encouraged to undertake environmental new product development projects (e.g. Charter et al., 2001).

The environmental concern may constitute a motivation to undertake a new product development project. In light of this, development teams within organizations may seek to create environmentally friendly products, which must satisfy some basic expected functionality. This may imply that the integration of environmental concern with other concerns, such as cost, market acceptance or product functionality, may influence the way project performances are assessed and supported.

Consequently, if the environmental concern is a primary objective for undertaking an NPD project, it may dictate the progress of the project. This may have relevant implications. First, given that greening is ill defined, the project may be difficult to evaluate according to environmental concerns. Second, the environmental concern may make decisions difficult for the development team when a tradeoff is necessary between environmental concerns and other concerns, for example, in case of material selection, energy efficiency, cost or convenience. Third, in the case of radical projects, project performances are unclear because, by definition, these projects incorporate parts that are unknown, uncertain and untested. Given the poorly defined performance criteria, development teams may emphasize environmental concerns while other concerns may be downsized.

Therefore, the main goal of this research study is to explore and explain how *the environmental ambition of environmental entrepreneurs influences their decisions in the new product development process*, to understand the challenges in environmentally driven innovation projects. The term "environmental ambition" is introduced here and may be defined as a specific intention to design, develop and implement new products and services with a lower environmental impact compared to the products and services that they aim to substitute.[7] The term "environmental ambition" is considered a better term here than "environmental concern" to indicate an effective manager's determination to act in the innovation domain. Most researchers from sociology and psychology view environmental concern as a general attitude toward environmental issues that does not always translate into a determinate response (e.g. Bamberg, 2003; Dunlap & Liere, 1978; Weigel & Weigel, 1978). Accordingly, many of these studies found that the relationship between environmental concern and behavior is weak (e.g. Diekmann & Preisendörfer, 1998; Weigel, 1983). Nevertheless, scholars in the environmental field have often used this term to describe and explain the responses of individuals to environmental issues. Unlike environmental concern, environmental ambition is more closely linked to actions that result in attempts to develop new environmental technologies, products or services.

To address the potential causal mechanisms between environmental ambition and the product development process, a closer link to existing product innovation theories and organizational studies is proposed. The underlying rationale is that these studies provide building blocks to build a conceptual model that may explain the environmental ambition in new product development (Berchicci & Bodewes, 2005).

To sharpen our understanding of the literature on product innovation, this research study restricts itself in several ways. Initially, it focuses on the new product development literature that has mainly studied how organizations specifically *generate* new products. The underlying rationale is that the product performance is considered to be heavily affected by how the process of innovation unfolds and how the activities are carried out (e.g. Cooper & Kleinschmidt, 1995a; Montoya-Weiss & Calantone, 1994). Moreover, this research study adopts an organizational perspective: the new product is seen as an artifact resulting from an organizational process (Krishnan et al., 2001). Therefore, organizational determinants such as management support, team commitment and competences are seen as having a direct influence on how activities are carried out and how products perform in the market. Finally, given its importance in the ENPD field, this research study will focus mainly on radical undertakings.

Furthermore, this study pays a great deal of attention to the organizational setting influencing the product development process (Van de Ven, Polley, Garud, & Venkataraman, 1999). Product innovation is rarely confined to the level of the product, but it often encompasses changes within the organization, such as a new project team or a new business venture, and between the organization and the stakeholders (Janszen, 2000). Progress has been made in understanding new product development within single organizations; yet research on product innovation within new entrepreneurial organizations and within interorganizational settings is limited but emerging (Van de Ven et al., 1999). The focus of this research study is on new product development projects within start-ups and networks of organizations rather than within single, established organizations.[8] The underlying rationale is that EPD and ENPD are traditionally focused on established organizations whereas very little is known about how environmental issues are addressed in other organizational settings. Moreover, it seems that environmental ambition is also playing an increasingly important role in starting new ventures, both within new organizations (Larson, 2000) and networks of organizations (Brown, Vergragt, Green, & Berchicci, 2003).

1.1.3 The empirical domain

This research study limits its empirical enquiry to the human-powered mobility sector. Specifically, it concentrates on new concepts designed and developed to provide new mobility solutions in the short-distance mobility sector. The underlying rationale is threefold. First, the mobility sector is considered one of the main sources of environmental and health problems such as pollution and congestion and it has been receiving a great deal of attention in the policy and business arena (WBCSD, 2001). Second, in the short-distance mobility sector new products and services are increasingly proposed to align environmental issues with market opportunities. For instance, although a niche market, car sharing is an example of perceiving an environmental challenge as a market opportunity (Meijkamp, 2000). On the contrary, it seems that in the car industry new environmental technologies such as fuel cells are driven by stringent regulation rather than by market opportunities (van den Hoed, 2004). Third, it seems that new entrepreneurial organizations in particular are proposing new mobility concepts. Velotaxi (see Box 2.2) or car-sharing systems are examples of new products and services exploited by entrepreneurs.

1.2 Research objective and research questions

This research study aims to gain better insight into the way that environmental ambition influences the new product development process. First, it attempts to conceptually integrate the environmental perspective into the NPD process. Second, it aims to enrich the theory on NPD by providing an understanding of the opportunities, risks and challenges of the integration of the environmental concern into NPD. Finally, it provides an empirical analysis and discussion of the short-distance mobility sector in the Netherlands. Within this research objective, this research question is posed:

> How does the environmental ambition of managers and product developers influence their decision making during the product innovation process?

To answer this question two lines of enquiry are proposed: a theoretical and an empirical approach.

The theoretical enquiry seeks to describe and explain two key concepts highlighted in the research question: the innovation process and the environmental issues within product development. First, it was felt that a better understanding of innovation theories would result from the evaluation and discussion of studies which have defined and measured the key constructs within the process of innovation. Therefore, literature on innovation, specifically NPD, is reviewed in Chapter 2 with an emphasis on the distinction between radical and incremental innovation processes, seeking to answer the first sub-question:

> a) What does the existing theory indicate or predict concerning conditions for successful radical and incremental NPD?

The relevance of the dichotomy of radical versus incremental innovation in this study is twofold. First, the ENPD literature stresses the importance of radical changes for the sake of the natural environment: the more radical the change, the better (see Chapter 4). Second, due to the greater uncertainty involved in radical projects, the extent to which factors are determinant for an NPD project is influenced by the nature and degree of the innovation (Balachandra & Friar, 1997). For example, detailed market research for a new product in a new market may be inconclusive because potential consumers may have difficulties valuing the product. Therefore, an in-depth analysis of radical innovation is needed.

The NPD literature is closely linked to the organizational innovation literature (Fiol, 1996). Both literatures theorize about how organizational factors influence the effectiveness of developing and bringing innovations to external markets. Given their importance for the process of innovation, studies investigating the way that innovation is organized in different settings are reviewed in Chapter 3 to answer the second sub-question:

> b) How does the organizational setting influence the process of innovation?

The relationship between three organizational forms, start-ups, established organizations and interorganizational networks, and the process of innovation is examined to highlight their own advantages and set of liabilities in innovation and their different decision-making processes.

The second key concept concerns environmental issues within the organization. Existing studies in the environmental field are reviewed in Chapter 4 seeking to answer the sub-question:

> c) How has the relationship between environmental issues and product development been addressed in the literature?

The inability to fully explore and explain the implications of environmental ambition in product development does not mean that previous studies are without merits. The literature review is essential to understand the current approach to the relationship between the natural environment and the organization especially regarding the integration of environmental issues with product development.

The literature review allows one to select key constructs for the building blocks of the conceptual model illustrated in Chapter 5. The underlying rationale for the selection of the constructs is twofold. First, to develop a model that attempts to explain how environmental ambition and the process of product innovation are related, parsimony is important. Parsimony requires selectivity, that is, only those factors that really add to our understanding should be included (Bodewes, 2000). This is strictly related to the second rationale: the empirical data.

The empirical enquiry is the natural following step. Although the literature review helps identify and select key constructs, these alone do not constitute a theoretical model unless clear relationships among them are established. To fully understand the influence of environmental ambition during the innovation process, that is, the relationship between these two key concepts, an appropriate research strategy needs to investigate the unfolding of events over time. The case study method has been chosen as the research strategy (see Chapter 5). The underlying rationale for choosing case studies is related to the kind of research question posed: how environmental ambition influences the product innovation process. According to Yin (1994), the case study approach is one of the most suitable research strategies when "how" questions are asked about a contemporary set of events and when the research attempts to elucidate a decision or a set of decisions. The theoretical and the empirical enquiries are not addressed sequentially, but an iterative process exists between the existing theories and data where discrepancies are reconciled in the subsequent iteration (Bansal & Roth, 2000). Moreover, to enrich or extend theory that is empirically grounded, an analytic induction methodology is appropriate (Yin, 1994) because it explicitly accommodates existing theories.

Here the selection of cases is important. In selecting cases, the recommended approach in analytic induction is theoretical sampling (Bansal et al., 2000; Eisenhardt, 1989). Cases are selected to highlight theoretical issues, to replicate or extend the emergent theory and provide examples of polar types (Eisenhardt, 1989). For the purpose of this research study, two new product development

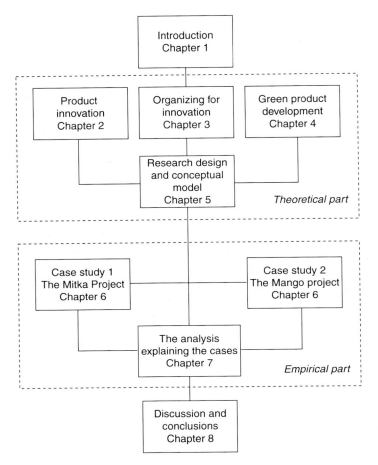

Figure 1.2 The outline of the research.

projects are examined: the *Mitka* project and the *Mango* project. The Mitka project is the main case study where a strong environmental ambition was the motivation to start such a project in an interorganizational network setting. Only after thoroughly examining the Mitka case, a second case of polar type was selected: the Mango project. As polar types, these cases present two extreme situations. They are polar types in their organizational settings and in their motives. The Mitka project was created by a set of established organizations with a high level of environmental ambition. The Mango project was set up by a new small firm with a low level of environmental ambition. They are similar projects in their objectives: the development and the implementation of a fast, three-wheeled, human-powered vehicle that is weather-protected for long distances and has commercial aspirations. The reason for choosing a sequential case to the first main case was to compare the decision-making process and the approach to the radical undertaking, attempting to answer the sub-question:

d) What are the differences in the decision-making process between high and low environmental ambition level projects?

In Chapter 6 the two cases are described and within- and cross-analyses of the cases are performed in Chapter 7. Finally, in Chapter 8 conclusions are drawn and the model is revised. Given the practical implications of this study, this chapter also discusses implications for scholars and product developers. An outline of the research in shown in Figure 1.2.

2 Product innovation

Many companies think innovation is a bit like Botox – inject it in the right corporate places and improvements are bound to follow. But too many companies want one massive injection, one huge blockbuster, to last them for the foreseeable future. Unfortunately, successful innovation is rarely like that.

(The Economist, April 24, 2004)

2.1 Introduction

This chapter presents a review of the product innovation literature. The sub-question this chapter attempts to answer is:

What does the existing theory indicate or predict concerning conditions for successful radical and incremental NPD?

The process of innovation is a multidimensional and complex phenomenon. Given this complexity, this chapter focuses on innovation literature on the micro-level, which specifically studies how organizations generate new products. This review highlights specific key constructs, which will be used as building blocks for the conceptual model illustrated in Chapter 5.

In section 2.2, definitions of innovation as an adjective of an idea, practice or artifact are reviewed and innovation typologies are illustrated. In section 2.3, success and failure factors in the new product development are examined. Section 2.4 explains the difference between the radical and the incremental innovation process from an organizational perspective. Finally, conclusions are drawn in section 2.5.

2.2 What is the essence of innovation?

The importance of innovation as a crucial means to create and maintain economic growth and sustainable competitive advantage has been largely acknowledged (e.g. Christensen, 1997; Drucker, 1985; Hamel, 2000). Schon (1967) describes the corporation as a miniature nation where the weapons are products and processes, its battlefield is the marketplace and innovation is essential to waging this war.[9] Nevertheless, there is no consensus in defining "innovation" exclusively. On the contrary, different typologies of innovation have been identified, such as radical, incremental, really new, discontinuous, imitative, architectural, modular and evolutionary innovations (for a recent review see Garcia & Calantone, 2002). However, the concept of innovation is not exclusively related to an adjective to stick to ideas, artifacts or services but also to the process through which the artifact is the outcome. Therefore innovation is perceived both as a process and an outcome of the process.

2.2.1 Innovation as an outcome

According to Johannessen et al. (2001) every definition of innovation is related to the concept of newness that may be investigated according to three dimensions: *What is new? How new? New to whom?*. A general definition of innovation as an outcome is that of Schumpeter: "the commercial or industrial application of something new – a new product, process or method of production; a new market or source of supply; a new form of commercial, business or financial organization" (Schumpeter, 1934). Other scholars, however, advise distinguishing between *something new* and *the application*, that is, invention from innovation (e.g. Freeman, 1982). Invention is defined as "an idea, sketch or model for a new or improved device, product or process" (Freeman, 1982: 7) or, more generally, it means "the process of bringing a new technology into being," where technology is any tool or technique, any product or process by which human capability is extended (Schon, 1967: 20).

The boundaries between invention and innovation have not been exclusively clarified. Some scholars argue that the invention does not become an innovation until it has been processed through production and marketing tasks and diffused into the marketplace (e.g. Freeman, 1982). Discoveries that go no further than the laboratory remain inventions. Therefore any invention brought into the market becomes an innovation. Others, on the contrary, argue that any invention that moves to the firm (Garcia et al., 2002) or that is put to use (Schon, 1967) would be considered an innovation. For example, Zaltman's definition stresses the adoption of any invention or innovation stating that "any idea, practice, or material artifact perceived to be new by the relevant unit of adoption" (Zaltman, Duncan, & Holbek, 1973: 10). Moreover, Green et al. (1999) suggest that "an invention may become an innovation not only with a commercial transaction, but also with its adoption into the social fabric in some other way" (1999: 782). Therefore invention and innovation shade into one another here because it is hard to specify the point at which a new product or process begins to be put to use (Schon, 1967).

Accordingly, in this research study the definition of invention and innovation are based on Schon (1967): the invention is defined as the process of bringing a new technology into being as result of a cognitive process, while the innovation is when the invention is put in use.

The above-mentioned definition does not specify to what extent something is considered new and new to whom. The degree of the newness, usually expressed as innovativeness, and the magnitude of the unit of adoption cause innovations to be perceived differently. For example, the use of titanium is common practice in the aerospace industry but relatively new for the bicycle industry.

Product innovativeness or newness refers to the degree of familiarity organizations or users have with a product. Addressing the question *how new*, products considered to be highly innovative are seen as having a high degree of newness and those with a degree of lower innovativeness are at the opposite end of the range. One common distinction based on the innovativeness is the *radical versus incremental innovation*. Utterback defines radical innovation "as change that sweeps away much of a firm's existing investment in technical skills and knowledge, designs, production technique, plant and equipment" (Utterback, 1996: 200). That means dislocation and discontinuity and a major departure from existing practices at the firm or industrial level, which goes together with radical innovations. It also encompasses changes in the organizational capabilities that force the organization to draw on new technical and commercial skills and to use new problem-solving approaches. On the contrary, incremental innovation expresses continuous improvement toward standardization within the firm and the industry, reinforcing organizational capabilities. In the same line of reasoning, Abernathy and Clark (1985) developed a matrix that focuses on competitive significance by mapping technology competence against market environments in the case of the car industry. Their classification of innovation is based on the conditions under which the innovation destroys or entrenches the current firm's competences and the market. Focusing on product development within the firm, Henderson and Clark (1990) classify an innovation according to its capability to overturn the existing knowledge of core concepts and components[10] and the knowledge of the linkages between them. The former is related to component knowledge and the latter to architectural knowledge.

Given the multidimensional character of innovation, these innovation classifications are unable to define innovativeness exclusively. For example, the Sony Walkman can be both a niche innovation (Abernathy et al., 1985) and an architectural innovation (Henderson et al., 1990) (Table 2.1). Several attempts have been made to give clarity to the degree of newness (e.g. Garcia et al., 2002; Johannessen et al., 2001), but arrival at a common and comprehensive definition seems unlikely. Furthermore, there is another question to be addressed: *new to whom*, which is closely related to *how new*.

The previously mentioned matrixes categorize the degree of newness in terms of knowledge, skills and competences in the organization (Abernathy et al., 1985; Henderson et al., 1990) and in the industry and market (Abernathy et al., 1985). According to Afuah and Bahram (1995), previous studies do not address the impact of the innovations on the capabilities and assets of suppliers, customers and suppliers of complementary products. They propose the *hypercube model*, where the Henderson matrix for the innovator entity (the firm) is expanded to the suppliers, customers and complementary inventors attempting to describe the impact of the innovation at various stages of its value-added chain.

Table 2.1 Typologies of innovation for the same device according to various scholars

	Type of innovation	Matrix elements	Author
Sony Walkman	Niche innovation	Existing technology competences/ disrupting market	Abernathy & Clark, 1985
	Architectural innovation	Core concept reinforced/linkages between core concept and components changed	Henderson & Clark, 1990
	Incremental innovation	Existing technology and market	Balachandra, 1997
	Commercially discontinuous	Existing technology competences/ disrupting market	Veryzer, 1998a

From this brief review of innovation as an outcome, the typologies of innovation seem to be tailored to specific domains, products and firms and/or users. Therefore, *is it useful to distinguish among innovations?*

Despite the intrinsic subjective perspective, the incremental–radical innovation dichotomy is still valid, both for the *firm* and for the *outside world*. A well-known typology categorizes new products along two dimensions of newness: *newness to the developing firm and newness to the market* (Booz, 1982). Mastering a new product into which resources, organizational and technical skills fit into seems to entail a lower degree of uncertainty than developing a new product that requires new skills, various resources and faces unclear information about the market. However, what may be seen by the innovation team as a really new product achieved through the accumulation of new skills and resources may be perceived by the "outside world" as a conventional product. Potential users may perceive the innovation as too radical, making the adoption difficult because the added value is unclear. Consequently, the perception of innovation impacts the innovation process itself. Downs and Mohr (1976) refer to the degree of novelty as a secondary attribute of the innovation. Secondary attributes are perceived by senses rather than being essential to the object. For example, some innovation may be seen as a minor change in routine by some organizations and a major alteration for others. Downs and Mohr (1976) suggest measuring the degree of innovativeness with respect to each organization and seeing it as a characteristic of the organization.

For the purpose of this research study the degree of innovativeness is related in primis *to the organization that develops, adopts and implements the innovation.*

2.2.2 Innovation as a process

Invention and innovation are best understood as features of a single continuous process rather than as steps or phases (Schon, 1967). The innovation process may start from a well-defined problem that requires a solution, or it may be derived from unexpected events or by chance. The innovation process has been illustrated either as sequences of steps and activities to carry out or as a non-linear process underlining the indeterminate nature of the innovation. They are two different perspectives of how the innovation may be described: the rational and the non-rational view of innovation (Schon, 1967). Keep in mind that here they are illustrated in their extreme form.

The rational view of innovation

According to this perspective, the innovation process at the firm level consists of a set of activities that are linked to one another through feedback loops. The process is visualized as a chain or sequence of steps starting with the perception of a market opportunity, a problem or a need, which is followed by the research, the analytical design of a new product or process and testing, redesign and production and commercialization (e.g. Buijs & Valkenburg, 1996; Fischer, 2001; Kline & Rosenberg, 1986; Landau & Rosenberg, 1986; Rogers, 1995; Roozenburg & Eekels, 1995). The innovation process is goal-oriented and orderly: first, the definition of the problem, then the identification of alternative routes to its solution and finally, the choice as to the most promising route. The generation of alternative routes is a divergent process, while the selection process is a convergent one (Roozenburg et al., 1995). A phase of "generation" precedes a phase of "idea screening", with the first stage calling for creativity and imagination and the second one for critical intelligence (Schon, 1967). Defining the problem is an analytic sequence in which the designer determines all elements of the problem and specifies the requirements that a successful design solution needs to have. Terms like the "management of innovation" suggest that we can foresee the dangers and rewards of projects where risks are controlled by mechanisms of justification and review. Here the rational view is presented in an extreme form but it is sometimes found in this "pure" state. However, what often happens in practice is more complex, and the rational view of innovation seems to oversimplify the complexity of the process. Although linear models may describe the process of innovation in general terms, experience tells us that organizations do not always *follow* or encompass all of the steps that the models try to depict (Buijs, 2003; McCarthy, Tsinopoulos, Allen, & Rose-Anderssen, 2006).

Innovation as a non-rational process

On the contrary, the non-rational perspective of the innovation process regards the innovation as a process in itself. It often moves not from a clearly defined goal to the discovery of technical means and then putting these into use, but from the observation of a phenomenon to the exploration of a use for it. "Once a process of technical development has begun it does not usually move in a straight line, according to plan but takes unexpected twists and turns" (Schon, 1967: 12). The innovation process reflects non-linear dynamics (Van de Ven et al., 1999) and may be illustrated as a learning process (Schon, 1967). Arrow stated that "the process of innovation is filled with uncertainty, it is a journey of exploration into a strange land" (Arrow, 2000). It involves sets of risks and uncertainties that are inherent to the process. The risk of an action is the likelihood that it will produce an unwanted result, and it is a quantitative expression based on probabilities (Schon, 1967). On the contrary, a situation is uncertain when it requires action but what needs to be done remains unclear. Taking decisions creates uncertainty when the situation is problematic and unfamiliar and there is too little or too much information. "A firm is not designed for uncertainty but is well-equipped for risks", accordingly, "the innovative work of an organization consists in converting uncertainty to risk" (Schon, 1967: 25). Thus the aim is to reduce uncertainty to permit decisions on the basis of defined information and to handle risks on clear alternatives of action.

Many scholars have drawn on the information-processing theory in which the product development is frequently described as an exercise in information processing (e.g. Moenaert, Demeyer, Souder, & Deschoolmeester, 1995; Tatikonda & Rosenthal, 2000). If the objective of the organization is to translate uncertainties into risks, the control of information becomes crucial when action is required (Schon, 1967). In this perspective, uncertainty is the difference between the amount of information required to perform a particular task and the amount of information already possessed by the organization/individual (Galbraith, 1973). Then the process of innovation may be seen as a process of uncertainty reduction (Souder & Moenaert, 1992).

For the purpose of this research study, the process of innovation is defined as a learning process through uncertainty reduction.

The innovation as an outcome is an invention put into use as the result of an experiential social process.

Common elements in the innovation process

The process of innovation as previously discussed is hard to describe as a sequence of stages or phases of activities over time. Instead the innovation process may be described as a much fuzzier and more complex progression of events in which uncertainties are expected to be converted into quantifiable risks (Schon, 1967). Notwithstanding the great deal of uncertainty, we can draw some general conclusions about how the uncertainty reduction progresses. For example, after studying 14 different innovations, Van de Ven et al. (1999) found some common elements pertaining to the *initiation, development* and *implementation periods* of the innovation.

The initiation period represents a gestation period in which a variety of intentionally or unintentionally related events, like new information, triggers awareness of technological feasibility ("technological push") or the recognition of the need for change (e.g. "market pull"). Although many ideas may be generated, it appears that concrete actions to start specific innovations are triggered internally or externally by shocks to organizations.[11] Many scholars call this period Fuzzy Front End (Khurana & Rosenthal, 1998; Kim & Wilemon, 2002).The Fuzzy Front End (FFE) is the period between when an opportunity is first contemplated and when the idea is evaluated ready for development. The FFE is intrinsically dynamic, uncertain and unroutine, where the ambiguity about the commercial potential of an idea prevents an opportunity from proceeding to the development phase (Kim et al., 2002). The ambiguity and uncertainty may arise from the novelty of the technology, new markets, the fact that new resources are required or lack of faith in a firm's capabilities (Verworn, Herstatt, & Nagahira, 2008).

The start of *the development period*, in which the inputs are bound to "be converted", is usually related to the event of the resources' acquisition. At the beginning of the development period, there is a relationship between the profitability of the innovation when it will finally be introduced and the amount invested in development (Arrow, 2000). Although this relationship is highly uncertain, plans are developed and submitted to resource controllers to obtain the resources. These plans often represent wishful thinking rather than realistic scenarios of innovation development. Therefore, formal plans are often bound to change. When the development period starts, the initial idea may proliferate in many divergent, parallel or convergent ideas, in which setbacks and mistakes often occur resulting in an alteration of pre-developed assumptions. Due to the intrinsic uncertainty of the process of innovation, some ideas are abandoned, others put on the shelf and others lead to important innovation spin-offs. Still some ideas converge, translating into an innovation. Proliferation may even be produced to leverage the risk "to bet only on one horse". As setbacks occur, the resource and the schedule lines, if these exist formally, often mismatch. Moreover, setbacks may influence the relationship within the team and between the team and the resource controllers. For example, escalation of commitment may occur within radical innovation processes (Schmidt & Calantoné, 1998) or interpretative barriers may emerge within the team (Dougherty, 1992). Accordingly, the innovative personnel may also change during the process. The innovation development period entails confrontation and interaction not only among the innovative team, managers and investors, but sometimes with other organizations.

The implementation/termination period occurs when inputs have been converted into outputs or when the uncertainties have been translated into risks (Schon, 1967). It begins when activities are undertaken to apply and adopt an innovation regardless of who is developing, implementing or adopting the innovation. Innovations stop when they are implemented and institutionalized or when the resources run out. The people involved in the innovation process may perceive and evaluate the innovation outcome differently. As Van de Ven et al. (1999: 62) state *"the success and failure of innovation adoption or development often represents a socially constructed reality* [rather than] *an objective reality"*.

As a result, the innovation process is a leap into the unknown where the desirable outcome is not controlled by entrepreneurs, managers or investors – they can only increase its odds of success (Van de Ven et al., 1999).

The findings of Van de Ven et al. enrich the definition of the innovation process: innovation as a process is defined here as a venture to develop, adopt and/or implement an artifact through a process of learning and uncertainty reduction.

It may be argued that not all organizations generate *and* adopt innovations. Innovations may be *generated* in one organization for their own purpose and sold to another organization, which *adopts* them (Damanpour & Gopalakrishnan, 1998). Then the generating process results in an outcome such as a technology or a product for the generating organization, while the adopting process delineates how the outcome is assimilated in the adopting organization (Damanpour et al., 1998). For the purpose of this research study, the focus is mainly on the generation of innovation within one organization. The same organization then adopts and implements the innovation.

2.3 New product development (NPD)

After defining what innovation is, the objective of this section is to identify factors influencing both the process and the outcome of the innovation. More specifically, it draws on a specific innovation literature that has mainly studied the generation of innovations and their performance in the market, such as the new product development literature (e.g. Cooper & Kleinschmidt, 1987; Rothwell et al., 1974) excluding the literature on adoption and diffusion of innovation widely studied in the last 30 years (e.g. Damanpour, 1992; Downs et al., 1976; Kimberly, 1979; Rogers, 1995). The rationale behind drawing on NPD literature regarding the generation of innovation exclusively is threefold. First, the focus of this research study is to examine and explain how environmental ambition influences product development. Therefore, the main concern is how organizations with environmental ambition develop products and services and what the implications are for product performance. Second, the product performance in the market is considered to be heavily influenced by how the process of innovation unfolds and how well activities are carried out (e.g. Cooper et al., 1995a; Montoya-Weiss et al., 1994). Third, the innovation adoption and diffusion literature has little direct relevance for the process of generating innovation (Damanpour, 1992).

Although technical and market changes can never be controlled, proactive new product development is considered critical for firms as a potential source of competitive advantage (Brown et al., 1995). The search for the factors influencing the effectiveness and efficiency of the product innovation has been the rationale of many studies. In the next subsection the most relevant ones are reviewed.

2.3.1 Success and failure in NPD

What makes product innovation successful? The existing literature on product development performance is extensive. The success of NPD is multidimensional (e.g. Griffin & Page, 1996). It can be viewed in time perspective (Hultink & Robben, 1995), such as in the long term or the short term; in market-oriented terms, such as customer satisfaction and market share; or in strategic terms, such the extent to which the new product allows the firm to enter a new market (Tatikonda et al., 2000). This research study attempts to cluster the relevant literature on the identification of determinants. More specifically, determinants of success and failure used to predict market success are categorized into two fundamental groups: 1) *project-level determinants* based on examining the specific compatibility of the process activities, product characteristics and market opportunities during the project; and 2) *determinants at the organizational level* examining the compatibility of company practices and firm characteristics that may be important for the success of the project but are not apparent at project level.

The project determinants

At the project level, the research focus is on the determinants that influence the performance of the project. Here, project performance is related to the financial success of a product development project. This school of research has investigated why new products succeed and why others fail by trying:

- To identify determinants of new product successes/failures (e.g. Cooper, 1975; Cooper et al., 1987; Hopkins & Bailey, 1971; Karakaya & Kobu, 1994; Link, 1987; Montoya-Weiss et al., 1994);
- to design and test new product development processes (e.g. Cooper, 1979; Cooper, 1985, 1992; Cooper & Kleinschmidt, 1991; Ettlie & Elsenbach, 2007);
- to establish relationships between NPD strategies and the product performance (e.g. Cooper, 1985, 1986; Cooper et al., 1995a; Karakaya et al., 1994).

The claim is that a product development project that is well planned with strong support has more chance of becoming a success (Brown et al., 1995). Montoya-Weiss and Calantone (1994) performed a meta-analysis synthesizing the results of empirical research on the determinants of new product performance. Their review and analysis resulted in 18 factors divided into four major categories capturing the essence of the research on the determinants of new product performance (see Table 2.2). These factors have proven to be helpful as screening or project selection and prioritization criteria (Cooper et al., 1995a). *Strategic factors* and *development process factors* were the factors most frequently included. For example, product advantage, referring to the customer's perception of product superiority, with respect to specific attributes relative to competi-

Table 2.2 Factors leading to new product success

Strategic factors	Development process factors
Product advantage Technological synergy Marketing synergy Company resources Strategy of product	Proficiency of technical activities Proficiency of marketing activities Proficiency of up-front activities Protocol (product definition) Speed to market Financial/business analysis
Market environment factors	**Organizational factors**
Market potential/size Market competitiveness External environment	Internal/external relations Organizational factors

tors, is considered the most important factor by far, although it is difficult to measure. Moreover, when there is a good match between the needs of the project and the firm's resources and skills with respect to market (the promotion, market research and customer service) and technological activities (research and development (R&D) and engineering), the product is likely to succeed. Note that the organizational factors mentioned in the table have received very little attention from this school of research.

On the other hand, *Why do products fail? And how many?* There is no consensus on the failure rate of new products or new projects. Many projects fail before the testing phase and others fail in the market (National Industrial Conference Board, 1964). Not surprisingly, much attention has been paid to the latter. Concerning product failure in the market, Crawford (1977) argues that a reasonable rate of product market failure is around 40% and the discrepancy of several studies is due to the wide range of research methodologies used (Biemans, 1989; Crawford, 1977). Based on existing schemes (Crawford, 1977; Karakaya et al., 1994; Montoya-Weiss et al., 1994), Table 2.3 summarizes the studies on the factors leading products to fail.

Many factors represent the reverse of the success factors – for example, lack of product superiority is the contrary of product advantage and deficiency of market or technological activities is the opposite of proficiency of the same activities. New products are not likely to reach their business objectives when one of these factors occurs, such as a lack of resources and managerial skills or poor planning.

The determinants at the organizational level

At the organizational level, the unit of analysis includes various aspects of the organization and several mechanisms within the organization that influence product performance. Here, product performance is defined differently in different research schools. The performance can be financial in nature as well as

Table 2.3 Factors leading to new product failure

Strategic factors	Authors
Lack of product superiority and a "me-too" approach	Cooper, 1975, Karakaya, 1994, Hopkins, 1971; Cooper & Kleinschmidt, 1987; Biemans, 1989 (Link, 1987)
Inadequate market analysis and effort	Cooper, 1975, Karakaya, 1994, Crawford, 1977; NICB, 1984; Cooper & Kleinschmidt, 1987; Link, 1987;, Biemans, 1989
Deficient resources	Cooper, 1975
Poor planning	Crawford, 1977 (Hopkins et al., 1971)
Lack of managerial skills	Cooper, 1975; Montoya-Weiss et al., 1994; Crawford, 1977; Hopkins, 1971; Cooper & Kleinschmidt, 1987
Poor distribution	Karakaya, 1994; NICB, 1964
Wrong pricing	Karakaya, 1994
Development process factors	
Deficient activities	Cooper, 1975; Cooper & Kleinschmidt, 1987
Poor timing	Cooper, 1975; Crawford, 1977; NICB, 1964; Hopkins, 1971
Higher costs than expected	Cooper, 1975; NICB, 1964
Market environmental factor	
Stronger competitors	Cooper, 1975; Karakaya, 1994; NICB, 1964; Link, 1987
Overestimated number of users	Cooper, 1975; Link, 1987; Biemans, 1989
Unexpected events and regulation	Hopkins, 1971
	Montoya-Weiss et al., 1994
	Crawford, 1977
Technical factor	
Technical difficulties	Cooper, 1975; NICB, 1964; Hopkins, 1971
Organization factor	
Poor internal communication	Crawford, 1977; Montoya-Weiss et al., 1994, Cooper & Kleinschmidt, 1987

related to the process and the effectiveness of the product concept (Brown et al., 1995).

The determinants used at the organizational level include aspects concerning the way firms organize their activities for new products, as well as the strategy and culture of the firm (Cooper et al., 1995a; Cooper & Kleinschmidt, 1995b; Ernst, 2002). Table 2.4 presents the main organizational factors influencing the product performance, based on Cooper and Kleinschmidt (1995a), Brown et al. (1995) and Ernst (2002).

To a certain extent, the factors at the organizational or project level are overlapping. Management support and the multifunctional team, for example, are viewed as an important measure of the performance of the new product at both levels. This may explain the importance of the project team consisting of members conducting the actual product development activities and the management supporting it at the very core of product development. The composition of

Table 2.4 Organization aspects influencing product performance

	Success factors for new products	Authors
How the firm organizes its activities with regard to new products	Cross-functional team	Cooper & Kleinschmidt, 1995a); Griffin, 1997; Dougherty, 1992
	A strong and responsible project leader	Cooper & Kleinschmidt, 1995a
	NPD team and team leader commitment	Thamhain, 1990; Dougherty, 1992
	Management involvement and commitment	Cooper & Kleinschmidt, 1995a
	Intensive communication	Cooper & Kleinschmidt, 1995a; Dougherty, 1992
Culture	Allow the emergence of intrapreneurs and risk-taking attitude	Cooper & Kleinschmidt, 1995a
	Product champions	Barczak, 1995
Strategy	Clear goal and strategic focus in NPD programme	Thamhain, 1990; Griffin, 1997; Cooper & Kleinschmidt, 1995a,b
	Market information and NPD programme	Balbontin, 1999; Cooper & Kleinschmidt, 1995a
	User involvement	Hippel, 1977

the team is therefore vital to the product development performance. Cross-functional teams are important, because functional diversity increases the amount and variety of information available for developing products as well as improving the internal and external communication (Dougherty, 1992). Strong support from senior management and good coordination by the project leader help create a positive climate for the product effectiveness and process performance. A fast (which means less time to product shipment) and productive (which means lower costs) process may lead to financially successful products. Moreover, product advantage, unique benefits and competences that fit the firm may also result in successful products (Brown et al., 1995).

2.3.2 NPD: summary

The NPD literature seems to suggest that the performance of a new product is influenced by a number of factors (Ernst, 2002). Thus far, it does not look like there will be a "unifying" theory that helps us explain and predict when a new product will prove successful. However, the review does yield some important factors, especially at the organizational level, which clearly have an impact on a new product's chance of success, such as the project team's commitment and competences, and management support. The emphasis on determinants on an organizational level has been underscored by scholars such as Brown and

Eisenhardt (1995), Cooper and Kleinschmidt (1995a, 1995b) Ernst (2002), Dougherty (1992), Pinto and Pinto (1990), mainly for two reasons.

First, determinants at the project level are directly influenced by determinants at the organizational level. Whether or not the product as a bundle of attributes will fit into the market depends on, to a certain extent, how activities during the project are performed and/or how an organization's resources are utilized. However, activities, resources and the overall decisions about the product attributes are crucially influenced by the organizational culture and the individuals' motivations within the organization. The product in other words is an artifact resulting from an organizational process (Krishnan et al., 2001).

An example may clarify this relationship in a better way. Within the wind power industry, the Danish wind turbines dominate the market because the quality of product (being cheaper or more reliable) gives them a competitive advantage compared to other products. Thus Danish wind turbines are more successful than other wind turbines such as the American ones (Garud & Karnoe, 2003). *Why do some products have these attributes while others do not?* It depends on the proficiency of market and technical activities, which in turn depend on how the network of organizations around the wind turbine has actually performed these activities. The decisions at the organizational level between and within the management network and the project team have actually influenced the project where the activities are performed. Therefore, the team composition, commitment and competences, together with the network management, strategy and internal and external communication have directly influenced the Danish wind turbine performance.

Second, studying determinants at the organizational level is a more recent phenomenon than doing so at the project level. For example, Cooper and Kleinschmidt, who are among the most active scholars in studying NPD success and failure, did not investigate the relationship between the organization and the NPD until their later work (Ernst, 2002). Accordingly, more research is needed to explore and explain the organizational characteristics influencing NPD performance (as suggested by Brown et al., 1995).

In the light of this, the management support for the project and the project team commitment and competences are the constructs chosen. These constructs may have a crucial role in understanding the challenges associated with ENPD:

1   Management support for new product development. The support for environmental issues in NPD is likely to affect product performance due to the complexity of greening. Moreover, this process may be even more complex when a radical approach is encouraged.
2   Coordination and commitment of the project team. The final product is the result of the effort of various team members, each with their own interpretation. Introducing environmental attributes into this process may introduce a different set of interpretations. The collective agreement with regard to the functional specifications may be influenced by a combination of environmental and other concerns.

The management support and the project team commitment influence how product attributes are chosen, the product innovation being an outcome of an organizational process. As a result, a third construct is selected:

3   Product attributes. As a set of attributes, successful products are "successful" because they meet market requirements, and provide functionalities valued by the market. Hence, the challenge is to understand what the implications are of the incorporation of environmental attributes into products when translating functional requirements into a product specification.

Beside the above-mentioned reasons, other explanations for the selection of these constructs are given in Chapter 5.

Before exploring the relationship between environmental ambition and management support, team commitment and design specifications, a better understanding of the selected constructs is needed. The selected constructs are important determinants for undertaking innovation projects successfully: clear goal and vision, strong management support, available resources and a strong, committed project team. Nevertheless, there is both theoretical and empirical evidence to suggest that it is important to distinguish among different degrees of innovativeness when undertaking new product development. Balachandra and Friar (1997) suggest taking a contingency approach for identifying contextual variables and their combinations that are likely to influence the process of innovation. Therefore, it seems important to understand the contingencies in which the process of innovation unfolds. For the purpose of this research study, the selected constructs are thoroughly investigated and examined with regard to the degree of innovation in the next section.

2.4 Incremental and radical product innovation processes

The extent to which the above-mentioned factors will actually result in successful NPD projects is influenced by the nature and degree of the innovation (Balachandra et al., 1997). This has to do with the fact that product newness is potentially linked to levels of uncertainty and risk (Schmidt et al., 1998), to new product development complexity and to new resources required when undertaking NPD ventures (Ali, Krapfel, & Labahn, 1995). For example, performing a detailed market analysis for radical products may be futile because the expected market may not yet exist (Balachandra et al., 1997) or consumers may find it hard to imagine the potential of a radical product (Veryzer, 1998a).

Therefore, it may be wise to compare two discrete forms of product innovation process: the incremental versus the radical, as illustrated in section 2.4.1. Section 2.4.2 defines and describes the decision process of managers and product developers under risk and uncertain conditions. Sections 2.4.3 and 2.4.4 illustrate how decisions, supports, commitments and coordination may be influenced by the degree of innovativeness.

2.4.1 The degree of innovativeness

Section 2.2 has illustrated the nature of the innovation process, comparing the rational and the non-rational view of the innovation process. The idealized and often after-the-fact linear process of innovation emphasized by the rational view is understandable for various reasons.

First, it is a useful device for attempting to describe innovation and for managing the uncertainties of the innovation. Many models of innovation have been carried out to deal with innovation. The process of planning and formulation of objectives may be helpful because they provide directions for efforts and stimuli for action although plans are bound to be inadequate and modified in light of discoveries made during the process. It is important to remember, however, that these innovation models are normative templates that suggest or prescribe how firms may innovate, but they do not actually *define* and *explain* the innovation process. The stage-wise models may oversimplify the innovation process (e.g. Cooper et al., 1991) while the feedback-loop models (e.g. Kline et al., 1986), although attempting to describe the complexity of the innovation process, do not enhance our understanding of the process. As a result, it may not be useful to arrive at a framework or a model of the innovation process that fails to explain it.

Second, the rational view of innovation may likely describe the process of incremental innovations. The more radical the innovation, the less rational and predictable the process (Schon, 1967). Accordingly, a well-planned process is desirable for incremental innovations and an accurate market analysis of the existing market is expected. The new product meets an existing need and the market uncertainty is relatively low (Balachandra et al., 1997). On the contrary, in the case of radical innovations, organizations undertake a journey in an unfamiliar land in which well-equipped practices may not be suitable. Note that the degree of innovativeness is viewed from an organization's perspective.

The process of innovation perceived as new by the organization has been widely studied. Danneels and Kleinschmidt (2001) suggest drawing on two bodies of literature: organization–environment relations studies and the resource-based theory of the organization. These theoretical perspectives allow us to distinguish two alternative conceptualizations of product newness to the organization: *newness as familiarity versus newness as resource fit* (Danneels et al., 2001).

Drawing on organizational theory, the *newness as familiarity concept* regards the relationship between the organization and its environment.[12] It is argued that all organizations establish a "domain", in which they are dependent on inputs from the environment. Normann (1971) argues that new products may enlarge the domain of the organization to such an extent that they make the organization face an unfamiliar domain. Therefore organizations are more confident in developing products in a well-known technical and market environment because of established channels of communication and existing structure. In contrast, developing products in different domains, where the market and/or technological environment are unfamiliar, may increase the uncertainties. Accordingly, many studies found that radical innovations pose greater challenges to firms and designers because of unspecific market opportunities (O'Connor, 1998; Rice, O'Connor, Peters, & Morone, 1998), uncertain technology (Veryzer, 1998a) without relying on familiar research techniques (Hippel, 1988). Moreover, the development of new products and businesses based on radical innovations requires management practices that differ significantly from those required for incremental innovation (Rice et al., 1998). For example, after following eight cases of radical NPD projects, Veryzer (1998a) found that radical innovations involve a "higher degree of technological uncertainty, long development time, a sequence of innovations, informal structure and 'unconventional' progression of the activities" (Veryzer, 1998a: 317).

The *newness as resource fit concept* draws on recent strategy theory referred to as the "resource-based view of the organization" which focuses on resources that firms control and the productive uses to which they put those resources. The organization is seen as a collection of resources (Wernerfelt, 1984). Resources that enable the organization to develop new products include R&D expertise, knowledge of customer needs and competitive situations, production facilities and so forth. The synergy of a project with an organization refers to how well the internally available resources fit the requirements for the new product project, that is, the extent to which the new product fits with the organization's resources and capabilities (Danneels et al., 2001). Moreover, product innovation requires the organization to have competences relating to technology (enabling the firm to make the product) and relating to customers (enabling the firm to serve certain customers). By undertaking an incremental innovation process, the organization can exploit internal resources and rely on existing competences of the technology and the market. A new product development that requires different technical and business skills is seen as a radical undertaking because such projects involve greater challenges and risks for the firm (Green & Welsh, 2003; Schmidt et al., 1998; Schoonhoven, Eisenhardt, & Lyman, 1990). Projects with more radical characteristics require larger resource commitments (Green et al., 2003), longer time-to-market periods (Schoonhoven et al., 1990), different organizational units (Christensen & Bower, 1996) and different capabilities (Green, Gavin, & Aiman-Smith, 1995).

It is also important to emphasize that radical projects may also encompass, to a certain extent, *new services* and not merely new products. For example, it may be a radical undertaking for a product manufacturer to be able to change part of their core business by investing in new services (De Brentani, 2001).

The French company Air Liquide, for instance, was a market leader in the supply of industrial gas. Its main revenues came from selling gas and building infrastructure. When gas became a commodity in the 1990s, with only price differentiating one supplier from another, its operating income plunged. Air Liquide then put all of its effort into radical projects, doubling R&D expenditure to create new products. The results, however, were negligible. It took several years before it realized that it could sell its skills, gained over years, to its

Table2.5 Differences between incremental and radical product innovation processes.

NPD	Incremental process	Radical process
Degree of uncertainty	Low	High
Process	Goal-oriented	Goal change
	Orderly	Sporadic death/revival
	Linear	Not linear
	Structured	Unstructured
	Formal	Informal
	More predictable	Unpredictable
Strategies and priorities	Planned	Dynamic
Execution of activities	Sequentially or overlapping	Not sequential/random
Key players	The same	New players in, old players out
Exogenous events/ Contextual factors	Critical	Influent
Market opportunities	Clear	Unclear
Market research technique	Suitable	Unsuitable
development time	Shorter	Longer
Information	Articulated	Unarticulated
Product attributes	Determinate	Indeterminate
Technological familiarity	High	Low
Market familiarity	High	Low
Resources	Fit	Unfit
Capabilities	Fit	Unfit

customers. An example of this would be the handling of hazardous materials and the maximization of energy efficiency. Through a massive program of retraining employees, Air Liquide was able to switch resources to these new forms of services. After selling gas for decades, Air Liquide became a provider of chemical and gas-management services as well. In 1991, services accounted for 7% of its revenues; in 2003 they represented close to 30% (Slywotzky & Wise, 2003).

Table 2.5 summarizes the differences between incremental and radical product innovation processes based on the findings previously discussed.[13] Furthermore, Box 2.1 illustrates an example of newness from the firm's perspective.

For the purpose of this research study, undertaking a radical innovation process involves the organization having to cope with a new and unfamiliar domain, where different technical and business skills are required.

Undertaking an incremental innovation process means that the organization copes with a familiar domain, exploits internal resources and relies on existing technology and market competences.

Exploration vs exploitation

One may ask: given these uncertainties, why should organizations pursue radical undertakings?

The reason firms do what they do is that they expect to reap the financial rewards at the end of the product development process. The development of new business and product lines based on radical innovation is critical for the renewal of an organization's competitive position (McDermott & O'Connor, 2002) and for its long-term survival (March, 1991). Drawing on organizational learning, March (1991) argues that organizations need to seek an appropriate balance between exploration and exploitation for their own prosperity. Exploitation entails refinement and improvement of existing knowledge and skills, while exploration entails search, risk taking, experimentation and discovery of new knowledge. Organizations that engage in exploitation to the exclusion of exploration are likely to find themselves "trapped" in a rigid and stable structure being unprepared to cope with a fast-changing market. On the contrary, "organizations engaging in exploration with the exclusion of the exploitation are likely to suffer the costs of experimentation without gaining many of its benefits" (March, 1991: 71).

Box 2.1 Newness from a firm's perspective

An example may provide a better explanation of the definition of radical versus incremental undertaking. An established company named Alfa in the bike industry has an existing product line made of "standard" bikes. A standard bike is a synonym of a safety bicycle, which has two wheels of equal size; pedals are connected to the rear wheel by a multiplying gear; and the rider is upright leaning forward.

The company Alfa is willing to develop a new bicycle concept: a recumbent bike (figure above). It is a bicycle that allows the rider to sit in a reclining position instead of leaning forward.

Beside the sitting position, design, balance, the steering systems and the wheel bases are different on recumbent bikes. There is great variety in how the recumbent bikes may look: using standard bicycles wheels, or

---

using one or more smaller wheels; and steering can be placed either above or below the seat. Moreover, there are few standardized parts for recumbent bikes, increasing the complexity of the product. Beside technical characteristics, developing a new product such as a recumbent bike also means focusing on a different market. Potential users may be different than normal customers and their requirements may differ as well.

From the *newness as familiarity concept*, for Alfa, developing such a bike entails enlarging the domain in which the company operates: looking for new suppliers and new potential users. Moreover, the current distribution might also be affected when regular retailers give recumbent bikes a lukewarm welcome. The more Alfa needs to change in the current technical, market and distribution environment, the better Alfa may cope with the unfamiliar environment. Thus developing a new recumbent bike might signify an exploratory entry into an unfamiliar technical and market domain.

The *newness as resource fit concept* in this case refers to the extent to which the internally available resources and skills fit the requirements for the development of such a new bike for Alfa. If the production and assembly of the new product require new competencies, capabilities and resources that depart from existing ones, the company is likely to undertake a radical innovation.

Radical or incremental projects: which leads to success?

Another question may arise: *What is the relationship between the degree of innovativeness and commercial success?* Previous research has struggled to find an answer to this question, attempting to identify a clear relationship between the degree of innovativeness and the product performance in the market. Many studies found that an innovative product has a greater chance of success in the market (e.g. Maidique & Zirger, 1984), while some scholars found otherwise (e.g. Rothwell et al., 1974). Others found that innovative products are much more likely to fail than less innovative products (Freeman, 1982). Kleinschmidt and Cooper (1991) found that the relationship between innovativeness and commercial success is not linear but rather U-shaped, while Franklin and Baylis (2003) recently found that the moderately new products tend to be more successful than the most or the least innovative ones. No matter how you see it, a simple relationship between product innovativeness and commercial success is still uncertain. As argued by Song and Montoya-Weiss, "there is very little conclusive evidence concerning the impact of product innovativeness on new product success" (1998: 127).

2.4.2 *Making decisions under risk and uncertain conditions*

In any project, managers and designers need to make decisions in their attempt to achieve the established specific goal. Decisions are here defined as a means to achieve some result or to solve problems (Gibson, Ivancevich, Donnelly, & Konopaske, 2003). There are several ways to classify types of decisions (Souder, 1980). Here the system suggested by Simon (1977) is adopted. He distinguishes two types of decisions: *programmed* and *non-programmed*.

Decisions are programmed when a particular situation occurs often and a routine procedure exists to work it out. Problems that require this kind of decision are frequent, repetitive and there is a certain cause–effect relationship. The way to solve these problems is dependent on certain policies, rules and definite procedures.

Decisions are non-programmed when they are unstructured and novel, concerning complex problems where definite procedures are not suitable. On the contrary, such problems deserve a procedure with tolerance for ambiguity, creativity and creative problem solving. For example, business organizations willing to diversify into new products and markets face non-programmed decisions.

In NPD projects, actors are likely to face non-programmed decisions, where a great deal of uncertainty and risk surrounds the outcome. Every decision is an outcome of a dynamic process that is influenced by a multitude of factors (Gibson et al., 2003; McCarthy et al., 2006). This process has been illustrated and explained by several scholars (see e.g. Gibson et al., 2003; Hellriegel, Slocum, & Woodman, 1992; Souder, 1980) as a sequential yet not fixed decision-making process: identifying problems, developing alternatives, evaluating and choosing alternatives, and implementing them. This process usually entails a problem (otherwise no decision is required) that is indicated by a gap between the organizational goal and objectives and the levels of actual performances, or by the complexity in measuring performances. However, it may be difficult to spot the locus of a problem due to misperception of the problem. After the problem is identified, decision makers need to develop alternatives, that is, potential solutions to the problem. Once alternatives have been developed, they need to be evaluated and compared with the most favorable outcome.

The relationship between alternatives and outcomes depends on whether the outcome is well known (condition of certainty), estimated (condition of risk) or unknown (condition of uncertainty). The goal of selecting an alternative is to solve a problem to achieve a predetermined objective (Mintzberg, Raisinghani, & Theoret, 1976). Unfortunately for most decision makers, an alternative rarely achieves the desired objective without impacting negatively or positively on other objectives (Gibson et al., 2003). Moreover, many decisions require trading off different objectives. For example, in certain situations an organizational objective may be achieved at the expense of societal-environmental objectives.[14] In any case, whether an objective conflicts with others or not, the values[15] of the decision maker influence the alternative chosen.

In general, Chapter 4 will discuss the concern for the natural environment as a value while Chapter 3 will explore how decisions are taken in different organizational settings.

To conclude this section, in any innovation project, managers and designers are required to make non-programmed decisions, which involves a comparison of alternatives and an evaluation of the possible estimated or uncertain outcomes according to a set of objectives (Gibson et al., 2003).

2.4.3 Decisions, team commitment and management support within NPD projects

To cope with intrinsic uncertainties, projects are periodically monitored and reviewed at multiple stages (Schmidt et al., 1998). This means that during the management's review the continuation and the direction of the project depend on the degree of support from project and management teams. If the project is not actively supported by key management actors, its prospects and priorities may be reassessed and even dismissed.

On the contrary, if a project is strongly supported, the chances that it will survive through ongoing reviews are greater. The survival chances of a new product development project are related to its expected strategic and economic values (Montoya-Weiss et al., 1994). In the same way, projects are constantly monitored along performance dimensions and evaluated, assessing their progress toward their technical and commercial goals (Steele, 1989).

Therefore, support from key management actors for NPD projects is crucial to process performance (Brown et al., 1995). When the level of uncertainty in NPD is low, the management support is likely based exclusively on performance evaluation. When the level of uncertainty in NPD is high and the project is perceived as radical, the support for the project may be driven by more than judgments about project performance (Green et al., 2003). Furthermore, radical projects may also be supported in cases of disappointing performance. Schmidt and Calantone (1998) found that managers are reluctant to shut down failing projects concerning radical products despite information indicating that outcomes are unlikely to be successful. They explained this phenomenon by adopting the escalation commitment theory.

Escalation of commitment situations are those where there is the tendency to invest excessively in a course of action to a greater degree than the information or circumstances should warrant (Barton, Duchon, & Dunegan, 1989; Staw, 1981). Decision makers appear to be locked into courses of actions that are unlikely to succeed, allocating resources such as time and money in the hope of attaining some goal (Brockner, 1992).

The escalation of commitment research is extensive and combines rational and non-rational explanations[16] for such behavior (for a review see Brockner, 1992; Staw & Ross, 1987; Zardkoohi, 2004). Escalation of commitment is a complex phenomenon, which lends itself to more than one explanation. Without going into details, there are three large categories of explanations, which are treated here as complementary and not mutually exclusive. First, the tendency to escalate may be explained by the prospect and expectation associated with continued commitment to the course of action. For example, Rubin and Brockner

(1975) discovered that individuals' persistence at a task at which they were failing was greater both when they sensed that they were drawing ever closer to their goals and when the goals were relatively high in value. Second, the escalation may reflect decision makers' unwillingness to admit that they were mistaken in having their initial commitment to the chosen course of action (Brockner, 1992). Third, psychological and social considerations are non-rational factors that may also influence the tendency to escalate commitments. Research has shown that cognitive processes are far from totally rational, because they are influenced by a number of sources of potential bias and error (e.g. Baron, 1998). They face situations characterized by high levels of uncertainty (Gilbert, Mcnulty, Giuliano, & Benson, 1992), emotion (Oaksford, Morris, Grainger, & Williams, 1996), novelty and time pressure (Fiske & Taylor, 1984). For example, individuals can and may bias information processing, as they are locked into previously held beliefs and preferences (Gilbert et al., 1992).

Prior research has investigated the non-rational factors leading to the escalation of commitment within new product development processes. While economic factors motivate the firm to develop new products, non-economic factors make it increasingly difficult to reassess and even stop an NPD project that is leading to an uncertain future (Schmidt et al., 1998). For example, people get emotionally involved in NPD projects, locked into a course of action that makes them reluctant to change despite clear signals suggesting that they should (Balachandra & Raelin, 1984; Hustad & Mitchell, 1982). Similarly, Boulding et al. (1997) found that, when managers were asked to review hypothetical financial information supposedly two years after the product commercialization, they remained committed to a losing course of action in the context of new product introduction.

Based on experiments, Schmidt and Calantone (1998) found that there is a greater likelihood that managers will forge on with a risky NPD project when the product is more innovative than when it is less innovative. Furthermore, their research showed that individuals inflate their perceptions of the chances of success for new products considered radical products than for incremental ones; causing individuals to become more psychologically committed (Schmidt et al., 1998).

Green et al. (2003) developed a more sophisticated theoretical model on factors influencing decisions to terminate NPD projects, adopting the performance threshold concept from the work of Gimeno et al. (1997) on entrepreneurial firm survival. During the NPD process, the project is evaluated according to performance judgments that influence the go/no-go decisions. If a project is seen as less likely to achieve performance goals, advocacy – that is, expressed support for the project and assessment of it as a higher priority –is likely to decline (Green et al., 2003). However, the advocacy is not only influenced by the performance judgments but also by non-rational factors, such as psychic income (Gimeno, Folta, Cooper, & Woo, 1997), which are likely to influence the performance threshold (Gimeno et al., 1997; Green et al., 2003; Schmidt et al., 1998). A low performance threshold means that key actors enthusiastically support a new project even in cases of poor performance. This implies a higher level of management support, regardless of how well the project performs. In contrast, a high performance threshold may lead to a premature termination of a new project that is considered not to be aligned with the core business. As a result, management support may dwindle irrespective of how well the project is actually doing. Green et al. (2003) found that when more radical NPD projects (technical and business experience is limited) were undertaken, the performance judgment thresholds were lower. That is, a higher level of advocacy may increase resource investments in a project for reasons other than expectation of economic returns.

In conclusion, when undertaking radical NPD processes, rational and non-rational factors may be equally important in the decision-making process (Green et al., 2003; Schmidt et al., 1998). High expectations and prospects, self-justification, psychological rewards and emotional involvements are some of the explanatory factors for escalations of commitment in (radical) NPD projects.

2.4.4 Decisions and team coordination within NPD projects

Product development is a complex process where decisions are made by a coordinated and competent cross-functional team that includes people from different functions (Brown et al., 1995; Dougherty, 1992). To a great extent, success depends on the communication and collaboration among the various members of the team (Brown et al., 1995; Cooper & Kleinschmidt, 1986; Cooper et al., 1995a; Dougherty, 1992). Remarkably, Dougherty (1992) found that in large firms differences in interpretation[17] between the members of a team may act as a barrier rather than a lubricant. This type of barrier may be one explanation for the poor performance of some new products. Different members of a development team will emphasize different aspects of innovation depending on their place and function within the organization. Due to the above-mentioned differences in interpretation, the development of new products for new markets[18] is even more difficult (Dougherty, 1990).

2.4.5 Product specifications

Product development is a complex process involving a number of decisions that have to do with the kind of attributes products should incorporate. Manufacturers and designers attempt to develop products whose unique attributes create value for customers. A successful product contains a set of attributes that are by definition balanced. From a design perspective, there are two discrete approaches to dealing with these attributes.

First, the common linear model divides the design process into two distinctive phases: problem definition and problem solution. The former is an analytic sequence in which the designer determines all the elements of a problem and specifies what is needed to solve the problem successfully. The latter is a synthetic sequence in which the requirements are combined and balanced against each other (Buchanan, 1992). In this case a set of criteria is established regarding the technical and process-related specifications, target costs and time-to-market period, which have to be carefully balanced.

Second, when market needs are unarticulated and information is insufficient, the attributes of the radical product are indeterminate. In such cases, the less common "wicked problems"[19] theory of design, might apply (Rittel & Weber, 1973). The set of criteria for the design process is *indeterminate*, meaning that there are no limits to design problems where the product is characterized by *n* requirements (Buchanan, 1992). Such design problems are defined as "wicked" because they are ill formulated and ill defined by decision makers with conflicting values and confusing available information (Rittel et al., 1973). The degree of innovativeness increases the indeterminacy of attributes creating risks and uncertainties in the design process.

2.4.6 *Radical projects: increasing product complexity*

Undertaking radical projects also means increasing the product complexity. In the product innovation context, uncertainties are intrinsic in the product development process and form part of the complexity of the product. Complexity is an attribute of new products and any idea or technology may be classified on a simplicity–complexity continuum (e.g. Kim & Wilemon, 2003; Rogers, 1995). The typical notion of complexity in the complex system literature revolves around the number of components in the system and their interactions with one another (Rivkin, 2000). For example, product complexity may be defined in relation to the number of functions designed in the product (Griffin, 1997b) or to the number of parts in the product (Murmann, 1994) or to the number of organizational subtasks and subtask interactions posed by the project (Tatikonda et al., 2000). These definitions, however, are clearly distinguished by the concept of radicality, which depends on whether the system includes new components and also on whether the combination/configuration is new (Henderson et al., 1990).

On the contrary, according to Novak and Eppinger (2001), the complexity of a product consists of three elements: the number of product components, their interactions and the degree of product novelty. Thus, they suggest that there is a relationship between the concept of complexity and the concept of radicality. When a product involves a new architecture, new technologies or the product is the result of a new task, there is no stable, well-understood set of interactions between components. The process of identifying and understanding these relationships adds to the difficulty of coordinating development. For example, in the design of the vehicle suspension system, occasionally a new configuration will be introduced that will affect the entire vehicle's dynamics. New interactions between components may emerge, resulting in lengthy development iterations to optimize the new suspension and to create the desired vehicle performance (Novak et al., 2001). Here the definition of complexity corresponds with Novak and Eppinger's definition because it captures the relationship between radicality and complexity.

The technological and/or market newness and development complexities influence the NPD process. The first impact of complexity is on the development time and cost, which are likely to increase (De Brentani, 2001; Germain, 1996). The speed of the process is then slowed due to the increasing number of tasks and resources required (Murmann, 1994). The communication and transferral of new ideas and the understanding of new technology may also increase the development time (Dougherty, 1992). The organization may also be affected by the degree of complexity of a product because the project may be misunderstood, creating cooperation and communication problems within the project and management teams. Moreover, excessive complexity could exacerbate the problem of unfamiliarity with the product (Veryzer, 1998b).

On the other hand, when the product is finally introduced in the market, its inherent complexity and highly specialized process technologies may prevent competitors from duplicating it, giving it a competitive advantage (Kim et al., 2003) and creating additional capabilities through a learning-by-doing process (Brown et al., 2003).

2.4.7 Approaches to radical projects: bricolage versus breakthrough

A radical project from an organization's perspective entails an exploration in an unfamiliar domain where the current resources and capabilities may not fit the project's requirements. Moreover, the organization may expect a long development time, a high degree of uncertainty and increased in the product's complexity. Having said that, the organization may adopt different *approaches* when undertaking complex and radical projects, which in turn may influence the development time, complexity and outcome of the innovation. After analyzing the wind turbine technology development process in the US and in Denmark, Garud and Karnoe (2003) found that a "*bricolage*" approach rather than a "*breakthrough*" one was more effective in completing complex technological projects.

The bricolage process connotes resourcefulness and adaptiveness among the actors involved in the development process (Baker & Nelson, 2005). It is also a "baby step" approach, a process of moving ahead on the basis of small feedback signals. In practice, practical experimentation coupled with thoughtful modifications allows the new system to emerge and gradually take shape.

On the contrary, the breakthrough approach "evokes an image of actors attempting to generate dramatic outcomes" (Garud et al., 2003: 279). Rather than adaptiveness, this approach favours the act of doing something radical or new through "leap-frog" advances. For example, actors in the US pursued an approach that attempted to generate breakthroughs in designing a high-tech, lightweight and high-speed turbine. Overconfidence on theoretical frames prevented these actors from truly understanding the complexities of wind turbines. Therefore, "they might have failed not despite but because of their pursuit of breakthrough" (296).

In contrast, the Danish actors took a bricolage path, scaling up from a heavyweight, low-speed, simplistic design to a well-functioning and sophisticated design, one of the most successful designs worldwide. With actors improvising and adapting, the emergent path was transformed to achieve higher functionalities (Brown & Eisenhardt, 1997; Garud et al., 2003).

In situations characterized by complex projects, the bricolage approach, through co-shaping and interactions among actors, seems to be particularly valuable. Moreover, another difference in the two approaches is in the perception of the market. The breakthrough approach emphasizes the revolutionary characteristic of the innovation, which is believed to be a blockbuster ready to diffuse rapidly in the uniform mass market. On the contrary, bricolage approach takes into account the fragmentation of markets or niches, in which everything has to be customized for a small group of consumers (Baker et al., 2005). Through the development of a series of innovations ready to be tested in niches, the bricolage approach emphasizes the adaptive character of the innovation (see box 2.2).

It is important to clarify that the bricolage concept should not be confused with the incremental approach. The reason is that the extent to which the organization faces exploration in an unfamiliar domain with a scarcity of resources means that the project in question is radical. Otherwise, if these characteristics do not apply to the actual situation facing the organization, the project is likely to be incremental. On the contrary, the bricolage or breakthrough approaches manifest themselves in radical projects.

Furthermore, it is important to stress that Garud's definition of bricolage is different from what bricolage originally meant. The evolution of the bricolage concept requires an attentive elucidation. Traditionally, anthropologists such as Levi-Strauss (1966) defined bricolage as the process of manufacture using current resources, creating new forms from readily available tools and materials (Baker, Miner, & Eesley, 2003). For example, one may decide to build necklaces with only materials left on the seashore. From this perspective, the bricolage approach would create only incremental, "just good enough" products rather than superior ones.

Recently, scholars see bricolage as a process that denotes a sequence of innovations, trial-and-error experimentation, fast development with resources at hand (Baker et al., 2005; Garud & Karnoe, 2001). From this perspective, the bricolage approach may create superior, radical products through incremental steps. The bricolage concept can be illustrated by this quote from a 3M director: "our approach is to make little, sell little, make a little bit more ... big ends from small beginnings..." (Peters & Waterman, 1982: 231).

These two approaches may have a moderate effect on the management support and team coordination. A breakthrough approach may even increase the likelihood of management supporting a failing project. Moreover, it may strengthen the escalation of commitments within the project team. On the contrary, a bricolage approach may achieve the reverse effect.

Box 2.2 Bricolage versus breakthrough approaches: an example

It may also be helpful, in this case, to give examples to better understand the difference between the bricolage and breakthrough approaches: the Velotaxi GmbH adopting the former and the Cree company the latter.

The successful entrepreneurial German firm Velotaxi GmbH, for example, is a bicycle taxi and advertising company based in Berlin. The firm developed an electric and human-powered tricycle to fulfill two main functions: a bicycle taxi and advertisement platform. As a fuel-free taxi, the Velotaxi represents an alternative to petrol cars (private or taxi cab) and public transport for citizens and tourists in the city centre of Berlin. As an advertisement platform, the external cabin was designed to host advertisement stickers. The main income of the company comes from the advertising: clients use the vehicle surface for promotion purposes.

Although the Velotaxi founder, an ex-manager of Daimler Chrysler, wanted a unique vehicle for his business model, he possessed limited skills and resources. He adopted a bricolage approach: he started the taxi-advertising service with redesigned Asian rickshaws, and, only after convincing venture capitalists, clients and the local authorities of the feasibility of the idea, was he able to find resources to build the new model. Furthermore, the Velotaxi company, with the help of the Berlin municipality, was able to convince the German authorities to change street regulations to recognize the legal status of Velotaxi-like vehicles as bicycles.

After four years of learning and business experience, Velotaxi GmbH was able to introduce the first version of the fancy tricycle. Other improved versions have been developed as well as customized for different countries. To date, the Velotaxi is the market leader in taxi-advertising services in an urban area (Berchicci & Brezet, 2003) in more than 40 cities around the world, demonstrating the validity of the concept.

The SAM is a three-wheel electric vehicle developed by Cree, a Swiss start-up firm. The vision behind the SAM was clear: to create an environmentally friendly compact vehicle that is electrically propelled. However, this was not new: it was the same vision shared within the Swatch-Mobile consortium (which resulted in the Smart car) in which the Cree founders were among the designers. After Daimler Chrysler departed from the original vision, they left in 1995.

Cree adopted a breakthrough approach: they were looking for the superior solution with few compromises to the original vision. The project was pure R&D, with no lead user and few partners involved. The search for technical superiority resulted in a new thermoplastic body with no need for paint (patented) and a new electric propulsion system with electronic control. After five years, in 2000, the first market test was done with 100 vehicles, part of the pre-industrial series. However, in 2002, the production had not yet begun, and the investments were exhausted.

2.4.8 Innovation processes and the degree of newness: summary

From this review of the degree of innovativeness some preliminary conclusions can be drawn. Incremental innovation processes entail harnessing existing organizational capabilities and resources to develop new concepts in a familiar environmental domain. The currently available skills and resources fit the innovative project. The degree of uncertainty is low, as is the complexity of the project. Planned activities may even progress as scheduled, keeping the development time under control. On the contrary, radical projects entail a higher degree of uncertainty and complexity during the process, requiring different capabilities and greater resources, with a direct effect on the development time. The effectiveness of the product might be unclear, especially when addressing new markets with untested technology. Despite the uncertainty, the organization may pursue different approaches to undertaking radical projects. The breakthrough approach, entailing very ambitious desired outcomes, may even enhance the product complexity, increase the resources needed, the development time and the escalation of commitment with uncertain outcomes. On the contrary, the bricolage approach entails adaptiveness and experimental, learning-by-doing activities, resulting in a sequence of innovations (Baker et al., 2005). The development time-cycle is shorter and the level of communication among the team is greater than with the breakthrough approach, resulting in the product being more effective.

2.5 Conclusion

This chapter discusses and defines the essence of product innovation from an organizational perspective, identifies factors influencing product performance, distinguishes radical from incremental innovation processes. To answer the sub-question pertaining to this chapter, formulated as "what does the existing theory indicate or predict concerning conditions for successful radical and incremental NPD?", three directions were taken.

First, definitions of innovation have been reviewed. Innovation as an outcome was defined as an invention put into use, while innovation as a process was defined as a learning process through uncertainty reduction.

Second, determinants of new product success and failure were reviewed. Given the multidimensional nature of success and the great number of factors influencing product innovation performance, management support and project team commitment have been selected as key constructs among the determinants because they entail crucial decisions for design specifications and consequently for product performance. Therefore, project team commitment and coordination and management support play a crucial role in the success of an NPD project. However, the novelty of the project may influence both the management support and the project commitment and coordination, and the conditions under which product attributes are understood, identified and selected.

Consequently, a third research direction has examined the dichotomy between radical and incremental innovation. Based on organizational theories, in this research study undertaking a radical innovation process involves organizations coping with a new and unfamiliar domain, where different technical and business skills are required. On the contrary, undertaking an incremental innovation process involves the organization operating in a familiar domain, exploiting internal resources and relying on existing technology and market competencies.

A radical undertaking has direct consequences on management support and team commitment and in general on decisions being taken during NPD projects. When the project is perceived as radical for the organization, besides performance judgments, escalation of commitment and psychic income may be important factors influencing the management advocacy. Two different approaches to the radical undertaking may influence the outcome: the breakthrough versus the bricolage. It seems that, by adopting a bricolage approach, the uncertainty of a radical undertaking may be reduced more effectively than with a breakthrough approach.

In the next chapter, the relationship between the innovation process and the organizational setting is described. In particular, decisions at management and project level are going to be examined in different organizational settings: established organizations, new organizations and networks of organizations. The comparison of these highlights the nuances, advantages and disadvantages of each organizational setting in pursuing innovation.

3 Organizing for innovation
How do firms innovate?

In the management of creativity, size is your enemy.
(Peter Chernin, President of News Corporation and Fox Entertainment Group,
The Economist, December 2, 1999)

In the end, size is not the only issue. In the future, the boundaries of a firm could become less important [for innovation].
(*The Economist*, July 19, 2001)

3.1 Introduction

This section aims to identify the extent to which the organizational setting influences the process of innovation.

The question of how the organizational setting relates to the ability and propensity to innovate has been widely examined by a large body of empirical literature[20] inspired by two contrasting statements of Schumpeter (1934, 1942). The first one states that entrepreneurship is a mechanism to create changes in the system through innovation and that entrepreneurs are the agents of creative destruction (Schumpeter, 1934). The second one states that large firms will be (more than) proportionately more innovative than small firms (Schumpeter, 1942). The existence of such a large literature does not seem to guarantee a clear interpretation of the findings due to the difficulties of measuring innovative activity (Cohen, 1995).

Previous research has extensively examined the relationship between the organizational setting and innovation along two dimensions: age and size. For example, firm age is perceived as an indication of external legitimacy, of staying power, or of the pervasiveness of internal routines (e.g. Stinchcombe, 1965). Firm size has often been associated with the extent of the firm's resources, with the existence of internal procedures such as formalization, controls or decision-making processes, with market presence and related network effects, and with competitive strength (e.g. Aldrich & Auster, 1986). The age and size of an organization, because of their relevance to both external relationships and internal arrangements, have direct implications for the process of innovation. The age and size of an organization are often treated as overlapping dimensions.

Young organizations are usually *small*, although the contrary is not always true. While *established* organizations are not *large* by definition, the opposite can still be valid. For the purpose of this research study, a positive relationship is assumed between age and size. This research study focuses on examining the extent to which the organizational setting influences the process of innovation by studying two discrete types of organization: start-up/small and established/large organization. For simplicity, a clear distinction is made between established organizations and young or new entrants, although there is a continuum defined by organizational age and size. Furthermore, a third form of organization is introduced: the interorganizational network. The interorganizational network setting is considered to be increasingly important for ENPD and NPD research.

The relevant literature for established organizations is reviewed first, followed by that for start-up organizations and the literature concerning interorganizational networks in the process of innovation is reviewed last.

3.2 Established organizations

How do established organizations innovate?

Innovation at the organizational level is governed by a set of organizational routines and search strategies (Hannan & Freeman, 1984). Organizational routines are repositories of organizational knowledge and, through the combination of these routines, organizations generate outcomes (Sorensen & Stuart, 2000). The potential of established organizations to perform well in the generation of innovations reflects a combination of their ability to refine and coordinate their organizational routines, here referred to organizational competences,[21] and the extent to which these routines are suited to the state of the external environment (Sorensen et al., 2000). The development of new products is one essential strategy helping firms to enjoy sustainable performance. Established organizations generate innovation by exploiting current or creating new knowledge.

3.2.1 Exploiting existing knowledge

Established organizations are well equipped to exploit current knowledge because they have already built technological and market capabilities. Technological capabilities refer to a system comprising 1) technical abilities in the form of people's skills; 2) managerial systems, supporting and reinforcing the growth of knowledge; and 3) values that serve to encourage or discourage the accumulation of different kinds of knowledge (Leonard-Barton, 1995). Market capabilities refer to how well established organizations know their current customers and possess market power, giving customers preferential access to distribution channels and sustaining market presence (Chandy & Tellis, 2000). Thus by exploiting existing knowledge, established organizations build up experience in production, in workforce, in stronger relationships with the vendors and customers (Hannan et al., 1984). Besides external communication, internal communication is crucial for the exploitation of knowledge. Communication patterns within the organization allow established organizations to use existing knowledge for further innovation (Cohen & Levinthal, 1990). Thus established organizations have perfected the routines, structures, incentive programs and other infrastructure needed to develop new products and bring them to market.

3.2.2 Exploring new knowledge

To create new knowledge, established organizations are able to allocate resources to a set of specific activities of research and experimental development aimed at the generation of innovation. These specific activities are under the umbrella of the R&D system. Rather than relying on individual intuition or chance, established organizations make every effort to pursue innovation systematically. It is assumed that R&D intensity positively impacts a firm's technological competence and the rate of new technologies it creates. For example, higher R&D investment increases the level of research activity within the organization and permits it to engage in basic research, which is essential for generating proprietary scientific information (Nelson, 1959), which results in specialized scientific/technological expertise (Rosenberg, 1990). The tangible outcome of basic research is the ability to develop several significant product technologies[22] (Hambrick and Macmillan, 1985). Then established organizations exploit patents and economies of scale in R&D (Porter, 1980). Moreover, the resources to undertake the process of innovation allow established organizations to tolerate an occasional unsuccessful R&D project (Damanpour, 1992).

3.2.3 Knowledge cycle

The cycle between the creation of new knowledge and the accumulation of existing knowledge within established organizations tends to be self-reinforcing (Cohen et al., 1990). Henderson (1993) argues that established organizations possess information-processing routines that facilitate incremental innovations along existing technological trajectories. Furthermore, the accumulation of knowledge enhances an organization's ability to recognize and assimilate new ideas as well as to convert this knowledge into further innovations.

The more established organizations have significant competitive strengths in terms of available internal resources, technological and market capabilities, managerial knowledge and ability to handle uncertainty in R&D, the better able they are to generate innovation through well-defined organizational routines. Furthermore, established organizations often enjoy external relationships and contacts, reputation, legitimacy and market positions, which further facilitate market transactions and new relationships (Damanpour, 1992).

3.2.4 Troubles in innovating

Although established firms may be successful in bringing innovations to the market, they may have trouble innovating and creating new knowledge (Abernathy & Utterback, 1978). The underlying rationales have been extensively studied from economic and organizational perspectives. Here three factors are described: perceived incentives, organizational rigidities and cognitive barriers.

1   *Perceived incentives.* An established organization with a large share in existing markets may have few incentives to develop products for a niche market (Ali, 1994). Such an organization's choice of product development is sensitive to the degree of uncertainty in the product of innovation. When innovation is highly uncertain, an established organization with a large market share is reluctant to invest (Ali, 1994). This is because such organizations receive profits for existing products based on current technology. When innovation is less uncertain, the opposite may be true. The established organization is willing to invest regardless of what resources are required, if the innovation is perceived to be a potential success (Ali, 1994) and if the new product addresses current customers (Chandy et al., 2000). Moreover, in the case of familiar markets, new products may represent a threat of *cannibalization* with the current business model. This threat may cause new projects to be managed suboptimally or even to be avoided because of inertia provided by mainstream operating units (McDermott et al., 2002).

2   *Organizational routines.* These allow established organizations to deal with the current product category because they enable the team to focus efficiently on current activities (Chandy et al., 2000). Organizational capabilities well suited to current challenges can easily turn into organizational rigidities when facing new challenges (Leonard-Barton, 1995). Organizational rigidities are the flipside of organizational capabilities or competences and are built on the same activities that create core capabilities. Moreover, as organizations age and grow larger, they are prone to inertia (Hannan et al., 1984), which may reduce their innovativeness (Chandy et al., 2000). Complex organizational structure, organizational formalizations and rigid communication channels may also lead to information loss (Arrow, 2000). Therefore, inertia, formalization of routines and internal processes, and institutionalization of the power structure may increase organizational rigidity and reduce the likelihood of adaptation and change for innovation.

3   *Cognitive barriers.* Established organizations are believed to be subject to "technological myopia" (Foster, 1986), which inhibits their ability to perceive the potential of newly emerging technologies and leads them to overestimate that of existing ones. This is because the organizational competences serve to direct managers' attention towards maximizing the utility of the current technology for current customers, filtering any

information not relevant for that purpose. This organizational filter (Chandy et al., 2000) may work between the external environment and the organization and also within organizational boundaries. Moreover, organizational routines and interpretative barriers strongly affect the development of a market understanding, which hinders the development of new products for new markets (Dougherty, 1990).

A combination of these factors leads us to consider the work of Christensen (1997), who argues that many things that established organizations do well, such as taking care of their current customers, can hinder the sort of innovative behavior needed to deal with disruptive technologies, which are simpler, cheaper and more convenient products that may seriously jeopardize the market position of established organizations (Christensen, 1997). For example, the invention of the personal computer can be seen as a disruptive innovation for IBM, which was once dominant in the computer market, because it put its very survival in danger (*The Economist*, 2004).

As a preliminary conclusion, established organizations have internal resources, legitimacy, competences and incentives to exploit existing knowledge and existing technology for existing customers and they do it in a very efficient way. Besides the accumulation of knowledge through systematic and formulated activities such as R&D, new knowledge is created that may lead to product technologies and patent exploitation. However, perceived incentives, cognitive processes as interpretative filters, organizational rigidities and inertia may hinder the understanding of new technologies, new markets and new ways of undertaking the process of innovation. Nevertheless, some established organizations are more successful than others at innovating.

3.2.5 Why are some established organizations more successful than others in the process of innovation?

Chandy and Tellis (2000) suggest two explanations: dynamic organizational climates and technological capabilities. Organizational climates refer to the extent to which some established organizations are able to overcome the bureaucratic inertia by creating small and autonomous organizational units. These units enable large organizations to respond to, and develop, technological innovation while maintaining resource advantages (Chandy et al., 2000). This decentralization also means creating competition among units. On the other hand, established organizations with strong technological capabilities are likely to be aware of scientific discoveries and nascent technologies. Moreover, thanks to their large resources, they are in position to undertake radical innovation.

Furthermore, successful established organizations adopt a common approach to overcoming interpretative barriers by creating cross-functional teams (e.g. encompassing functions such as marketing, R&D and manufacturing) together with less routine procedures and improved communication channels (Dougherty, 1992; Griffin, 1997a).

It seems that successful established organizations are successful because they have organizational climates, flexible structure and communication channels that are believed to resemble those of *small* firms (Chandy et al., 2000). *Why do organizations that mirror small and young firms seem to be more innovative than established organizations?*

In the next section the process of innovation in start-ups is discussed.

3.3 New organizations

The creation of new firms is an important mechanism through which entrepreneurs use technology to bring new products, processes and ways of organizing into existence (Schumpeter, 1934). The process through which individuals discover and exploit opportunities is defined here as entrepreneurship (Shane & Venkataraman, 2000). New organizations are born as a consequence of this process, which involves exploiting opportunities and converting them into products and services. The phenomenon of entrepreneurship has been examined by several social science disciplines and applied fields of business.

For the purpose of this research study, this section examines specific elements of the process of entrepreneurship that have influenced the process of innovation. Accordingly, the definition of what constitutes an entrepreneur and their decisions to exploit opportunities through a firm's creation are examined *in primis*. The underlying rationale is that the individual characteristics of the entrepreneur and the nature of the opportunities may influence the success of the start-ups and the outcome of the innovation process (Van de Ven, Hudson, & Schroeder, 1984). Second, crucial factors for developing and implementing the innovation are explored. Finally, this section discusses why some young firms are more successful than others in the process of innovation and surviving.

3.3.1 The entrepreneur and knowledge creation

Although entrepreneurship has been the subject of many studies, there is no common definition of who is an entrepreneur. One reason is that entrepreneurship has been studied from different perspectives, such as economics, sociological or psychological dimensions, emphasizing different attributes.

For example, Amit et al. (1995) take an economic/psychological approach, explaining that individuals become entrepreneurs because it is economically advantageous (lower opportunity cost). Such individuals represent a sort of nothing-to-lose person who gains less than their colleagues (Amit, Muller, & Cockburn, 1995). On the other hand, according to Carroll and Mosakowski's sociological perspective (1987), being an entrepreneur is a temporal characteristic – an individual's choice to be self-employed depends upon prior self-employment experience. In both approaches the definition of entrepreneur is related to the circumstances under which individuals become self-employed.

On the contrary, Stevenson, Roberts, and Grousbeck (1989), argue that it is flawed to define individuals as entrepreneurs by considering only their desire to become self-employed. Accordingly, they define entrepreneurs, on their own or inside organizations, as individuals who pursue opportunities regardless of the resources they currently control.

Rather than "what they are", Drucker (1985) defines entrepreneurs in relation to "what they do" and asserts that an important activity of entrepreneurs is the search for systemic innovation and the exploitation of opportunities (Drucker, 1985). Entrepreneurial actions involve creating new resources or combining existing resources in new ways to develop and to commercialize new products, to move into new markets and/or to service new customers (Hitt, Duane, Ireland, & Camp, 2001).

"How they do what they do" is also an important characteristic of entrepreneurs. According to van Mises (2000), the entrepreneur is someone who is able to predict or to judge future prices of products before and/or more correctly than other persons; then he/she buys at lower prices than he/she expects them to be in the future. The entrepreneur is an *alert agent* who is able to spot opportunities and inefficiencies in the market (Kirzner, 1997), based on his prior knowledge and information asymmetry (Shane, 2000). Rather than an alert agent, Schumpeter views the entrepreneur as a *creative destruction agent* who is able to destroy old paradigms and beliefs (Schumpeter, 1934), thus performing the function of innovation. Entrepreneurs are "outsiders" who create changes within the industry due to their ability to see possibilities unlike other existing players in the field (Larson, 2000). The non-entrepreneur defines everyone else who do not carry out new innovations. The entrepreneur can lose this characteristic, becoming a non-entrepreneur, when he/she ceases performing the function of innovation. Being an innovator, the entrepreneur changes the economy in some way or another, "enabling the liberal system to persist by going beyond its contradictions" (Schumpeter, 1934).

It seems that the distinction between the alert agent and the destruction agent may be related to the degree of innovativeness. The alert agent performs moderately new activities, spotting "holes" in the market. In contrast, the creative destructive agent performs new activities through profound changes in the system.

Summarizing, entrepreneurs are individuals who perform the function of innovation, discovering and recognizing opportunities, through information asymmetry and prior experience, and exploiting them. The decision to exploit the opportunities through firm creation is reviewed in the next section.

3.3.2 Exploiting opportunities through a new organization

Entrepreneurs may or may not create a new firm to exploit new opportunities. Accordingly, they can sell these opportunities or they can simply abandon them prior to exploitation (Roberts, 1991). Here the focus is on the exploitation of opportunities by new entrepreneurial firms. The pre-organizational period is vital in the organization's life because decisions about industry, location, market and product technology may be made during this time (Katz & Gartner, 1988).

Previous research has identified three categories of explanations for the exploitation of the opportunity through firm creation: *individual characteristics, nature of the opportunity* and *nature of the industry organization.*

The first explanation is that organization formation depends on the individual characteristics of an entrepreneur, such as career experience or psychological traits. The entrepreneur assumes that the expected value of the entrepreneurial profit will compensate the opportunity cost of other alternatives (Shane et al., 2000). Individuals who have experience in firm creation, creativity (Schumpeter, 1934), a risk-tolerant attitude (Khilstrom & Laffont, 1979), counterfactual thinking (Baron, 1998), optimism and a strong need for achievement (Roberts, 1991) tend to form new firms to exploit opportunities.

The second explanation is that firm creation depends on the nature of the opportunity. Here technological opportunities are emphasized – when opportunities are more uncertain (Casson, 1982), do not require complementary assets (Teece, 1996), destroy competence (Tushman & Anderson, 1986) and when the new technological discovery is radical, relevant for the sector and the appropriability information cannot be protected (Shane, 2001), entrepreneurship is more likely to take the form of a new organization.

The third explanation is based on industrial organization research, which shows that firm formation is likely to occur when the demand for new products is high (Schumpeter, 1934); when industry profits are high and the technology cycle is young (Utterback, 1994), with moderate competition (Freeman, Carroll, & Hannan, 1983), populated by firms that are not R&D intensive (Audretsch, 1995; Shane, 2001).

However, it is important to remember that these explanations might represent the chance to exploit opportunities but they do not guarantee the success of such exploitation. In the next section, the firm formation is illustrated.

3.3.3 Firm formation: organizing for the new venture

Previous research has studied firm formation, examining mainly entrepreneurial (e.g. Bruyat & Julien, 2001) and environmental[23] characteristics (e.g. Aldrich & Martinez, 2001). Here the focus is on functions and activities necessary for firm formation.

The *new firm formation* process is defined as "the process that takes place between the intention to start a business and making the first sale" (Gatewood, Shaver, & Gartner, 1995: 380). This process is initiated by a nascent entrepreneur, who is engaged in activities and actions in order to develop a business structure and operational procedures for the purposes of creating a new firm (Reynolds & White, 1997). The nascent entrepreneur by definition is an entrepreneur and an innovator. The creation of new ventures also entails the development of and management of the functions and skills necessary to exploit the innovation in the marketplace. In this formative stage there is a set of assumptions about market needs, product specifications, resource availability and production and organizational capabilities that needs to be tested in practice.

Since entrepreneurs rarely possess all the resources and capabilities required to seize an opportunity, the vital entrepreneurial task of assembling the resources is often a "trial-and-error" process because the exact resources needed are as yet unknown (Starr & Macmillan, 1990). Accordingly, informal, multifunctional, interpersonal and interorganizational relationships are seen as ways through which entrepreneurs gain access to a variety of resources held by external actors (Hoang & Antoncic, 2003). Moreover, innovation is a collective phenomenon (Freeman, 1991). The individual cannot develop and implement new products/service systems alone; links with external actors are needed to get the required resources or capabilities to exploit the innovation.

The network approach is useful here to define the context and the boundaries of the entrepreneurial activities. Through formal and informal linkages, the entrepreneur acquires the necessary *information, resources* and *legitimacy* in the firm-formation process (Elfring & Hulsink, 2003). A key benefit of networks for the entrepreneurial process is the access they provide to necessary *information* prior to and during the exploitation phase. The network of the start-up gives the entrepreneur access to relevant information about markets, ways to serve these markets and ways to deal with customers (Elfring et al., 2003) – for example, where to find experts in a needed area or new channels to acquire resources.

In the early phase firms must access, mobilize and deploy *resources* to exploit the opportunities that they have spotted. The network can provide the necessary resources (human, technical and financial) to entrepreneurs through formal and informal agreements so that the entrepreneurs do not have to own all of the resources needed to compete in the market. Young firms usually have neither the capital nor the cash position of better-established firms. Given the uncertainty, the resource constraints and the survival challenges, entrepreneurs often deploy the minimum assets needed to achieve the desired results and secure the resources to do this at minimum cost (Starr et al., 1990).

Entrepreneurs also seek *legitimacy* to reduce perceived risks by associating with or by gaining explicit certification from well-regarded individuals and organizations (Hoang et al., 2003). Aldrich and Fiol (1994) define two kinds of legitimacy: the cognitive and the socio-political legitimacy. The first refers to acceptance and understanding of the new concept and its intrinsic value by actors such as competitors, customers and universities. The second refers to the acceptance of a new venture by key stakeholders in terms of conforming to rules and standards through negotiations and marketing in a specific industry (Aldrich et al., 1994).

Summarizing, to exploit the opportunity, the new organization requires capabilities, resources, competences, expertise and legitimacy, which are sought by entrepreneurs through formal and informal structured networks.

3.3.4 Many are called but few are chosen: the trouble of surviving and innovating

Not all new ventures succeed in their efforts to acquire the required resources, market and technological capabilities and legitimacy to survive and grow. As

Aldrich and Martinez state, "In entrepreneurship, as in the biblical story, many are called but few are chosen ... a universal constant is that no matter how many entrepreneurs emerge, most do not succeed in creating lasting organizations" (Aldrich et al., 2001 p. 42). Stinchcombe (1965) argues that most of new firms have a high propensity to fail due to a *liability of newness*, which entails both internal and external obstacles that make survival difficult. Barriers to entry into a new domain are the major external obstacles for new firms including, among others: (1) product differentiation; (2) technological barriers; (3) licensing and regulatory barriers; (4) illegitimate acts of competitors; and (5) experiential barriers to entry (Aldrich et al., 1986). In addition to these, there are also *liabilities of smallness*, including (1) problems raising capital; (2) major disadvantages in competing for labor with larger organizations; and (3) limited abilities to obtain benefits from specializations and economies of scale (Van de Ven et al., 1999). Despite liabilities of newness and smallness, many new firms manage to overcome these barriers. The next section attempts to explore the factors that increase or decrease the likelihood of survival in the process of innovation.

3.3.5 Why are some young firms more successful than others in the process of innovation?

Previous research has attempted to answer this question. It is important to remember that, in the case of new firms, survival is directly linked to the ability to develop and introduce new products in the market. Success is usually referred to as the survival of the new firm able to incorporate technical, marketing and production expertise into the new product. Van de Ven et al. (1984) examined the start-up success and early development of 14 companies through day-long on-site interviews and questionnaires with people dealing directly with the new firms. By analyzing the data from different theoretical approaches, they found that entrepreneurial characteristics such as competence, confidence, prior experience, imagination and commitment are associated with successful start-ups. From an organizational perspective, (1) implementing a start-up on a small scale with incremental expansion; (2) having a single person in command; (3) active involvement of top management and board members in decision making; (4) strong internal and external communication channels; (5) a clear and brief business plan; and (6) a lower yearly rate of expenditure were all associated with successful start-ups (Van de Ven et al., 1984). Although the multi-perspective approach helps us understand the new firm performance, the limited number of samples and the use of retrospective historical data might only in part explain the success of new firms (Bacharach, 1989).

A more sophisticated approach has been adopted by Schoonhoven et al. (1990), in which historical data and longitudinal studies are combined to analyze 98 start-ups in the semiconductors industry. The research examined the speed with which new firms dispatch the first product for revenue. This factor is seen as a crucial performance criterion for new organizations because getting products in the market fast means gaining cash flow, legitimacy and market share sooner, increasing the likelihood of survival (Schoonhoven et al., 1990). Their conclusions are interesting for several reasons.

First, firms that were faster in shipping their first product did not explore new knowledge or synthesize existing knowledge in a new way, rather they created a relatively low level of new knowledge. Accordingly, the greater the extent of new knowledge created, the longer it takes for the first product to enter the market. This seems to suggest that entrepreneurs seeking a fast first product shipment should select less radical and less technically ambitious projects. Rather than developing technically *superior* solutions, technically *elegant* solutions should be preferred during the development process.

Second, the joint existence in the organizational structure of marketing and manufacturing positions decreased the time before the first product shipment. This demonstrates that these elements in the organizational structure constitute important functional expertise that seems to make a difference in outcomes for new organizations.

Third, the greater the monthly cash flow, the longer it took to ship the first product. That is, well-financed start-ups took longer to ship their first product than did new organizations with less money. So, firms that spent less were faster in introducing the first product in the market. This is an interesting finding because it challenges conventional wisdom, which considers that, the greater the external power of outside investors, like venture capitalists, the greater the pressure is on new organizations to generate revenues sooner (Pfeffer & Salancik, 1978).

Fourth, the findings point to an unexpected role for competition. Although previous research stated that competition decreases environmental munificence and impedes performance, such as product differentiation (Aldrich et al., 1986; Stinchcombe, 1965), Schoonhoven et al. (1990) found that a greater number of competitors has the effect of reducing the time before the first product shipment. This finding suggests that new firms tend to target existing markets, in which competition already exists, addressing a current need of customers. Another explanation suggested by the authors refers to the presence of competitive threats, which increases the impetus to speed the development and shipment time of the first product (Schoonhoven et al., 1990).

Taken together, these findings suggest that new firms that started their business as on a shoestring in a competitive environment, creating relatively new knowledge, were faster to ship their first product. These entrepreneurs, opportunistic in spotting opportunities and innovative when necessary, better evoke the image of the alert agent described by Kirzner (1997), and less the destructive agent illustrated by Schumpeter (1934) who achieves dramatic outcomes. Pursuing more technically ambitious and complex projects means longer development and shipment time, with higher expenditure and more risks for the survival of the new firms.

Does this mean that new firms pursuing less ambitious projects are more successful than new firms pursuing more radical ambitious projects? The answer is not clear because these findings directly conflict with many studies that, although not directly testing the factors influencing the survival of new technology firms, state that new technology firms are likely to survive if they exploit radical technologies that cannot be imitated in the founding period (Christensen et al., 1996; Tushman & O'Reilly, 1996; Utterback, 1994). However, it seems that the industry and technology characteristics might have a moderate effect on the firm's survival. For example, Nerkar and Shane (2003) found that the exploitation of radical technology as a way for a new firm to compete only works in fragmented industries. In concentrated industries, the exploitation of a radical technology fails to deliver an advantage to new firms.[24]

As a preliminary conclusion, it seems that new firms that pursue less technically ambitious projects, with limited money, that incorporate functional expertise and spot market opportunities in competitive environments, are likely to be faster in shipping the first product than other new firms. Therefore these new firms are likely to gain legitimacy, revenues and market share, thus increasing their chances of survival. On the other hand, new firms pursuing more radical projects need more time, money and functional expertise, factors which are crucial for their survival. In a fragmented industry their efforts are likely to be rewarded.

3.4 Interorganizational networks

Over the last decade, the innovation studies and the organizational and strategy management literature have increasingly focused their attention on networks, coalitions and other collaboration agreements (Doz , Olk, & Ring, 2000; Gulati, 1999; Afuah, 2000; Porter, 1996; Powell, 1990, etc.), to explore organization performance and the ability to innovate through relationships with other organizations.

Networks can be described as a number of organizations with different interests that depend upon one another for the achievement of their goals (see for example Bruijn & Heuvelhof, 2000). According to Powell (1990), a network is a form of coordinating social activities, defined as a third form of cooperation beyond market and organization. It suggests some kind of special organization form at an aggregate level above that of individual companies. Other authors have focused on a firm's strategic choice to become part of a network because the potential profit from cooperation exceeds individual strategies to maximize benefit (e.g. Ireland, Hitt, & Vaidyanath, 2002).

Using Teece's metaphor, (1996) no organization is an island, every organization needs vertical (supply-chain) and horizontal networks to develop and commercialize new technologies.

Here the focus is only on *the horizontal networks*, which entail interactions among two or more organizations linked by formal agreements to access or share resources. These organizational arrangements include joint ventures, equity partnerships, collaborative research pacts of large-scale research consortia, reciprocity deals and satellite organizations.

Organizations pursue cooperative agreements to improve their competitive position and performance by sharing resources (Ireland et al., 2002), increasing their market power, entering into new markets or enhancing their capabilities (Hagedoorn & Duysters, 2002). They also look for cooperative agreements to utilize sources of know-how located outside the boundaries of the firm and to share risks for activities that are beyond the scope or capability of a single organization (Powell, 1990). Examples are the collaborative agreements between small firms possessed of entrepreneurial commitment and expertise in technology innovation and large-scale corporate organizations with marketing and distribution power (Christensen, 1997). *Strategic technology alliances* are those modes of interfirm cooperation for which a combined innovative activity or an exchange of technology is at least part of the agreement (Hagedoorn & Duysters, 2002).

3.4.1 Characteristics of network formation

The definitions of a network are various and have been used for different kinds of relationships and for different purposes. As stated by Coombs et al. (1996), two main approaches deal with networks in the innovation process: the *sociological* and the *economic approach*.

The first approach encompasses a large number of interdisciplinary studies focusing on the interactions between actors within and between organizations. The emphasis is on the *informal network* between individuals, on the exchange of tacit knowledge, on the nature of the linkages and the process of their creation and development between individual actors, users, buyers, suppliers, regulatory authorities and potentially competing firms (Callon, Laredo, & Rabeharisoa, 1992; Coombs et al., 1996; Powell, 1990). Additionally, the establishment and maintenance of linkages are essential for the success of innovation. In this view, incomplete networks or weak linkages are associated with failure.

One of the main theories in this field is the social network theory, which tries to apply the sociological approach to strategic alliance formation. This approach suggests that a firm's strategic actions are affected by the social context in which the firm is embedded (Ahuja, 2000; Gulati, 1999; Harrisson & Laberge, 2002; Kale, Singh, & Perlmutter, 2000; Uzzi, 1997) and focuses on the network properties rather than on simply individual (dyadic) links within the network (Angel, 2002).

In this context, the kinds of ties among actors are emphasized. For example, Uzzi (1997), building on the work of Granovetter (1985), introduced the concept of embeddedness. This concept entails two kinds of ties: arm's-length (weak) and embedded (strong) ties (Uzzi, 1997). The first one refers to sporadic interactions and/or economic transactions, the second to established relationships between actors. Although arm's-length ties provide greater information flow than embedded ones, they increase the risk of opportunistic behavior. On the contrary, embedded ties generate trust, discourage opportunism and facilitate the creation of knowledge. Embeddedness, however, can also act as a constraint, such as one incurred by the unforeseeable exit of a core network player or, in cases of overembeddedness, when social aspects of exchange replace economic imperatives (Uzzi, 1997).

The economic approach focuses on the organization itself and the role of the business firm as a central institution through which the innovation is commercialized (Coombs et al., 1996). The *formal network* is therefore the main concern: formal collaborative agreement involving legal contracts between organizations. From the economic perspective, two different theoretical approaches are usually discussed.

The first, known as transaction cost economics theory (TCE) is concerned with the nature of the transaction and the cost incurred in managing the transaction. TCE arguments suggest that alliances are preferable and more efficient than market or hierarchy cooperation if they minimize the firm's costs in the transaction (Ireland et al., 2002). In other words, when transaction costs are high, firms will tend to carry out technology development activities inhouse, rather than partner with external firms (Teece, 1996).

The second approach is resource-based view (RBV) theory. RBV theory suggests that the establishment of alliances derives from the resource needs of the firm. Managing these resources can provide a competitive advantage over its rivals. Thus, firms form alliances to obtain access to needed assets (Hagedoorn & Schakenraad, 1994; Ireland et al., 2002; Porter, 1985; Powell, 1990; Teece, 1996), learn new skills (Baum, Calabrese, & Silverman, 2000), manage their dependence upon other firms (Pfeffer et al., 1978), or maintain parity with competitors (Garcia-Pont & Nohria, 2002).

The literature mentioned suggests two different ways to define networks, which nevertheless complement each other. They differ in their level of analysis: TCE theory views firms from an outside-in perspective and tend to explain and predict transactions among firms. On the contrary, RBV theory views firms from an inside-out perspective and focuses on firms' resources allocation and acquisition. Some important concepts emerge for the innovation process, such as weak/strong ties. On the one hand, to gain new information and new resources, the organization needs to have a great number of heterogeneous, weak ties. The organization will essentially benefit from such sparse networks to the extent that the organization is seeking to pursue exploration of new knowledge or radical innovations (Burt, 2000; Elfring et al., 2003). On the other hand, commitments, trust and experience, being expressions of dense networks with strong ties, may facilitate the innovation process in exploiting existing knowledge and pursuing incremental innovation (Burt, 2000; Elfring et al., 2003).

3.4.2 The process of network formation

Doz et al. (2000) suggest that the formation process of R&D networks may be dominated by three kinds of initial conditions. First, changes in the organization's environment. These changes may involve: 1) new governmental regulations; 2) rapid changes in the market; 3) new entrants into existing markets; 4) foreign competition (R&D in industry collaboration). Second, the presence and identification of common interests among potential members may increase the likelihood of forming collaborative agreements: 1) pre-existing relationships; 2) common industry origin; and 3) similar organizational characteristics. Third, the intervention of a triggering entity may also encourage the formation of networks. This role is played by, for example, government agencies, individuals acting as champions or specific firms.

Pressure from the environment or the presence of a triggering entity create two kinds of process formation. Doz et al. (2000) call these the emergent and engineering processes, respectively. In the first, collaboration is driven by responses to common threats or a perceived need to gain access to similar resources. Accordingly, members with similar interests can generate consensus on the domain of their R&D consortium, leading to a strong expectation of continuity. On the contrary, the engineering process is started by triggering entities in the case of dissimilar interests and low interdependence. A "hub-and-spoke" approach to member solicitation will be employed in the initial stages. The triggering entity is likely to be an individual with strong personal connections.

Risks and challenges in developing effective alliances

Although popular, alliances often fail (Van de Ven et al., 1999). Factors such as goal divergence, partner opportunism, improper partner selection, and cultural differences may contribute to alliance failure (Doz, 1996; Kale et al., 2000). Research shows that different expectations can lead to either major changes or dissolutions that are unplanned by one or more partners (e.g. Das & Teng, 2001). Moreover, selecting partners with different or conflicting expectations may lead to opportunistic behavior or to alliance failure (Kale et al., 2000). For example, opportunistic behavior may take the form of a learning race, that is, when a firm's primary motive is to quickly learn (acquire) a partner's skills and then underinvest in the alliance after achieving its learning objectives (Alvarez & Barney, 2001).

Thus in all kinds of collaborative agreements there are risks that can lead to subsequent instabilities. According to Das and Teng (2001), there are at least two types of alliance risks – relational and performance risks. Relational risk is concerned with the probability, and consequent actions, of a partner who does not appropriately commit to an alliance and fails to behave as expected. Performance risk refers to factors that may impede achieving alliance objectives. For example, in interfirm modularity projects, in which the component products of different firms work together to create a system, firms were frustrated at their lack of control over the definition of their own products (Staudenmayer, Tripsas, & Tucci, 2005). Thus, performance risk is common to all strategic decisions, while relational risk is idiosyncratic to individual strategic alliances (Ireland et al., 2002). Ensuring cooperation, avoiding competition and developing trust between partners are the major challenges in building alliances.

3.5 How does the organizational setting influence the process of innovation?

Conventional wisdom suggests that young and small firms have a greater advantage in innovation (e.g. Ács & Audretsch, 1990). In general those firms possess capabilities such as niche-filling and flexibility, seeking out protected market niches that are too small to engage larger organizations (e.g. Chen & Hambrick, 1995). Moreover, these organizations are also seen as being quicker than established organizations due to structural simplicity, streamlined operations, lack of structural inertia, faster decision-making processes and targeted innovation (e.g. Dean, Brown, & Bamford, 1998). The result is a quicker response to the dynamics of industry environments.

These arguments seem to be supported by many recent studies, which tend to find that small firms have introduced a proportion of innovations larger than their share of employment. This finding has frequently been interpreted as showing that small firms are more innovative than large firms, or more efficient innovators, achieving greater outputs per unit of R&D input (Ács & Audretsch, 1991; Cohen, 1995).

In contrast, there are arguments in favor of established organizations in relation to innovation. The advantages of established organizations, as we previously discussed, include their market power over customers and suppliers, the exploitation of patents and scale economies in R&D, accumulation of technological knowledge and capabilities, competitive strengths in terms of available resources, managerial knowledge and ability to handle uncertainty (e.g. Aldrich et al., 1986; Cohen, 1995). Furthermore, established organizations often have external relationships, contacts and reputations that expose them to new competitive tools and technologies. For example, after a historical analysis of a relatively large number of radical innovations, Chandy and Tellis (2000) found that the established and large organizations introduced a majority of the radical product innovations in the last 50 years.

Just as small and established organizations differ in the advantages they have, they also differ in their weaknesses. While start-ups may be more innovative, they frequently have trouble bringing innovations to the market in a successful way. On the contrary, while established organizations have more trouble innovating, they enjoy greater success bringing innovations to the market (Abernathy et al., 1978). The established organizations are believed to be constrained by organizational rigidities, structural inertia, technological myopia and poor incentives to pursue radical innovations. On the contrary, young and small firms, due to liabilities of newness and smallness, are subject to lack of market recognition, weak financial positions and lack of internal structure. They will be more likely to succeed when entering industry environments in which speed, flexibility and niche identification are rewarded or when pursuing radical innovation in a fragmented industry.

It seems that an answer to the question of this section is unlikely to be exhaustive, because, as Aldrich and Auster said, "the obstacles faced by new,

Table 3.1 Liabilities and advantages of different organizational settings in the process of innovation

	Advantages	Disadvantages	Solutions
Established organizations	Organizational routines Technological and market capabilities Market power and position Available internal resources R&D investment Managerial knowledge Reputation/legitimacy	Few perceived incentives Organizational rigidities Inertia Rigid formalization Cognitive barriers Technological myopia Organizational filters Interpretative schemes	Organizational climates Flexible structure Cross-functional team Technological capabilities
New firms	Flexibility Adaptation Spot inefficiency in market Niche filling Creative destruction agent External network Information asymmetry	Liability of newness and smallness Product differentiation Technological barriers Experiential barriers Over-optimism Few resources Legitimacy	Less technically ambitious projects Business on shoestring Functional expertise More radical projects likely to be rewarded in fragmented industry
Collaborative network	Flexibility New information Interdisciplinary/functional Integration Resource Legitimacy	Liabilities of double parenting and conflict New knowledge synthesized Antitrust Sovereign conflict Intellectual property conflict Losses of autonomy and control High rate of failure	Trust-building relationship Ensuring cooperation

small organizations can be easily overcome by the established and large one, whereas the constraints faced by larger and more established organizations can often be easily overcome by new and small ones" (1986: 168). Moreover, industry characteristics, technology appropriability and organizational capabilities have a moderate effect on the relationship between the organization size/age and its ability to innovate (see Table 3.1).

The network of various organizations, representing an intermediate form of organization to that of new, small and established organizations, may provide a more conducive environment for product innovation or new business creation (Van de Ven et al., 1999). In theory, it can overcome the liabilities of newness, smallness, bigness and aging. However, we saw in practice that the problems in managing joint ventures largely stem from having more than one parent organization. Thus the problems of communication and conflicts found in large organizations are likely to increase in networks. Moreover, sovereign conflict, antitrust, intellectual property and appropriability conflicts and losses of autonomy and control are liabilities of "double parenting and conflict" (Van de Ven et al., 1999).

Also, decision-making processes have dissimilar characteristics in different organizational settings. In start-ups, decisions are made by one or a few individuals (with similar values and interests) aiming for specific established objectives. Decisions are usually fast and responsibilities for outcomes are clear. On the other hand, a group decision-making process (likely to take place in larger organizations) is usually slower, but it brings specialists and experts together, whose interactions result in better decisions. However, different interpretation schemes, motivations and interests may hinder the decision process. This phenomenon is particularly emphasized within interorganizational networks.

Table 3.2 Advantages and disadvantages of different organizational settings in decision-making processes

	Advantages	*Disadvantages*
Established organizations	Interaction of different expertise has benefits in identifying, evaluating and choosing alternatives Greater knowledge available to the group	Slow process Interpretative barriers Different individual values
New firms	Fast decision process Clear responsibility for implementing	Limited knowledge for nonprogrammed decisions Individual values and motivations as guidelines
Collaborative network	Greater knowledge and competences within the group	Different motivations, vested interests Organizational and individual objectives inconsistent with the network's objectives

Despite the ability of heterogeneous actors to better identify and evaluate alternatives, different individual and organizational values, vested interests and different motives may create problems for choosing among alternatives. Moreover, one actor's objective may be different from another's objectives which could create tensions and conflicts in the very identification of the problem (see Table 3.2).

However, many of the supposed liabilities of the new companies may not be totally accurate as Schoonhoven et al.'s (1990) findings, previously discussed, suggest. New and small firms are able to develop and implement relatively new products without large resources in a competitive market. Further, functional expertise, fast decision making, flexibility and allocating resources through external networks increase the likelihood of developing and implementing moderately new products. Moreover, the degree of innovativeness of the project is likely to be more radical for the outside world than for the innovate team in the new firms – prior experience seems to play a crucial role in recognizing and exploiting the opportunities (Shane, 2000; Van de Ven et al., 1984). So here it is assumed that new and small firms have greater advantages in the process of innovation than established organizations.

4 Environmental product innovation

Some things in nature are irreplaceable – literally priceless. Even so, it is essential to consider tradeoffs when analyzing almost all green problems.

(The Economist, April 25, 2005)

4.1 Introduction

In the last decades, an enormous amount of knowledge has been created on the impact of human activities on the natural environment in the environmental field. This concern has been translated into new policies, new research programs, tools and methodologies to decrease the environmental burden of firms' activities. This chapter reviews the literature on the relationship between the natural environment and the organization, encompassing different units of analysis from the organizational level to the product level. The purpose of the review is threefold. First, it highlights how scholars have made use of existing theoretical frameworks, which may explain and predict the phenomenon under study. Second, it emphasizes the complexity of EPD and ENPD. Third, it shows how environmental ambition has evolved from optimizing production processes to radically changing products and services. Section 4.2 gives an overview on how the relationship between the organization and the natural environment has been addressed, highlighting the theoretical background. Section 4.3 focuses on EPD, illustrating the status quo in research and in practice and the future challenges especially for ENPD.

4.2 The greening of business

During the last decades environmental issues have become crucial for industries, corporations, government policies and various stakeholders. After the disasters in the 1960s and 1970s, such as industrial pollution and oil spill, public concern and government authorities realized that industrial processes could have negative effects on human health and on the natural environment. Driven by regulatory and societal pressures, industry became "greener", adopting new technologies and managerial systems to monitor, control and reduce the environmental impacts of industrial activities. At the beginning of the 1990s some firms within industry moved beyond just complying with the legislation to actually exceeding regulatory emissions requirements (Roome, 1992). Currently, environmental issues have been integrated into firms' activities and the greening of business seems to have achieved unexpected levels.

Scholars have investigated the role of corporations in society, arguing that, rather than the conventional technocentric paradigm, an alternative "ecocentric" paradigm should be proposed (Starik & Rands, 1995). This paradigm advocates an ecologically centered conception of interorganizational relations and internal management activities (Shrivastava, 1995a). Others argue that a synthesis of the two opposite paradigms is preferable, where the two paradigms are integrated (Gladwin, Kennelly, & Krause, 1995; Shrivastava, 1995a). Numerous studies have addressed the relationship between the organization and the natural environment at different levels of analysis (e.g. Starik et al., 1995) and investigated the greening of business through the lenses of existing theories.

4.2.1 At the industry level

Scholars at the industry level have investigated how and to what extent existing industries are embracing environmentally responsible conduct, often referring to "self-regulation" (Berchicci & King, 2007; Ostrom, 1990; Russo, 2003; Starik et al., 1995). One recurrent example is the chemical industry, whose leading firms have decided on a set of rules under the name of the "Responsible Care Program". Nevertheless, it has been shown that non-members improved their environmental performance more quickly than did the program's members (King & Lenox, 2000). Besides existing industries, new industries are getting in line with environmental and social issues. Russo (2003) defines *sustainable industry* as a collection of organizations with a commitment to economic and environmental goals, whose members can exist and flourish, permitting other entities to do the same (Starik et al., 1995). An example of a sustainable industry is the fast-growing wind energy industry, where institutional environment, geographic concentration and natural capital have positively influenced the growth of the sustainable industry (Russo, 2003).

4.2.2 At the organizational level

Most of the studies have addressed environmental issues at the organizational level in relation to the strategic management and capabilities of the firm. Some studies argue that, by going green, corporations may reduce costs through ecological efficiencies, capturing emerging markets, gaining first-mover advantage and improving the corporation's image (Hart, 1995, 1997; King & Lenox, 2001, 2002; Porter et al., 1995; Roome, 1992; Shrivastava, 1995c). These studies are often defined as the "pays to be green" literature.[25] Others dispute the "win-win" logic of being green and competitive, affirming that the economic and environmental goals are distinctive and the actions needed to achieve them are not the same (e.g. Walley & Whitehead, 1994). Moreover, many firms still frame environmental issues as a one-dimensional nuisance, involving regulations, increased costs and liabilities (Hart & Milstein, 2003). Rather than being mutually exclusive, some scholars affirm that the economic and environmental performances seem to be positively correlated (Gilley, Worrell, Davidson, & El-Jelly, 2000; Klassen & McLaughlin, 1996; Russo & Fouts, 1997). Others argue that there is a non-significant (McWilliams & Siegel, 2000) or mixed (Hillman & Keim, 2001), or even negative (Wright & Ferris, 1997) relationship (for a review see Margolis & Walsh, 2003).

Furthermore, some scholars suggest that environmental practices are similar to other managerial practices. For example, Christmann (2000) proposes that firms should not blindly follow recommendations on environmental management and expect to be green and competitive but that they should select environmental practices that fit with their existing resources and capabilities. Accordingly, Andersson and Bateman (2000) emphasize that, within the firm, treating the environment like any other business issue, may engender successful environmental champions. Similarly, Reinhardt (2000) suggests the framing of environmental issues as a business problem, taking into account the type of industry, sector and market in which firms are operating.

These scholars have been analyzing environmental issues in the organizational setting – integrating, combining and improving existing theoretical frameworks and models. Many authors adopt the resource-based view of the firm approach (e.g. Aragon-Correa & Sharma, 2003; Christmann, 2000; Hart, 1995; Russo et al., 1997; Sharma & Vredenburg, 1998; Shrivastava, 1995c) because it provides a theory to explain the competitive advantage as an outcome of the development of organizational capabilities associated with a proactive environmental strategy (Aragon-Correa et al., 2003; Hart, 1995; Sharma et al., 1998) and to link the proactive environmental strategies to environmental performance (Russo et al., 1997; Sharma et al., 1998).

4.2.3 Why become greener?

Other studies have investigated in depth the question was to why firms respond to ecological issues. Scholars have identified three main driving forces of corporate responsiveness to environmental issues, two institutional forces and one economic rationale (e.g. Bansal et al., 2000). First, the role of legislation in stimulating firms' environmental responsiveness has been largely recognized. Firms seek to comply with legislation to avoid penalties, fines, legal costs and market and social pressures (Cordano & Frieze, 2000). Proactive behavior and earlier adoption of environment-related activities take place in firms to anticipate regulatory allegations and keep competitive (Aragon-Correa, 1998). However, in the absence of explicit sanctions, firms may respond more slowly to environment-related activities and undermine environmental performances (King et al., 2000).

The second driver is social pressure. Customers, local communities and environmental interest groups encourage firms to take their environmental impacts into account (Bansal et al., 2000; Starik et al., 1995). The Shell–Brent Spar accident and Nike child-labor issues are well-known inductive examples that have persuaded firms to respond. These two institutional forces increase legitimation and appropriateness of their actions within an established set of regulations, norms and values or beliefs (Bansal et al., 2000; Starik et al., 1995; Suchman, 1995).

The third driver is economic. By adopting eco-efficient practices, firms may reduce operating costs by reducing waste, conserving energy, reusing materials and focusing on life-cycle costs (Porter et al., 1995; Shrivastava, 1995c). Besides cost reduction, environmental response is considered a source of competitive advantage (Bansal et al., 2000; King et al., 2002a), by addressing green consumers, preempting competition, building a corporate reputation and creating value for the firms (Hart, 1995; Russo et al., 1997).

Besides the RBV approach, authors have adopted the institutional approach[26] to explain how organizations become more aligned with the institutional environment due to coercive, mimic and normative pressure (Bansal et al., 2000; King et al., 2000; Oliver, 1991; Starik et al., 2000; Suchman, 1995). Other authors have investigated individual decisions to embrace environmental issues by adopting theories of planned behavior (Cordano et al., 2000; Flannery et al., 2000).

4.2.4 At the micro-level: a firm's product development activities

Another stream of research has focused on the micro-level, specifically on the firm's product development activities where the integration of environmental issues into products and services is the main concern (e.g. Baumann et al., 2002; Brezet et al., 1997; Charter et al., 2001; Chen, 2001; Graedel et al., 1995; Handfield, Melnyk, Calantone, & Curkovic, 2001; Hart, 1995; Lenox et al., 1997; Lenox, Jordan, & Ehrenfeld, 1996; Pujari et al., 2003; Shrivastava, 1995b; Shrivastava, 1995c). Green product development, which intends to decrease the environmental burden through product design and innovation, is emerging as an innovative systematic means to deal with environmental problems (Chen, 2001). The next section reviews and discusses the literature and emergent topics in this field.

4.3 The environmental issues involved in products and services

Products affect the natural environment during their life cycle, from the extraction and production phase to the disposal phase and during usage. Product designers are the interface between the "user" and the "product", and they have a crucial role in integrating environmental requirements into the product design (Charter et al., 2001). Driven by ecological concerns such as increasing waste and the depletion of natural resources, product designers and practitioners have developed a new design philosophy called *ecodesign* or "Design for the

Environment" (DfE).[27] DfE is defined as a systematic process or approach by which environmental considerations are integrated into products in order to design environmentally conscious products (Graedel et al., 1995). Environmental requirements in the design process encompass several aspects of the product life cycle, like minimizing raw materials, choosing materials with a lower environmental impact, reducing energy consumption and increasing recycling opportunities.

Within the ecodesign literature evolutions in the terminology and in the scope of research have occurred. Over the last years, the terminology has evolved from green design, eco-redesign and ecodesign, to sustainable product design, environmental product innovation and product service system (PSS). If ecodesign or DfE is concerned about the environmental issues in product design, sustainable product design integrates social and ethical aspects of the product's life cycle alongside environmental and economical considerations (Charter et al., 2001). On the contrary, environmental innovation encompasses new technologies, new products and services, while PSS focuses on functions rather than products.

Accordingly, the research in the environmental arena has widened its scope. The approach for addressing environmental issues has been extended from the optimization of existing products to the creation and development of new technologies, radical products and services.

This change in scope has important implications. Several scholars, practitioners and managers have realized that the concern for the natural environment was not only the reason to optimize existing products and processes, but also the driving force for creating new business opportunities through new products and services. As a consequence, environmental ambition has been translated into the intention to develop new products and services, and to search for new ways of fulfilling product functions.

This shift in environmental ambition can be explained using an example. A famous saying often heard at conferences in the environmental field is "why redesign a chair when you can design the whole office?" The redesign of the chair entails an optimization of the product, while the design of the whole office leaves room for creativity and innovation, where changes may occur encompassing different aspects of the office system and their specific functions. It is assumed that the larger the changes in the system (e.g. the office), the greater the benefits for the natural environment (Hart et al., 2003; Weterings et al., 1992).

This assumption originates from "factor" thinking. According to the Brundtland report (Brundtland, 1987), in which the term "sustainable development" was coined, to give next generations the same opportunities as our generation has today, present consumption needs to be reduced by a factor of 10 or 20 in the next 50 years. This factor is based on the doubling of the world population, combined with a fivefold increase in wealth per capita while halving the total global environmental burden. Factor-thinking has gained legitimacy in the environmental arena. To achieve a reduction of the environmental burden, a classification of different innovations was proposed. Such a classification

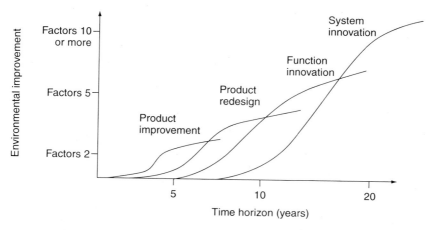

Figure 4.1 Levels of environmental innovation (based on Brezet & Rocha, 2001; RAND, 1997; Weterings & Opschoor, 1992).

system, as displayed in Figure 4.1, enables opportunities for environmental and economical profits, yet requires larger and more fundamental changes.

Product improvement involves product optimization while *product redesign* entails process improvements and replacements of product components. *Function innovation* entails new products and services and changes in the way existing products function; PSS is part of this type of innovation. The shift from physical products to dematerialized services is an example of function innovation. *System innovation*[28] requires technology development, but also implies changes to the social (adoption by consumers) and structural environment (infrastructure development) (e.g. Ashford, 2000). Major changes usually take more time than minor changes.

For ease of communication, in this research study DfE, ecodesign and sustainable product development (SPD) processes represent the broad umbrella of EPD regarding product improvement and product redesign. ENPD denotes a more recent evolution in the literature, including environmental product innovation and PSS and it focuses mainly on function innovation and to some extent system innovation. This distinction is necessary because many scholars refer to EPD or ENPD indiscriminately (see for example Baumann et al., 2002; Pujari et al., 2003).

In the next section EPD is discussed, followed by a discussion of ENPD.

4.3.1 EPD as a research agenda

Although EPD is a relative new discipline, in the last decade scholars from environmental studies have yielded hundreds of publications contributing to a better understanding of environmental product development (for a comprehensive review see Baumann et al., 2002).

One research stream encompasses both industry and academic studies, using success stories to prove conceptually that there are opportunities to combine environmental issues in products and also improve market performance (e.g. Charter et al., 2001; Cramer & van Lochem, 2001; Dutton, 1998). Several companies, like Xerox, Electrolux, BMW and 3M, have been heralded as ENPD pioneers, and are said to have benefited from the approach (Gutowski et al., 2005; Mackenzie, 1997). Another stream of research offers engineers and managers guidelines, manuals, tools and advice for integrating environmental concerns into the product design process (e.g. Brezet et al., 1997; Burall & Design Council, 1996; Huisman, 2003). The purpose of these tools[29] is to identify environmental and cost implications of alternative materials or process decisions (Handfield et al., 2001; Huisman, Boks, & Stevels, 2003) and help firms to develop greener products. There are various typologies of tools at different stages of development for this purpose (for an extensive review of tools see e.g. Boks, 2002; Tischner & Tukker, 2002).

Third, several studies were carried out to examine and to identify factors that promote green product development (for a review see e.g. Johansson, 2002). The role of an environmental coordinator (Pujari et al., 1996), the integration of environmental professionals (Ehrenfeld & Lenox, 1997), the involvement of customers (Pujari et al., 1996) and suppliers (Pujari et al., 2003; Stevels, 2001b) and top management support (Ehrenfeld et al., 1997; Handfield et al., 2001; Pujari et al., 2003) are considered crucial factors. Empirical studies have investigated the ways that firms have tried to engage in EPD (e.g. Gutowski et al., 2005; Handfield et al., 2001; Handfield, Walton, Seegers, & Melnyk, 1997; Hemel, 1998; Lenox et al., 1996; Pascual, Boks, & Stevels, 2003; Stevels, 2001a; Tukker et al., 2001).

Although these studies have increased our understanding of EPD and contributed to the development of a systematic approach to dealing with environmental issues in product development, all but a few fail to draw on existing theoretical frameworks in NPD and the organizational innovation literature (as suggested by Baumann et al., 2002; Lenox et al., 1997; Pujari et al., 2003). Few studies have adopted existing theories to explain how to manage the development of green products (e.g. Handfield et al., 2001; Johansson, 2002; Lenox et al., 1997). One of the few examples is the promise manual (Brezet et al., 1997) based on product development methodologies developed by Roozenburg and Eekels (1995) and Buys and Valkenburg (1996).

It also looks as though the discussion in the academic literature has been largely normative and prescriptive (Baumann et al., 2002; Pujari et al., 2003). Scholars seem to have mainly drawn on normative templates, attempting to build new knowledge rather than integrating existing knowledge and resources from contiguous research fields (as suggested by Lenox et al., 1997). Remarkably, publications mainly describe new tools rather than evaluating and improving existing ones (Baumann et al., 2002).

Not surprisingly, the great deal of tools and methods built on this specific knowledge did not prevent some crucial drawbacks of EPD from surfacing.

The complexity of greening

Greening itself is not a well-defined concept (Chen, 2001) and degrees of greening are perceived differently by consumers, producers and government (Kleiner, 1991).

For example, in the academic circle, there is an ongoing debate about what is considered a green product. One distinction is between products that have been systematically designed to reduce their environmental impact (for example with ecodesign methods) and products that achieve the same result and environmental quality without using any specific tools or methods, thanks to autonomous technological development such as digitalization, miniaturization and energy efficiency. For example, mobile phones have changed drastically in the last decade; their eco-performance has increased, they weigh less, use less energy, carry less hazardous batteries and incorporate more functions for customers.[30]

The fact that the concept of greening remains ill defined also manifests itself from a market perspective. Many scholars and practitioners seem to assume that consumers are willing to pay a premium for green products when they indicate that they care about the natural environment or look for environmentally friendly products or brands (Ottman, 1998). Unfortunately, people's attitudes towards the environment may not always materialize in their purchasing behavior (Simon, 1992). In 2000, Shell, for example, introduced Pura, a more environmentally friendly fuel that contained fewer pollutants. Although Shell assumed that its customers would pay a premium for the environmental aspect of the new fuel, Pura proved to be a failure. When Shell subsequently introduced a new fuel, with even fewer pollutants than Pura, and marketed it as a fuel that would increase engine performance, not even mentioning its environmental advantages, they managed to turn it into a commercial success (Op Het Veld, 2005).

The complexity of greening is also reflected in the challenging tasks for producers trying to deal with environmental attributes. Incorporating levels of both green and regular attributes in one product might occur through the design process in terms of material selection, energy efficiency or toxic waste, for example (Chen, 2001). However, integrating environmental attributes should not conflict with traditional product attributes or performances such as safety and convenience. Environmental attributes are seen as distinct from the more traditional ones like price and quality[31] (Chen, 2001; Prakash, 2002). As suggested by Chen (2001: 252), "typical environmental attributes that are listed on various green consumer guides include recyclability, recycled content, fuel efficiency, toxic content reduction, and emission-related performance", and others like efficient packaging.

Moreover, the increased degree of complexity opens up a larger set of possible tradeoffs (Hemel, 1998). Keeney and Raiffa (1993) argue that, in cases of multiple objective decisions, the improvement of one attribute might be achieved only at the expense of other attributes. For example, cars with electric propulsion result in an improved emission rate but the speed and distance rates are forgone (De Neufville et al., 1996). Not surprisingly, Handfield (2001) found that requirements that have immediately observable effects in terms of profitability, customer needs and market share might take precedence over environmental goals.

The ill-defined nature of the concept of greening also concerns the extent to which product optimization is achieved through ecodesign methods and tools. On the one hand, to design a product, the designer might rely on DfE tools to choose environmentally better materials or to design a product with energy-efficient attributes. Then the DfE tools are used as a tradeoff method to select and choose specific product attributes. On the other hand, the designer is required to design products without a specific material banned by regulation because it is harmful for health and environmental reasons. A checklist might help the designer select proper materials. As result, both end-products are considered eco-products although the designer's willingness and the degree of product optimization are different. For example, in Japan and in Europe the use of cadmium is banned in many manufacturing products and any cadmium-free product is seen by many firms as a green product. Therefore, firms such as Toyota and Epson claim that all of their newly developed products are green products (Yamamoto, 2003) because they are cadmium-free. Due to the lack of a clear definition of greening, firms can claim their products as green regardless of their environmental ambition and the extent to which products have been optimized.

Despite these heterogeneous interpretations, in this research study greening is defined as the (explicit) attempt to reduce and minimize the environmental impact of the development, manufacturing, use and disposal of products and services.

4.3.2 EPD as a practice

The intrinsic complexity of greening may explain why firms that have tried to develop more environmental products have had mixed experiences. For example, after studying ten firms seen as proactive in integrating environmental issues into their business, Handfield et al. (2001) found a gap between the advocates of DfE tools (environmental managers) and the users (designers) of these tools in terms of expectations, perceptions and orientations towards DfE practices and tools. Weak research foundation and barriers in the interpretation of DfE principles between these two groups seem to have created uncertainties in the process and outcome of DfE. According to Gloria et al. (1995), due to the complexity of DfE issues, some of the barriers to the use of DfE tools are intrinsically related to the tools themselves, which feature poor data availability and quality together with high implementation costs.

Moreover, many companies cited in the literature as examples of corporate environmentalism have employed the tools sparingly and, when they have done so, they were used as an addition to the regular product development with marginal effects on overall environmental impact reduction (Handfield et al., 1997). For example, a survey in 1996 found that 25% of manufacturing companies had a corporate program for incorporating environmental concerns into design (Lenox et al., 1996). However, designers did not seem to use environmental database and design software extensively and even fewer organizations have adopted environmental analytical tools such as life cycle analysis (LCA) or full-cost accounting. Consequently, guidelines and checklists are the tools most commonly employed. Similarly, though environmental targets are added to a set of fundamental product requirements, they are often not prioritized and are given less weight than costs or time-to-market criteria (Handfield et al., 2001). It looks as though environmental improvements are mainly accomplished thanks to stricter regulations (Ashford, 2002). Moreover, the assumption that green products resulting from DfE processes might lend them a competitive edge is still to be proven. For example, Ehrenfeld et al. (1997) found that firms that have been successful were successful without relying heavily on tools.

4.3.3 Green products in the market

Are green products successful in the market? The answer is not straightforward. Well-known examples of champions of successful environmental products in the market are often cited, like the energy-saving lamp, and the successful diffusion of environmental technologies such as photovoltaic cells is slowly but inexorably occurring. It seems that the number of green products among all US new product introductions rose from 1.1% in 1986 to 13.4% in 1991 (Ottman, 1998) but decreased to 10% in 1997 (Fuller, 1999). These numbers need, however, to be carefully handled because, as explained earlier, there is ambiguity about the definition of green products. However, the Ottman and Fuller rate is taken as a "barometer" of green products' success. According to some authors, this rate is low (Baumann et al., 2002; Pujari et al., 2003). The effort to make better products in environmental terms does not always convert into a viable business case creating new and/or expanding markets (Hall et al., 2003a). As a result, many green projects end up with products in niche markets, or at the prototype stage; or they have failed to introduce any products, stopping prior to that stage (Hall et al., 2003a). Surprisingly, whereas the number of green products is rather small, the number of tools to design and develop them has been rapidly increasing in the last few years.

4.3.4 Current research in ENPD: the call for radical undertakings and PSS

Recently, scholars have emphasized that the development of new products and services rather than the optimization of existing products is a necessary condition to achieve consistent improvements in eco-efficiency[32] (Charter et al., 2001). It is assumed that greater "factor" gains can come through the development of a new product (and a new business) based on a critical reassessment of the consumer (or market) needs that are to be fulfilled (Ryan, 2003). The achievement of such leaps forward in eco-efficiency demands a different approach from companies than continuous improvement processes; rather than incremental steps, new radical approaches are required (Green & Vergragt, 2002; Jansen & Vergragt, 1992; Weiszäcker et al., 1997). Furthermore, a strong role is attributed to technology in achieving increased levels of eco-efficiency (Weaver et al., 2000).

Accordingly, the ecodesign might only accomplish incremental improvements to current products rather than reinventions or fundamental innovation (Hart et al., 1999). Consequently, focusing on DfE processes might be one of the elements distracting companies from pursuing radically different products and business models (Senge & Carstedt, 2001).

Such thinking has led to an increasing interest in new products and services development and the idea of "product service systems" as business strategy and policy development (Mont, 2004; Roy, 2000; Ryan, 2003). PSS is defined as tangible products and intangible services designed and combined so that they are jointly capable of fulfilling specific customer needs (Mont, 2002; Tischner et al., 2002). The underlying assumption is that the development of services together or in substitution of products leads to an environmental improvement of the current production and consumption pattern.[33] For example, it is argued that substituting tangible products, such as answering machines, with intangible services, such as electronic mailboxes, affords a substantial environmental gain. According to Senge et al. (2001), providing services rather than just selling products creates a potential new alignment between what is economically sound and what is environmentally sound.

Scholars have developed tools and guidelines to design and implement PSS (for a review of these tools see e.g. Beerepoot, 2004; Tischner et al., 2002) and used several cases to prove the potential of such a PSS concept (Beerepoot, 2004; Brezet, Vergragt, & Horst, 2001b; Goedkoop, van Halen, te Riele, H., & Rommens, P., 1999; Hawken, Lovins, & Lovins, 1999; Manzini & Vezzoli, 2003; Mont, 2004; Tischner et al., 2002). Nevertheless, it seems that experimentations with business organizations resulted in mixed success (Beerepoot, 2004).

The PSS approach emphasizes the systematic innovation in which new products and services may be developed (e.g. Fussler et al., 1996). Although this approach calls for the adoption of unorthodox conduct, that is, radical undertaking, few studies have examined what radical undertaking entails for the organization – for example, explaining to a project team how to deal with the higher degree of uncertainty intrinsically linked to project radicalness.

Furthermore, PSS scholars suggest designing and developing products and services beyond organizational boundaries (Mont, 2004). Given the environmental ambition, scholars affirm that the PSS model "implies new types of stakeholder relationships and/or partnerships, new convergence of economic interests, and a concomitant systemic resources optimization" (Manzini et al., 2003: 856). Accordingly, the larger the network of committed stakeholders, the greater the chances of attaining system innovation. However, PSS seems to overlook the higher risks of innovating in interorganizational settings (Van de Ven et al., 1999).

4.3.5 EPD summary

How have the environmental issues been addressed in the literature?

What emerges from the literature review on green product development is a rather contradictory picture. Although EPD is high on the policy and business agenda and previous research has significantly contributed to explanations of how to incorporate environmental issues into new products (e.g. Chen, 2001; Handfield et al., 2001; Lenox et al., 1997; Pujari et al., 1996; Pujari et al., 2003), it seems that EPD and ENPD are not without pitfalls.

Within EPD, the ill-defined nature of the concept of greening increases the complexity involved in successfully incorporating environmental issues within product development. Furthermore, the overemphasizing focus on building tools, while overlooking links with existing product development and innovation theories, make this task even more complicated. The reason is that treating EPD without taking into account the context in which it is embedded can lead to a conflicting and complex situation.

These drawbacks might even increase within ENPD for two main reasons: the call for radical undertakings and interorganizational cooperation.

For example, although there is a call for a radical approach in the environmental field to address the environmental imperative (e.g. Hart et al., 1999; Senge et al., 2001), the effect of the radicalness in the process of innovation has not been sufficiently explored. Adapting normative templates from redesigning methodologies to build tools for radical undertakings might be ineffective. This is because radical undertakings entail a much higher degree of uncertainty than less ambitious projects. Moreover, new highly environmentally ambitious products and services need to meet market demands. This entails a better understanding of new product development and radical undertakings. NPD provides an understanding of the complexity and radicalness of product development.

The same argument can be made about interorganizational cooperation. Scholars have investigated EPD and ENPD within established firms. Undertaking (radical) projects with an interorganizational cooperation might present different mechanisms and challenges. Moreover, the entrepreneurial start-up is seen as a relevant setting for the creation of environmental innovations (Larson, 2000).

Summarizing, the literature previously discussed in Chapters 2 and 3 on NPD and organizational settings provides the theoretical framework to examine what environmental ambition implies for product development and performance. The underlying rationale is that these theories give better insights into how new product development projects unfold, identifying factors that might create risks and uncertainties during the innovation process.

Integrating EPD and ENPD literature in regular NPD and organizational literature should also strengthen the legitimacy of ENPD within the more mature NPD and organizational field. A better integration of the two disciplines seems plausible and desirable. This brief review highlights the need for a deeper understanding of environmentally driven projects and an integration of ENPD within the larger umbrella of existing innovation and organizational theories.

5 Theory-based conceptual model and research methodology

5.1 Introduction

Chapters 2, 3 and 4 have discussed the innovation, organizational and environmental literature to better understand the process of innovation, its relationship with the organizational setting and the relationship between environmental issues and product innovation. This chapter will present a conceptual model that is based on the constructs previously discussed. This model will serve as the research methodology for the empirical part of the book. Section 5.2 explains the selection of constructs chosen for the conceptual model and presents and explains this model. It also enumerates and illustrates the research propositions. The constructs and their relationships serve as a guide for the selection and analysis of the empirical data. Section 5.3 explains the case study approach as a research strategy and also illustrates the selection process and data collection process.

5.2 Building blocks of the conceptual model

The process of innovation is a complex phenomenon. Many factors influence the process of innovation, both outside and within the boundaries of an organization. In the literature review in Chapter 2, the focus is on factors within an organization's boundaries because the aim is to discuss various components of different theories regarding new product development projects, that is, specifically how organizations innovate. When we examine or develop a theoretical framework, however, we need to use specific language devices that help us organize a complex empirical world. Therefore, "factors" need to be translated in units of theoretical statements, that is, constructs and variables. Accordingly, the components of a theory[34] are constructs and variables in which constructs are related to each other by propositions and variables are related to each other by hypotheses. This whole system is bounded by assumptions such as value, time and space. As nicely formulated by Bacharach (1989: 500), "the constructs may be viewed as a broad mental configuration of a given phenomena [*sic*] while the variables may be viewed as an operational configuration derived from the constructs". The primary difference between propositions and hypotheses is that propositions involve concepts, whereas hypotheses require measures (Whetten, 1989).

Given the qualitative and explorative character of this study, constructs and propositions rather than variables and hypotheses are discussed. Therefore, "if the purpose of proposition is to communicate the relationship between two or more constructs the only performance criterion which these constructs must meet is that they have good clarity and parsimony" (Bacharach, 1989: 503).

Accordingly, the focus on specific literature does not prevent the number of constructs and their relationships from being rather large, making it difficult to study and evaluate the very components of the theories. Given this complexity, only some key constructs are chosen. The selected constructs are the building blocks for the preliminary conceptual model. In Chapter 2 three constructs were selected because of their crucial importance as determinants of product performance. In addition, other explanations are noted in this section. The underlying rationale for the process of selection is threefold.

First, as explained in Chapter 1, selectivity is an important criterion in social science. Only key constructs that really help to understand the phenomenon under study should be incorporated (Bodewes, 2000). Furthermore, propositions should be limited to specifying the logically deduced implication of a theoretical claim (Whetten, 1989).

Second, from the literature review some constructs and variables have been extensively studied, while others have been poorly defined and occasionally lead to conflicting results. Thoroughly examining these poorly defined concepts and their unclear relationships may yield a better understanding of the phenomenon under study. For example, studies on new product performance have focused on the identification rather than the explanation of success and failure factors (Cooper et al., 1987; Montoya-Weiss et al., 1994), and have not provided sufficient predictions (Brown et al., 1995). To be "useful", a theory should be able to explain and to predict (Bacharach, 1989). Thus the understanding of these determinants and questions like "why did it occur" (or "why not?") might indeed improve the theory on success and failure (Whetten, 1989).

Third, the qualitative aspect of this research study suggests that the theoretical and the empirical enquiries are not addressed sequentially, but that an iterative process exists between the existing theories and data where inconsistencies are settled in successive iterations (Bansal et al., 2000). Whereas the research strategy will be discussed later in this chapter, it is important to emphasize that the constructs chosen were also selected because they are substantially supported by empirical data.

5.2.1 Selection of the building blocks

In Chapter 2, two typologies of the innovation process were defined: the incremental and the radical. The key difference was related to the level of uncertainty and newness for the outside world and for the organization undertaking the innovative projects. Note that the focus here is mainly on the organization's view of the innovation process.

Incremental innovation processes are characterized by a low level of uncertainty because the organization is familiar with developing products in a well-known technical and market environment and boasts resources, capabilities and competences that are well suited to the requirements of the new product project. Radical innovation processes are characterized by a high level of uncertainty; the organization is unfamiliar with developing new products in a new technical or market environment because greater resources, different technical or market capabilities and competences are needed.

In this research study the new product development process, which is seen as a radical undertaking for the organization, is examined.

The underlying rationale is twofold. First, although radical NPD has received a great deal of attention, our understanding of radical undertakings is limited (e.g. Veryzer, 1998a), which has also occasionally led to conflicting results (e.g. Balachandra et al., 1997). Second, there is a demand for radical innovations. As seen in Chapter 4, many scholars argue that, to reduce the impacts on the natural environment, new radical solutions based on new technologies are needed (e.g. Hart et al., 1999). Assuming this to be correct, a better understanding of radical undertakings is needed.

The selected constructs are: *environmental ambition* and *the organizational setting*. They influence the product and the process characteristics expressed here by four constructs: 1) *management support*; 2) *project team commitment*; 3) *product attributes*; and 4) *product performance*.

Environmental ambition

The construct of environmental ambition is defined as a specific intention to design, develop and implement new products and services with a lower environmental impact compared to those that they aim to substitute. The extent to which environmental ambition influences the process of radical innovation is far from clear. As previously discussed, there is a tendency to emphasize the radical approach in innovation to address important societal problems (e.g. Hart et al., 1999; Senge et al., 2001). However, previous research has barely defined and examined the relationship between decisions taken during the radical undertaking and concern for the natural environment. This gap in the literature requires empirical data, discussed later in this chapter.

Environmental ambition, as a driver to start an ENPD project, may set up qualitative or quantitative objectives. For example, the former may be evident in the actors' willingness to contribute to a better sustainable society, while the latter may be noticeable in clear, formalized goals like improvements by a factor of four in energy efficiency. However, remember that environmental ambition cannot be the only driver to start a new project. Organizations engage in ENPD to create value. Commercial and/or technical goals such as profits, sales, growth and R&D, are the main motivations behind any decision or action.

Here two discrete forms of environmental ambition are defined: high and low levels of environmental ambition or eco-ambition. The former identifies an environmental ambition clearly and explicitly expressed from the beginning of a project. For example, clear statements concerning the environmental imperative in the business plan, which are recurrently addressed in meetings, in public or through formal requests for subsidies concerning environmental projects. Therefore, measuring environmental ambition may rely on observable variables such as statements in the business plan, in the project development description and the mission. Moreover, the level of eco-ambition is high when decisions during the innovation process may be influenced by the environmental ambition. On the other hand, a much lower eco-ambition level is denoted when concern for the natural environment represents an opportunity to innovate but does not influence decisions during the innovation process. It may manifest itself *after* product implementation in the market as a marketing tool rather than as an objective.

The organizational setting

In Chapter 3, the relationship between the process of innovation and the organizational setting, which could take the form of a start-up, established organization or network of organizations, was discussed. It was briefly decided that no clear conclusions could be drawn about the comparative merits of alternative organizational settings for innovation. Each organizational setting has its own benefits and unique liabilities, such as liabilities of *newness*, *bigness* and or *double parenting* (Van de Ven et al., 1999). The decision-making process is influenced by these organizational structures. In this study two discrete organizational structures constitute the construct of organizational setting: start-ups and the interorganizational network. There are differences between the decision processes in new product development projects within a coalition of firms and entrepreneurial firms. The former, rather than the latter, entails decisions during a new product development project frequently being made by a group of managers representing the firms' interests. The strategic alliance, rather than a single entrepreneur, holds ownership of the project.

Management support

The management advocacy for a project was defined in Chapter 2 as expression of support for projects (Green et al., 2003). The *decision maker* has the faculty to lend support to projects. Any project's survival within one firm or a network of firms is inextricably linked to management support. This means that a high level of management advocacy for a project will result in it being assigned a higher priority, while a lower level of support could lead to the project's demise. Previous research has found that management advocacy appears to be driven by both performance judgments, evaluating the progress of projects toward their commercial and technical goals, and non-rational factors, such as psychological income or excitement about radical projects (Gimeno et al., 1997; Green et al., 2003). Therefore, a decision about a project's evaluation may be influenced by factors independent of performance judgment. Then the questions are: *Does the environmental ambition of decision makers shape the management support for ENPD projects? Is the environmental ambition a non-rational component of the support process?*

Project team commitment

Organizational aspects are crucial for product innovation. The commitment of the project team is the chosen construct for the conceptual model. Here the project team consists of the members responsible for the actual product development, the *decision takers*. As discussed in Chapter 2, it is important to take the project team into account because it is considered to be the core of product development (Brown et al., 1995). The team's commitment is therefore vital for product development performance because aspects such as communication, coordination, information within and outside the team strongly influence the process performance (e.g. Dougherty, 1992). In radical undertakings, the decision takers may get emotionally involved and escalate their commitments due to psychological and social considerations (Schmidt et al., 1998). The question is whether decision takers may escalate their commitments to a course of action because of environmental ambition. *Do non-rational factors like psychological and social considerations play a bigger role when environmental concerns are incorporated into decision making?*

Product attributes

The complex process of product development involves a number of decisions related to functionality and attributes of the product. The product attributes are the result of decisions made by managers and product developers. The reason for taking "product attributes" as a building block is related to the effects of integrating environmental issues into products. In Chapter 4, it was suggested that it may be difficult to fully understand and evaluate environmental performance. Two rationales were discussed. First, greening is an ill-defined concept (Chen, 2001), because it has different meanings according to different actors. Second, many environmental attributes, such as fuel economy and recyclability, may conflict with traditional product attributes or performances, such as safety and convenience (Chen, 2001). The question is whether environmental ambition influences product specification decisions and product performance.

Product performance

The main goal of new product development is to have a new product or a combination of product-service whose performance enhances the benefits for the organization directly or indirectly (in terms of profits, learning or legitimation) (Brown et al., 1995; Cooper et al., 1987, 1995a; Montoya-Weiss et al., 1994). If the product does not perform as expected, it is likely that some aspects were overlooked during the NPD process. The above-mentioned constructs may directly or indirectly influence the product performance. Note that in a radical undertaking there is a great deal of uncertainty, which increases the difficulties for new products trying to match market requirements.

5.2.2 The preliminary conceptual model

The constructs selected are the building blocks of the preliminary conceptual model illustrated in Figure 5.1. Note that the model is underdeveloped. These constructs and their relationships are guidelines for the analysis of the data through which a better and well-suited model will emerge. In the final well-tuned model, relationships among existing constructs will be reinforced and new relationships between constructs may emerge.

As the literature review in the previous chapters has shown, all of the constructs and their relationships presented in the model have been investigated by scholars to some extent. What the existing literature has overlooked is the existence of a new key construct, named here as environmental ambition, and its relationships with the other constructs in the model. Therefore this research study proposes a new construct and new relationships to demonstrate how and why environmental ambition changes the accepted relationships. This research attempts to generate new theoretical insights, demonstrating how the addition of a new construct significantly alters our understanding of the phenomena by reorganizing the causal model (as suggested by Whetten, 1989).

In the next section the relationships among the constructs are explained.

5.2.3 Propositions

This section discusses the propositions, that is, the relationships among the selected constructs. These propositions are, however, *tentative* but they are useful for guiding the empirical exploration. Given the fact that the empirical exploration might reveal additional insights, the propositions may be provisional.

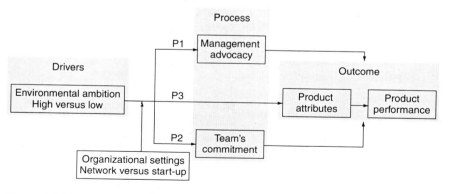

Figure 5.1 The preliminary conceptual model for the influence of environmental ambition in radical undertakings.

The escalation theory and Green's theoretical model may explain and predict how radical projects with a potential environmental gain may be pursued and supported despite poor financial and process-related performances. Unlike prior research, this study suggests that environmental ambition may be seen to act as a non-rational factor in the decision-making process.

Environmental ideology may influence the project support, resulting in a reduction of the performance thresholds, depending on the contextual settings. In situations with similar performance indicators, environmental ambition may influence the go/no-go decision in different ways.

In the first case, a radical project with a high potential for environmental gains may be supported enthusiastically by decision makers concerned about environmental issues. Consequently, the threshold for the performance indicators may be lowered. This implies a higher level of management support, regardless of performance. In another extreme situation, a project with a high level of environmental ambition may receive a lukewarm reception because the team may perceive intrinsically complex environmental issues as too alien and unfamiliar to the organization. Despite management support, the project team may be reluctant to undertake such a project. This reluctance may take the form of a higher performance threshold. As a result, management support may decline regardless of how well the project is actually doing. Considering environmental ambition as a non-rational component of the support process, the first proposition is:

P1 Decision makers with a high level of environmental ambition will support environmental projects and thus lower performance thresholds.

The effect of the radical undertaking on the team's commitment might be twofold. First, the commitment of the team might be escalating (Schmidt et al., 1998), making any performance judgment difficult (Gimeno et al., 1997; Green et al., 2003; Schmidt et al., 1998). Improper methods for evaluation and psychological rewards (Gimeno et al., 1997) for doing radical projects are likely to lower the performance judgment thresholds. Second, commitments may turn heterogeneous within the team during the project – some members will be more committed than others, especially in large organizations and networks of organizations. This may result from different interpretative schemes (Dougherty, 1992) or different/changed interests. These effects are moderated by the kind of approach taken toward radical undertakings. The escalation of commitment (Schmidt et al., 1998), different interpretative schemes (Dougherty, 1992) and divergence in commitments (e.g. Ireland et al., 2002) may delay the development process, increasing the risk of having a product unfit for the market (Montoya-Weiss et al., 1994). Given its non-rational nature, environmental ambition in decision-making processes may provide psychological rewards and high expectations associated with continued team commitment to the course of action regardless of performance. Previous literature has overlooked the role of environmental concern in dictating the innovation process and its potential ability to emphasize psychological and social considerations in product development. This research study suggests that environmental ambition may act as a non-rational factor and one of the mechanisms underlying escalation of commitment.

P2 In a radical undertaking, decision takers with a high level of environmental ambition are likely to escalate their commitments.

New product development is a complex process that entails a number of decisions related to the kind of attributes the product should include. Incorporating new attributes such as environmental ones may increase the product complexity. The rationale is threefold. First, as discussed in Chapter 2, new attributes, by definition, increase the product complexity because they entail new interactions between new components and the existing ones (Novak et al., 2001). Furthermore, in cases of conflicting attributes, giving a higher priority to environmental attributes at the expense of other parameters (like customer requirements) may affect product performance. Second, when environmental attributes are ill defined, the integration of these with other attributes may create difficulties in the decision making process because the information at hand is confusing. In such cases, the set of interactions between components is unclear. Third, the environmental motto suggests that radical solutions rather than incremental ones may engender substantial improvements for the natural environment. Product developers with high environmental ambition may favor new attributes regardless of their effects on coordinating development. This may result in increased product complexity.

P3 A high level of environmental ambition will likely increase product complexity.

5.3 Research design

The purpose of this book is to understand how environmental ambition shapes the NPD process. As we saw hitherto, previous research but has poorly addressed this specific relationship. The lack of sufficient understanding of this phenomenon requires a qualitative empirical line of enquiry. This type of enquiry is well suited to *exploring and discovering* new substantive areas about which little is known (Strauss & Corbin, 1999).

In this section the research design is discussed. This discussion addresses case selection, data collection and data analysis methods.

5.3.1 Case study research

This research project utilizes the case study strategy. The underlying rationale is based on some key features well suited to the purpose of this study.

First, it allows investigation of how product innovation unfolds in a real-world environment in which decisions actually take place (Yin, 1994).

Second, the case study method is well suited to studying the overall picture of the research object as a whole. It allows for the in-depth identification of a variety of contextual factors when the phenomenon under study is dependent on a large number of factors (Verschuren & Doorewaard, 1999). As emphasized in the words of Montoya-Weiss et al. (1994: 413):

> Case studies must play a new role in the future.... Case studies can contribute to the field in terms of identifying new factors (of new product performance) or developing new methodological approaches. Also, new branches of new product performance research are primary candidates for case study.

Third, it is an appropriate strategy for enriching or extending theory, yet also accommodates existing theories through an iterative process (Yin, 1994). Fourth, compared to other methods, the case study method provides evidence in a situation in which all of the relevant behaviors cannot be manipulated through experimental design. Moreover, it may elucidate and explain a decision or a set of decisions too complex for a survey or experimental strategies (Yin 1994). Finally, it allows the incorporation of a variety of different sources of evidence, including archival documents and interviews (Yin 1994).

Table 5.1 briefly illustrates the summary of case study characteristics, based on Verschuren and Doorewaard (1999).

An important component of case study research is the *unit of analysis* (Yin, 1994). It reflects the core of the phenomenon studied, which occurs in a bounded context. The case is actually the unit of analysis (Miles & Huberman, 1994). In this research study the unit of analysis is the new product development project within an organizational setting.

5.3.2 *Case selection*

The selection of cases is an important aspect of qualitative studies and crucial for later analysis. Qualitative sampling, unlike quantitative sampling, tends to be purposive rather than random. The choice of informants, episodes and interactions are being driven by a conceptual question, not by concern for "representativeness" (Miles et al., 1994). Sampling in qualitative research is usually not wholly pre-specified, but it evolves once fieldwork begins.

Regarding this research study, the author had the opportunity to step into a project begun in the Netherlands in which the objective was to design and

Table 5.1 Case study's characteristics

Small number of research units	Selective, i.e. strategic sample
Labor-intensive data generation	Qualitative data
More depth than breadth	An open observation on site

develop a new, three-wheeled, human-powered vehicle. One of the motivations behind the Mitka[35] project was to provide *a sustainable mobility solution* for individual transport over short distances. The project aimed to reduce the amount of kilometers individuals traveled by car. Although it started as an R&D experiment, the project team and the network management soon realized that the Mitka could be an attractive product for the market.

Therefore, the project was considered an extremely interesting case study for various reasons. First, the environmental concern was a strong driver behind the project – the idea of a new alternative for commuters to car use. Second, there was a strong belief that, to address the environmental imperative, a radical approach was needed. Third, a heterogeneous coalition of organizations established to develop and implement such a concept existed.

The Mitka project was considered a crucial case for understanding the influence of environmental ambition on decision making during the NPD process.

A second, sequential case was chosen to gain an even deeper understanding of the phenomenon under study. The reason was to be able to *compare* decisions during the innovation process within a similar technical and market environment. Given the limited number of cases that can usually be studied, according to Pettigrew (1990), it makes sense to opt for cases with extreme situations and polar types in which the phenomenon of interest is "transparently observable". The advice of Pettigrew was followed in choosing polar types but variations in specific settings were restricted.

To restrict variations, the cases needed to have a similar *context* and to present a high level of uncertainty in the innovative undertaking. It was felt that the selected cases needed to be a new product development project in the *mobility context*, with similar technical characteristics to the Mitka. Specifically, the new venture's objective needed to be the development and the implementation of a new human-powered vehicle.

The new venture should also represent a *radical* undertaking for the organization and to some extent for the market. The development of a three-wheeled, human-powered vehicle was considered a radical undertaking because the competences involved in its development, production and manufacture were sensibly different to those required for a two-wheeled vehicle. Thus a great deal of uncertainty influences the choice of actors during the venture development process.

On the other hand, the selected cases were required to be polar types with respect to the *organizational setting* and to *the degree of environmental ambition*. As discussed earlier, two discrete forms of organizational setting were chosen: small/young organizations and a network of organizations. A better understanding of the influence of these two discrete forms on new product development will enrich the theoretical discussion on the topic.

The presence of cases where high and low levels of environmental ambition are identifiable are extremely important for understanding how decisions in the innovation process are more or less influenced by the environmental imperative.

Given the explorative nature of the study, beside the Mitka project, new cases were pre-selected and proposed that responded to the sampling parameters (see appendix I). Keep in mind that some of the cases not selected are used as illustrations of conceptual statements such as in Boxes 2.2 and 6.1.

However, only one case was selected to be compared with the Mitka case: the Mango. This case was chosen because it met the selection criteria such as technical similarities with the Mitka and motivational and organizational setting differences (see Table 5.2).

They are polar types: the Mitka project, through a network of organizations, started with a high level of eco-ambition; the Mango project was started by entrepreneurial individuals with a low level of eco-ambition. On the other hand, they have similar technical characteristics and functions, were designed for the same Dutch market and were developed simultaneously.

Besides being polar types, the two cases present methodological differences. The study of the Mitka case resembles longitudinal research in *real time*, meaning that the researcher lives with an organization over time or carries out periodic interviews (Pettigrew, 1990). In a period of more than two years, real-time data were gathered through observation, meetings and interviews. On the contrary, for the Mango case, selected after the Mitka case was chosen, real-time data collection over the whole innovation process, although desirable, was not feasible. *Ex post facto* investigations were needed to reconstruct the product development process. Thus *retrospective data collection* was the main source for this case study. However, interviews carried out in January, February, June and October 2004 allowed for the identification of patterns and dynamic processes through retrospective study, while lending the opportunity to gain at least some verification through a real-time close-up view (Leonard-Barton, 1990: 248). Thus the Mitka case is by far the most in-depth case studied over a two-year time-horizon. The Mango case in comparison was much more focused, consisting of five interviews over eight months that were used to verify the insights and theory elements that had emerged from the Mitka case. Analyzing only two cases allowed for a much deeper and more detailed analysis than would have been possible if a wider sample of projects had been studied. Thus richness of description makes up for the disadvantages associated with a small sample size.

One may ask why so few cases were examined. In management science there

Table 5.2 Selection of cases based on motivation and organizational setting

		Motivation/opportunity	
		Environmental ambition and market	*Profit/market*
Organizing for innovation	Individual entrepreneur		Mango
	Interorganizational network	Mitka	

is an ongoing discussion with regard to the in-depth study of a single case versus the study of multiple cases (see e.g. Dyer & Wilkins, 1991; Eisenhardt, 1991).

The main advantage of in-depth study of one or two cases is related to the ability to deeply understand and fully describe the context of the phenomenon under study. Otherwise, the more contexts investigated, the less contextual insight is communicated (Dyer et al., 1991). By taking into account the details of a particular context, the researcher increases the accuracy of the theoretical relationships, because he/she understands the "deep structure" of social behavior (Light, 1979). On the contrary, with a larger number of studies, "the descriptions will be rather thin, focusing on surface data rather than deeper social dynamics" (Dyer et al., 1991: 615). Furthermore, in-depth cases allow a researcher to highlight a construct by showing its operation in an ongoing social context, with the result that the case study becomes a much more coherent story (Dyer et al., 1991). With regard to product development projects, another advantage of in-depth study of few cases is associated with the ability to thoroughly examine the decision-making process of the development team. In this research study, deep understanding of the context and the decision-making process was considered a necessary condition to examining the phenomenon under study and to produce new theoretical insights.

5.3.3 *Quality criteria for case study research*

To evaluate the quality of the case study design Yin (1994) suggests various criteria such as construct validity and internal validity. Construct validity refers to the extent to which the phenomenon under study matches the constructs supposedly representing the phenomenon. It requires an iterative process involving 1) refining the definition of the construct; and 2) building evidence that measures the construct in each case (Eisenhardt, 1989). To enhance construct validity Yin (1994) suggests 1) using multiple sources of evidence/data; and 2) having key informants review the findings. In this research study the iterative process involved data from multiple sources: semi-structured interviews with key informants, participant observation and archival documents.

Internal validity refers to the extent to which the emergent relationships between the constructs fit with the evidence in the case (Eisenhardt, 1989). Moreover to increase the internal validity it is important to discover the underlying theoretical reasons as to why the relationship exists. The structured analysis technique *pattern matching* (Yin, 1994) is used in this research study. It compares empirical patterns with constructs' relationships proposed a priori; the more the patterns match, the higher the internal validity. According to this technique, an independent construct has a causal relationship with a set of constructs. If all the outcomes are consistent as predicted, strong causal inferences can be made. However, if just one of them does not support the data, it is preferable to have another case that could augment the first case. Then the independent construct is the reverse and the outcomes predicted should follow a different pattern using the same set of constructs.

5.3.4 Data sources

Case study research privileges qualitative and unstructured ways of gathering data (Verschuren et al., 1999). In this study the empirical focus was on the research objects: the Mitka project and the Mango project (Table 5.3). Moreover, the context in which those projects had unfolded was given a great deal of attention; in particular, the bicycle industry has been extensively analyzed. To elucidate the propositions different data sources were used: semi-structured interviews with key informants, archival documents and participant observation (see appendix II).

Interviews

Regarding the two projects under study, the selection of key informants was based on their knowledge of the project and their proximity to the decision-making process. Thus, members of the project team were identified as primary key informants and, adopting a snowball method, additional relevant key informants involved in the projects were interviewed. The interviews were semi-structured and lasted from one and a half to three hours. Informants were first requested to describe the historical timeline of the project, its main players and decisions taken during the process.

The initial interviews were kept broad in scope in an effort to expose a wide range of motivations, decisions and competences. As the research project progressed and the theory was refined, interview questions became more focused in an effort to ascribe more details to the emerging patterns. To build internal validity inconsistencies were probed further (Eisenhardt, 1989).

With regard to the bicycle industry, interviews were conducted with managers of the leading, large bicycle-manufacturing companies and with some entrepreneurs from small and young bicycle-manufacturing organizations in the Netherlands. The reason was to understand how these organizations innovate and build internal validity given the "the small world" of the bicycle-manufacturing industry, where people know about each other's work.

Participant observation

During the period 2001–2003, the author had the opportunity to participate in the product development of the Mitka project, observing the team at work.

Table 5.3 Data collection source based on Yin (1994)

	From individuals	*From an organization*
About an individual/ entrepreneur or a team	Behavior, motivation, decisions	Archival records
About the NPD	How NPD proceeds	NPD outcomes

Although these observations were not coded, they were instrumental in shaping initial conceptualizations for the preliminary model. Several discussions and informal conversations occurred with the team members regarding technical development as well as market research. The author's role was active in the project with regard to the market research, in particular the test preparation and implementation.

Archival documents and press releases

In qualitative case study research, corroboration of interviews through archival records is important to validate information (Yin, 1994). Therefore, the interview data were supplemented with information from archival documents and press releases. Internal reports, archival information, newspaper and magazine articles were used to confirm the reliability of the interviewees' responses and also permitted directed and detailed probing in the interviews.

Procedure for case description

The data collected formed the backbone of the case description. All the sources of evidence were reviewed together; consequently the case description was based on the convergence of information from different sources. The use of different sources enables crosschecking of findings using the triangulation method, which increases the reliability of the conclusion (Yin, 1994). As illustrated in Figure 5.2, all the various sources were used to write the first draft of the case study description. In the Mango case, only the interviews with the founders, press releases and surveys among a limited number of Velomobiel's users were used for the case study description. The draft of the case study description was checked by key actors, who also gave further comments on the project. After the check, the final descriptions of the cases were written.

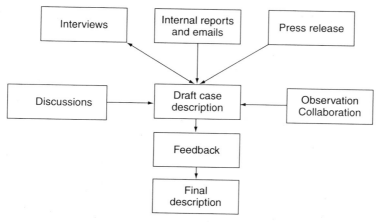

Figure 5.2 Case description procedure.

In the Mitka case, the identity of the actors is kept anonymous and only the function and organization are given. Moreover, a limited number of quotes from interviews were integrated into the case description for privacy reasons.

5.3.5 Data analysis

Data analysis adopted approaches common to qualitative, inductive research studies (i.e. Miles and Huberman, 1994; Eisenhardt, 1989; Yin, 1994). For each case a *detailed written case history and timeline* were prepared along with a schematic representation of the main phases and events (as has also been used, for example, by Van de Ven et al., 1999). The descriptive *time-oriented* display is utilized, arranging a series of concrete events by chronological time periods. These periods are based on the categorizations made by Van de Ven et al. (1999), who identified three major periods during the innovation process: the initiation period, the development period and the implementation period. These periods are then sorted into three categories that represent the levels of analysis: management support, project team commitment and product attributes.

It is important to mention that, while in the Mango case decisions were taken by two individuals within a start-up firm, in the Mitka case decisions during the process were taken by a network of heterogeneous actors. The coalition was established formally by the different organizations through formal agreements (e.g. contracts). Each member in the coalition represented their direct company in the coalition. The question is who is making the decisions? Decisions within a network may be examined at three levels of analysis. First, from the individual perspective, each member expresses his or her opinions which may not necessarily be aligned with the parent company. From a group perspective, decisions are the outcome of a compromise process among heterogeneous actors where discussions act as the means to reach agreements. Finally, from an institutional perspective, each member's decision in the coalition is the expression of their company's mission and rules. Each decision in a coalition is the manifestation of these three different perspectives. Here the actors are treated as a group (the project team and the management team) rather than as institutions or individuals: "organizations do not make decisions, individuals do" (Liedtka, 1991: 543), on their own (as solitary entrepreneurs) or more often in groups.

Procedure

Initial versions of the interview schedule were written following the first couple of interviews. These were then used to identify blank spots and inconsistencies that could be probed in later interviews. In general respondents agreed on key issues, such as what were the main phases of product development, or the major disruptive events.

Following each timeline, *within-case analyses* (Yin, 1994) were conducted by studying the key research issues, such as environmental ambition, the innovation approach, and the key resources and competences.

The perspective an author has on a topic is obviously strongly influenced by his or her personal development. To control for researcher bias a process of *consensus validation* was employed, whereby informants were invited to comment on the general description of the study. This feedback is a valuable reality check and has triggered a return to the data to find more substantiating evidence. In other cases the feedback has been dismissed when informant bias emerged due to inconsistency between "what was said" at any point of time and assertion a posteriori.

In the *cross-case analysis*, finally, the findings from the cases were compared through tables and graphical mapping. From this, a revised version of the conceptual framework will result. This model is once again contrasted with the case data, thereby continuing the iterative process between data and theory.

6 Description of the Mitka and the Mango cases

This chapter begins with a brief introduction to the human-powered vehicle sector (HPV), and then describes the Mitka and Mango cases.

6.1 The human-powered vehicle sector

Although the bicycle industry is more than 120 years old, it seems that the design of the present-day bicycle has remained much the same as that originated in the 1880s, when J. K. Starley developed the Rover Safety Bike in 1885 (for a review of bicycle history see Bijker, 1995).[36] This bike is regarded as the archetype of modern bikes, setting the trend for future technical development and commercial production (Figure 6.1).

Figure 6.1 A detail of a Penny Farthing bicycle about 1870.

Before the safety bicycle became the dominant design in the 1880s, there was great diversity in bicycle designs and diverse developments were possible. For instance, an 1886 catalogue of all British cycles described 89 different bicycles and 106 tricycles (Bijker, 1995). With the establishment of the safety bicycle development and the rise of automobiles,[37] the number of "unconventional" human vehicles declined drastically. Moreover, the growing success of the car from the 1950s on coincided with a decline in the popularity of the bicycle and a gradual disappearance of bicycle producers. For example, in the Netherlands the increased competition and the decline of bicycle use[38] (de la Bruhéze et al., 1999) forced many companies to close down or to be taken over by other companies. Today, only a few well-known old Dutch brands such as Gazelle, Batavus, Union and Sparta have managed to survive from the 45 companies listed with the Dutch Chamber of Commerce in 1962.[39]

Over the last century, these bicycle producers also changed their core activities. Before, design, development and production were performed within the company, now these activities are almost entirely outsourced. The bicycle design is commissioned to design bureaus, the frame production is outsourced to Asian countries and other parts such as the wheels, gears, suspensions and brakes are provided by suppliers. The modern bicycle brands seem to be more like assemblers than manufacturers. Moreover, it seems that most bicycle manufacturers in the Netherlands (Giant company included)[40] tend to adopt similar innovations once they are available in the industry. The first adopter is usually followed by the others after a relatively short period of time.[41] In light of this, it is not surprising that suppliers and small entrepreneurial firms are the ones developing new technological concepts.

For example, in the early 1970s the emergence of the mountain bike as a new product was due to some bikers riding sturdy unsophisticated bikes for off-road cycling in California. From the late 1970s, some of these lead users began to make a business out of it, selling custom-made mountain bikes, 5,000 of them in 1982 alone (Berto, 1999). Traditional American bicycle producers reacted late to the mountain bike boom, and only after that bicycle component makers, such as Shimano and Suntour, introduced groups of components particularly designed for off-road terrain in mountain bikes (Berto, 1999).

6.1.1 New forms of HPVs

Despite the almost unchanged design of regular bikes, much of the development has gone into refining geometry and all the components – looking for better functionality, efficiency, new materials, better manufacturing processes, lower weight and lower cost. For example, high-end bicycles feature highly sophisticated designs with frames and components made from advanced aerospace materials, including titanium, carbon fiber and metal-matrix composites (Roy, 1994).

Over time, some hybrid bikes have been introduced in niche[42] markets to address various needs. Such bikes include folding bikes, recumbent bikes,[43] tricycles, cargo trikes and electric-assisted bikes.[44]

For example, the Velotaxi (described in Box 2.2), and the Smarttrike, alias the RoodRrunner, are two new concepts that were developed and introduced in the market as a new passenger trike and as a new transporter respectively (see Box 6.1).

Box 6.1 The RoodRunner

The RoodRunner[45] is a specially designed mail-delivery vehicle for the Dutch mail service company. It was designed by Springtime (a design bureau located in Amsterdam) to help postmen deliver a large volume of mail with less effort. The RoodRunner has an electric engine that provides 50% more driving power to the driver while cycling.

The RoodRunner was commissioned by the Dutch mail service managing director, who was eager to have this type of new carrier in a short period of time. Springtime had one year to develop the design and build a working prototype. This implied a simple and attractive design without any fuzziness to keep the price low, around €2,500. The consequences for the design were choosing well-known and affordable production processes and avoiding sophisticated and costly technological solutions. In 2000, the first ten prototypes were ready and tested. After an enthusiastic acceptance by the postmen, the trike presented some technical problems. For example, the tires were perceived to be small and fragile for cycling up and down the sidewalk and the batteries were discharging more quickly. Because of these problems, Springtime decided to keep on improving the concept, for example, making the frame more robust, providing more battery power, and increasing the capacity for the carrier. The solutions proposed increased user acceptance. The great deal of attention aroused by this novelty went beyond the post company. New companies such as GranTurismo saw in the RoodRunner an opportunity to meet different mobility needs. The name was changed to Smarttrike. To encompass different purposes, Springtime built it in a modular system, so that its individual parts could be adapted to the particular company or private-use function. The versatility of the concept offered the scope for customization of the tricycle to suit company users like postal or cargo carriers or private users transporting children to school. In 2004, the first vehicles were launched at €2,000 and €3,400, human and human-electric version respectively.

Intriguingly, the Roodrunner's popularity was the reason the Dutch mail company terminated its purchase contract. The managers felt that the RoodRunner was their own "creature", and therefore not to be exported to other companies.

Among new forms of HPVs, the *velomobiles* are increasingly proposed (Walle, 2004) as the missing link between the automobile and the bicycle due to their ability to fulfill commuting and recreational needs, and to offer protection from the weather. The next section provides a brief description of the velomobile.

6.1.2 What is a velomobile?

The term "velomobile" has recently appeared in numerous websites, articles and debates among producers to denote a new kind of bicycle. The definitions vary, but it is usually understood to mean a fully or partially faired, human-powered vehicle, almost always three-wheeled for stability (for a recent history of velomobiles, see Walle, 2004). Unlike fully faired machines, which set speed records, velomobiles are designed for practicality, weather protection and utility use in traffic in addition to pure speed and efficiency (van der Laan, 2004). The sitting position is low and comfortable like that on a recumbent bike and the body is protected by the streamlined fairing, which allows low air resistance, equalling more speed, and provides a large dry luggage unit (Eick, 1998). The term velomobile covers a wide range of vehicles (see for an example Figure 6.2),

a)

b)

Figure 6.2 Some velomobiles in the market: a) Versatile from Flevobike. b) Cab-Bike.

Table 6.1 Strengths and weaknesses of velomobiles

Strengths	Weaknesses
Comfort	*Heavy weight*
Relaxed sitting position	Heavier than bikes
Full suspension	Between 25 and 45 kg
No balance problems	
Speed	*Cost of purchase*
Good aerodynamics	Between €3,000 and €8,000
Lower air resistance	
Safety	*Position*
Stability	Lower position perceived as unsafe
	by some potential customers
Low centre of gravity	
Fairing protecting the body	
Low maintenance	Space needed for parking
Drivetrain enclosed and drum brakes	
Weather protection	*High steering ratio*
The body is usually totally sheltered,	Cumbersome driving in cities
with the head out	
Luggage capacity	*Original design*
	Attracts too much attention

which includes vehicles that have removable fairings and those with a mono-coque[46] design. Table 6.1 illustrates the perceived strong and weak points of the velomobiles, compared with regular bicycles, compiled by users and velomobile experts (Eland, 2002a, 2004; Walle, 2004).

Since these attributes are a combination of a bike's characteristics with many of the features of a car, velomobiles are often promoted as car-replacement vehicles (van der Laan, 2004). An email survey completed by Velomobiel[47] clients confirms that velomobiles are primarily used to replace other means of transport for commuting (see Table 6.2).

It is important to emphasize that the Mitka concept was not viewed as a velomobile by the coalition, but as a completely new concept. Nevertheless, the Mitka concept shares some similarities with the velomobiles, such as weather protection, speed and luggage capacity.

The futuristic look of velomobiles does not come cheaply. Velomobiles cost between €3,000 and €8,000, due primarily to production costs, but also to the cost of materials and unique parts. Velomobiles are produced in very small series, which makes the production very expensive. Moreover, velomobiles represent only a small portion of the recumbent bikes market, which itself totals about 1% of the total bike market in the Netherlands.[48]

The velomobile and the recumbent bike producers form a small community where almost everyone knows each other at the national and the international level. Specialized magazines such as *Velo Vision*, dedicated competition events,

Table 6.2 Results from the email survey conducted among Velomobiel's drivers

Questions	Variables	Results
Purpose of using the HPV	Commuting	100%
	Recreational	65%
Commuting with Velomobiel's vehicles	Distance (average)	54 km
	Days per week (average)	3.8 days
Commuting by alternatives (multiple choices)*	Public transport	46%
	Car	28%
	Bike (other than Quest and Mango)	19%
	Motorbike	3%
	None	3%
Car sold or not bought due to NPV purchase (from the total)		17%
Commuting before buying the HPV (multiple choices)	Public transport	37%
	Car	36%
	Bike (other than Quest and Mango)	24%
	Motorbike	2%

Notes
* It is intended to cover the remaining days in which alternative means of transport to the HPV were used. Due to variety of working days (4 or 5) these percentages should be seen as a rough estimation.

In January 2005, an email survey was sent to 50 drivers of Velomobiel's products (the Quest and the Mango). The questionnaire included both open questions (e.g. Why did you buy a Mango? What are the barriers for velomobiles' market diffusion?) and structured questions (e.g. How many days a week do you use your HPV for communing?). Twenty-three (46% of the total) questionnaires were fully completed and returned.

such as *Cycle Vision*, touring trips such as *Oliebollentoertocht*[49] and many internet websites like www.ligfiets.net, help inform the community about the latest technical developments, enable its numbers to exchange opinions and information and create publicity aimed at a wider public. However, combining the passion for making and riding these special bikes with the need to sustain a profitable business in this niche market is not an easy task for most of the producers.

6.2 The Mitka case

Zo kind, je nieuwe Pausmobiel? (Oh boy, your new Pope Mobile?)[50]

This section presents an in-depth case study of the Mitka project. The study is based on two years of participatory observation between January 2001 and January 2003, 25 formal interviews carried out between January 2001 and March 2005, several discussions with project participants on different occasions and archival documents, which included meeting reports, research documents, product development and business plans and emails (see Appendix II). The main events of the Mitka history are reviewed in Box 6.3.

6.2.1 What is the Mitka?

The Mitka (an acronym derived from "mobility solution for individual transport over short distances", in Dutch, *Mobiliteitsconcept voor Individueel Transport op de Korte Afstand*) is a roofed, three-wheeled, human-powered vehicle with an electric engine that doubles human pedaling power. It has a maximum speed of 25–40 km/hour and automatically tilts during steering. The Mitka has an innovative shape that works with the natural position of a driver's body (Figure 6.3). It is intended as an alternative to a car for commutes of up to 25 kilometers, since 80% of the car trips made in the Netherlands are between five and 20

Figure 6.3 The Mitka, May, 2003.

kilometers (Flipsen, 2000). The aim is to reduce the number of kilometers that people travel by car. Its environmental impact (especially CO_2, local emissions and resources used) is estimated to be one-third that of a car (Luiten, Knot, & Horst, 2001a). The Mitka concept is based on the assumption that people will take the Mitka instead of the car and thus use less energy on their regular trips (home–work, shopping, visiting).

The project described in this section was developed through the joint efforts of several actors. Here the actors are treated as individuals rather than as organizations. Decisions are expressions of the group constituted by these individuals. The coalition of partners behind the Mitka is formed by:

- The *Sustainable Product Innovation group* of the TNO Institute of Industrial Technology (TNO). TNO is a major Dutch organization conducting applied research in technological innovation in industry. The group's core business is product development with a considerable reduction in environmental impact. The Sustainable Product Innovation group has been the Mitka project leader. The team included the director of the group, three project managers and other individuals.
- The director of *Gazelle*, a major bicycle company. Gazelle is the bicycle market leader for the Netherlands, selling more than 400,000 bikes per year (Bovag-RAI, 2003). The director's role in the Mitka project has been in business development and distribution.
- The director of the *Peter van der Veer Designers* bureau (Vd Veer) has been the product development designer. He is the lead designer for Gazelle Company.
- The director of *Freewiel Techniek* (Freewiel), an engineering company specializing in three-wheel configuration.
- The facility manager of European *Nike*. Some Nike employees were the lead users for the new sustainable mobility concept.
- The *Design for Sustainability* (DfS) group, located in the faculty of Design, Engineering and Production at Delft University of Technology (TUDelft). This group was asked to design detailed features of the Mitka concept and a set of services. More crucially, DfS's role was to conduct consumer research, examine user acceptance of the Mitka and to design different Mitka accessories through students' projects. This and several other projects in product-service innovation have been carried out through a cooperative agreement between TUDelft and TNO under the umbrella of the Kathalys project (Brezet et al., 2001b). The group included the leading professor, a senior researcher and two junior researchers.
- A project manager of *Novem*, a government agency funded by the Dutch ministries of environment and economic affairs, has subsidized the Mitka project.[51]
- The business developer from a one-person consulting firm.
- The managing director of *BOM* (Brabantse Ontwikkelings Maatschappij, in Dutch), a regional development agency.

For a project that has lasted more than seven years, the project and the management teams' members have inevitably changed. In the following sections these changes are described according to a timeline of events similar to van den Ven's scheme (Van de Ven et al., 1999). The events are described according to four phases: initiation period, early development period, late development period and implementation. A list of the important events is given at the end of the section (Box 6.3).

6.2.2 Initiation period: vision and coalition building

The idea for a new concept in transportation able to combine a number of car and bicycle attributes such as speed, rain protection and comfort with a significant reduction in environmental impact was formulated during a three-year process called the initiation period. This phase contemplates all the ideas, research studies and failed network coalitions that led both to the Mitka's coalition and to the first concept design of the Mitka. During the initiation period, much of the information was scattered. There is no precise reference to one business organization's strategy but more to a combination of the interests, expectations and opportunities of different organizations during different timeframes. Moreover, the final concept of the Mitka is the result of many ideas brought together by some key actors during the whole process. Three major events between 1996 and 1997 can be identified as the beginning of the initiation period. These events are referred to as "TNO & Batavus", "TUDelft" and "TUDelft & TNO" to highlight the *locus* of the major activities. The TNO team was highly committed to starting a PSS concept, which this research study refers to as the "Bike Plus".

TNO & Batavus

In 1996, a manager from TNO and two managers from Batavus bicycle company came up with an idea for a new bicycle concept. This concept envisioned a bicycle suitable for longer distances than generally covered in normal bike use. A proposal for subsidies to develop a sustainable concept was submitted to the EET. The basis for the proposal was a "renovate" bicycle concept, but the proposal was not accepted. As a research institute, TNO industry started to invest resources in studying the opportunity to develop such a concept. The team moved in two directions, finding partners for a likely project and defining the product characteristics for a new "Bike Plus" vehicle.[52] The Stork company (engineering development in automotive industry) decided to join the project with a commitment from its R&D unit. However, it withdrew in 2000 after the EET-KIEM program was submitted.

TUDelft

Simultaneously, at Delft University of Technology several students' projects were focusing on sustainable solutions to substitute the car for short-distance travel. In particular, one project used the VIP[53] approach (Hekkert, 1997) to develop a new concept for short-distance travel in 2005 (Maas, 1998). Moreover, to get a first impression of the acceptance of these ideas, a concept test had been carried out. Abstract sketches were presented to potential future users utilizing the Future Conditioning technique (Urban, Weinberg, & Hauser, 1996). The concepts encompassed rain-protected bikes as well as trikes with child seats. The final concepts resembled the "ideal" bike: comfortable in all weather conditions, suitable for distances ranging from five to 20 kilometers with an incorporated luggage unit or child seat incorporated.

TNO & TUDelft

In 1997 a new cooperative agreement was established between TUDelft and TNO under the umbrella of the Kathalys project (Brezet et al., 2001b). The mission of this project was twofold: first, to help companies explore market opportunities for sustainable product innovation; second, to develop promising sustainable concepts in collaboration with one or more organizations. Some workshops during this period helped create the conditions for a sustainable vehicle concept combining car and bicycle characteristics.

The four years of collaboration resulted in the development of a method for sustainable product innovation – the Kathalys method, which was refined and tested during the Mitka Project. See Box 6.2.

Box 6.2 The Kathalys method

The Kathalys method is an approach for developing sustainable product service systems (SPSS). It distinguishes five tracks, which should all be simultaneously worked upon throughout five project phases. See the table below for an overview of these tracks and phases, and the expected deliverables per phase and per track.

The five phases in the SPSS development process, as distinguished in the Kathalys method are:

1 *Future exploration.* Environmental information is combined with needs, consumer trends and/or technological potentials. This results in a vision of the future. Often scenarios are built to explore the possibilities and to generate sustainable ideas. The result of this phase is one or more ideas for likely sustainable system innovations.
2 *System design.* In this phase the boundaries of the system to be developed are defined in more detail. Building a partnership and reaching commitment is very important in this phase. The result is a project plan that is supported by a consortium of partners.
3 *Product/service specification.* The products and services are developed in this phase. A concept model with a mockup of the

Tracks phases	The product/ service system	Sustainability	Organization	The user	The economical feasibility
1 Future exploration	Innovation vision	Environmental bottleneck(s) and vision on the environmental opportunity	Actor overview	Vision on needs and consumer trends	Economic opportunity
2 System design	System definition	Quantitative environmental targets	Commitment by partners to the project plan	User profile	Turnover target
3 Product/ service specification	Testable product/ service combination	(Hypothetical) environmental assessment	Partner agreement	Evaluation of acceptance	Economical assessment
4 Drawing in detail and testing	Tested product/ service combination	(Practical founded) environmental assessment	Business agreement	Practical foundation for acceptance and use behavior	Investment and exploitation estimation
5 Implementation	Developed product/ service combination	Environmental gain	New business	Fulfillment of needs in a sustainable way	Profit

product(s) and a conceptual idea of the services is the result of this phase.

4   ***Drawing in detail and testing.*** Because the solutions are often rather new to the user, a practical test period is necessary to be able to really evaluate the customer added value and the environmental impact of the solution.

5   ***Implementation.*** In this phase the final development of the system takes place. All specifications are set and the system, not in its final stage but as close to reality as possible, has been tested and evaluated. Now all separate elements of the system individually can be fully developed in more detail. It is assumed that this will not differ much from "normal" product or service development tasks.

The Kathalys method is a result of the new research field within the environmental arena, the product service system, which is considered different from the regular product development, and the ecodesign approach.

The TNO project manager explained why PSS is necessary and how it is different from other approaches by stating that (Luiten et al., 2001a: 1):

To reach sustainability, so [it] is argued, the environmental efficiency of production and consumption should be improved by a factor 4 (Weiszäcker et al., 1997) to even a factor 20 (Weterings and Opschoor, 1992). This represents enormous efficiency improvements, which cannot be reached by mere technological innovations alone or by new use-patterns as such.... Thinking from existing solutions is not sufficient to reach these radical changes. There is a need for creative new thinking to generate ideas for fulfilling needs in an alternative way. Solutions that are sustainable often go beyond one product or one service. They are more often on a system level, with a system being defined as a combination of products, services, organisations, rules, policies, (infra) structure, etc. that all together enable the user to fulfil a certain need.... The result is in most cases not only one product, but moreover a system of product(s) and services. Therefore current methods for EcoDesign as described ... are not appropriate for dealing with SPSS [Sustainable Product Service System].

The "Bike Plus"

In 1998, the TNO team started to characterize the future concept of the "Bike Plus". The key characteristics of the new vehicle, selected by the initial participants through several creativity visioning workshops, included speed higher than a regular bicycle (about 18 km/h), power assistance, youthful athletic appearance, resemblance to a bicycle yet innovative design, safety and comfort and low environmental impact (Oskam, 1999). Electric power assistance was needed to reach high speeds around 30–40 km/h. The TNO team also calculated two scenarios for the environmental gain – the first one entails 924 million kilometers driven by car per year substituted by a new vehicle concept; the second one, less optimistic, around 109 million kilometers per year. Such a vehicle should have the flexibility of a bike with the comfort of a car (rain protection, safety, seat position, etc.). TNO made an inventory of original individual transportation concepts on two and three wheels, such as the Swiss Twike or a recumbent bike, to understand their penetration in the market. They found that none of them had a significant market share.

The question was why these alternative methods of transport to the car are not successful. According to the TNO team, the answers generally revolved around:

- *Bad image.* Electric bikes and man-wide cars are perceived by many people as transportation for elderly persons or for individuals with physical disabilities.
- *Conservative consumers.* Many bike users perceived new kinds of bikes, such as three-wheeled bikes or recumbent bikes, as too innovative. They do not think that these innovative bikes respond to their needs. These vehicles are also considered unreliable, uncomfortable and sometimes unsafe.
- *No marketing.* Many vehicles are made by "amateurs", developed in garages and are known by only a few people (Van Gemert, 2001).

As a result of this phase of the project three actors became involved in "Bike Plus" – TNO, Batavus and Stork product engineering.

The new concept was for a faster than normal bike (thanks to power assistance), which was also flexible and reliable, safe and comfortable. It was to have a highly customized profile with high-tech innovative solutions and a low environmental impact. A flexible modular system was desirable, such as interchangeable modules for the frame, steering mechanisms and brakes, which could be customized to individual preferences. The result should have been the development of different modules to build up several "Bike Pluses" to reach a large target group.

For the TNO team, a new product service system ought to have been in place. This meant that the new PSS was not bound only to new product development, but that it required the development of new services and infrastructure. As further explained by the TNO manager, as project leader, in a conference paper:

> The present mobility-system based upon the car with [a] combustion engine is strongly interwoven with society. Designing only a new vehicle probably will not yield a solution that is attractive enough to supersede the car. Moreover, if a solution is sought in new products only, in this example [the Mitka concept], these should comply with current means of infrastructure. The innovation space for sustainable solutions then would be unnecessarily small, and hence the environmental gains possibly lower than could be. Therefore the innovation space was enlarged, to include the surrounding system of (infra) structures, (organisational) arrangements and services.
>
> (Luiten et al., 2001a: 4)

After a second attempt was rejected by the EET committee, a third attempt failed to get subsidies. This time the Batavus company withdrew from the proposal. According to the TNO manager, there were the following interdependent reasons:[54]

1   *The innovative factor.* The idea to build a bike with characteristics closer to the car (speed, longer distance, privacy, status) was thought to be too innovative by the Batavus company, whose managers could not foresee a serious market for it.
2   *The core business.* The project was considered to be too far from the core business of the bicycle company – bicycle production.
3   *New president in charge.* The company had financial problems and a new president took control, deciding not to invest money in the project, in contrast to the former president, who had been enthusiastic about it.

While the ideas for features of the new vehicle were brewing, the TNO manager, whose enthusiasm, commitment and energy kept this initiative alive, pursued two essential objectives: funding for the project and links with viable business partners with a high potential for production and marketing and a willingness to carry on with the project. The way out would be to find an immediate mobility problem that Mitka could solve. In short, the sustainability solution was searching for an immediate problem to solve.

The opportunity came along during a meeting with the environmental commissioner of Nike, who was at the Nike European headquarters in Hilversum (in the Netherlands) on an official visit. The TNO team leader asked the commissioner for a joint partnership to create a new sustainable vehicle. The reaction was enthusiastic. In addition to the recognizable "big name", Nike offered a valuable opportunity to test the new vehicle among the employees at its European headquarters in Hilversum. Nike was running out of car parking space and welcomed alternative solutions. As explained by the facility Nike manager:

> Being part of this project, it is related to the company's culture [Nike] for three reasons:
>
> 1 Innovation. The Mitka is something new and it can be trendy, sportive and attractive for young people.
> 2 Moving. Nike started to make shoes, that's moving and the Mitka is about moving too.
> 3 The logo of Nike is "doing the right thing", and it looks that Mitka is about environment and mobility.[55]

The decision to involve Nike in the project was based on the need to find a client for a sustainable vehicle concept. In this way, the Nike employees were considered the lead users, the final customers for such a vehicle. The new vehicle needed to be developed according to the needs of these lead users (Luiten et al., 2001a). The next step was to involve a company that had the resources and knowledge to develop the new sustainable vehicle. The choice was the Gazelle company, a competitor of Batavus's in the bicycle market. Gazelle's reaction was positive, the managing director saw an opportunity to cooperate both with TNO engineers and with Nike, which is considered a successful and well-known company. To develop a new sustainable bicycle concept, the managing director asked Vd Veer Designers to work on the product design.

The basis for the fourth proposal to the EET-KIEM was established, submitted and accepted, TNO receiving €226,000. Meanwhile, the name "Bike Plus" was changed to the Mitka. Another change was the project leader. Within the TNO team, another manager became the project leader, under the supervision of the former project leader. The aim of the project was:

> To develop a family environmental friendly compact vehicle which is more comfortable and functional than the bicycle and with better production techniques that allows us to produce the vehicle on a large scale.[56]

At this point, after three years of incubation, the parameters of a flexible modular bike-plus vehicle emerged, along with a coalition of actors ready to develop and pilot it in a specific "real-life" context.

6.2.3 Early development: from vision to design concept

To understand the technological, economical and ecological potential of a new mobility vehicle, TNO performed two market studies in the European Nike headquarters in Hilversum. The first study consisted of several tests lasting for a couple of weeks with different bicycle concepts, from regular safety bikes to electric ones, recumbent bikes and trikes as well. The reason was to get feedback and comments on the different bikes' aspects and characteristics (Joore, 2000a).

The second study, in March 2000, was launched through an internet-based questionnaire given to Nike employees. The respondents were asked to describe their current mobility situation and to "build" on a computer screen, out of individual components, a vehicle that would meet the general set of specifications defined earlier by the Mitka coalition and their own preferences as future Mitka users. The respondents were able to construct their own ideal product service system by combining elements, like two or three wheels, a rain-protection shield, a luggage unit or a child seat.

Furthermore, since the project was meant to constitute a product service system, the respondents had the opportunity to express their concerns on the service development. In the questionnaire three service packages were presented:

1 Service package A: "*Damage control*", which focused on maintenance and the repair of the vehicle. Possible services are an "on-site" repair shop, helpdesk, insurance, etc.
2 Service package B: "*Comfort for you*", which encompassed supplementary services like shopping service, call-a-car, rent-a-car services, children to day-care transport, etc.
3 Service package C: "*Comfort at work*", which included showers and changing rooms with lockers.

According to the project manager, the goal of the questionnaire was to create awareness about the project among Nike's employees.

Some important findings emerged from the questionnaire. Based on a total of 88 respondents, 27% perceived the Mitka as a reasonable alternative and 17% saw it as a good alternative to their current means of transport (Table 6.3). Among car drivers the percentage was at 2.2% and 35% respectively[57] (Broeke van den, Korver, & Droppert-Zilver, 2000). These percentages were seen by the TNO team as positive confirmation of the value of the Mitka concept. The majority of car drivers found that the Mitka was not a good alternative for car use, unless they would be required to walk for more than 15 minutes to reach their workspace from a parking space or they had to leave home two hours earlier to find a parking place. None of the respondents who tried the electric trike (the Twike) during the bike tests chose the three-wheeled version, probably because it was perceived to be difficult to maneuver at high speed (Flipsen, 2000). The average daily distance that people thought that they could cover with the Mitka was between five and 15 kilometers one way and the speed was around 25 km/h. Moreover, one of the central findings from this exercise was the users' preference for a two-wheeled over a three-wheeled vehicle (table 6.3).

In May 2000, the coalition decided to develop a three-wheeled Mitka.

Three interwoven factors were mentioned during discussions and interviews

Table 6.3 Findings based on the Nike questionnaire (Broeke van den et al., 2000)

Mitka as an alternative for the current means of transport	Good	Moderate	No choice	Bad	Very bad
Respondents					
Total population (N = 88)	17%	27%	23%	17%	16%
Car drivers (N = 45)	2.2%	35%	62.8%*		

Mitka version	Two-wheels vehicle	Three wheels vehicle
Total population (N = 88)	66%	34%
Car drivers, alone in their car (=33)	60%	40%
Car drivers, traveling between 5–15 km (N = 6)	50%	50%
Car drivers, traveling between 5–30 km (N = 18)	50%	50%

Note
*This is a cumulative percentage of the three choices.

that may explain this decision. First was the appeal of the sleek, innovative appearance. The three-wheeled concept was considered more innovative than the two-wheeled one. The challenging task stimulated the design team as well as the management. As the designer explained:

> Making a two-wheeled version meant another recumbent bike, therefore nothing new. On the other hand, a completely new mobility solution was needed, something really new. It was much more interesting for us as designers to make a completely new kind of vehicle than to redesign hundreds [of] bikes.[58]

Second, the Gazelle manager was clearly positive about this solution,[59] while most of the other coalition members were doubtful which to choose. This was especially true after the option to develop both versions was considered to be too expensive and time-consuming. In choosing the three-wheeled version, the project leader's intention was to stimulate the Gazelle manager to increase his commitments.[60]

The third reason was because it was "better for the environment". The ultimate goal of the Mitka was to be an environmentally friendly substitute to car use for commuters. The team's strategy was to make drivers interested in the Mitka and the people who chose the three-wheeled version concept seemed to take the car as a frame of reference when reflecting upon the Mitka. On the contrary, those who chose the two-wheeled version seemed to be more oriented towards the bike concept. A two-wheeled version would be likely to attract cyclists, with unwanted and disastrous consequences from an environmental impact view. Cyclists moving from the bike to the Mitka would have increased the environmental impact. On the contrary, car drivers moving from the car to the Mitka would have a positive environmental impact, estimated at a factor of 3 (Oskam, 1999; Weiszäcker et al., 1997). As explained by the project leader: "in this way [the three wheeled vehicle] it is hoped to encourage car users to switch to the Mitka."[61]

After this important decision, the design team worked on the model. The product characteristics had to encompass the various features identified in the questionnaire:

> The three-wheel vehicle is comfortable in all weather types due to the various coverings, it is easy to maneuver and park and it has a modern aura about it. An electric motor doubles the pedaling power, so the driver always has "a following wind".[62]

According to the Nike facility manager, the design needed to be attractive and sportive to match the Nike culture and engage the curiosity of young people. For example, the choice to have two wheels in front and one behind and not the other way around is related to the sleeker, more innovative appearance.

The first 1:3 model

Finally, in July 2000 a model (scale 1:3) was ready to be revealed to the public. The occasion came on September 20. The model was presented at the Nike European head office in Hilversum. It was the project leader's intention that the presentation would promote the Mitka to potential investors. At the presentation, many people, including journalists, were overwhelmed by curiosity and reacted very positively to the Mitka model. In the following days, there was a significant amount of enthusiastic press coverage concerning the futuristic vehicle.

The enthusiasm was contagious. The coalition resolved to explore the Mitka concept with the objective of developing a prototype. The coalition brought in Freewiel Techniek company, specialized in electric and three-wheeled configuration vehicles, to build the prototype. The decision of the Freewiel Techniek director to join the coalition was influenced by the challenging task of the project and the occasion to work again in collaboration with Vd Veer Designers. At this point the necessary financial resources were the main problem. The coalition resolved to take advantage of an opportunity to obtain subsidies, the MOVE program. This program would cover around 50% of the total cost of the project.

The MOVE program was set up in two phases: MOVE I (October 2000–July 2001) and MOVE II (August 2001–September 2002).

The goal of the MOVE I (Joore, 2000b) program was threefold:

1   determine the technical feasibility of the Mitka vehicle;
2   build a full-scale mock-up of the Mitka vehicle;
3   develop the market for the Mitka, build a strategic alliance around the Mitka and find partners for phase 2.

In the MOVE I project proposal there is reference to MOVE II as phase 2:

> The realization of these purposes is necessary for the realization of phase 2, in which the MITKA will be implemented on several testing positions. In phase 2 (following after this project) several MITKA vehicles will be placed on about 10 testing spots, totaling about 50–100 vehicles. Among the testing positions will be the European Headquarters of Nike Europe.
>
> (Joore, 2000b)

The cost of the MOVE I program was estimated to be around €300,000 (50% of the figure was subsidized).

The coalition consisted of the Kathalys team (TNO & TUDelft), the Nike manager, Vd Veer designer, the Gazelle managing director and the Freewiel Techniek managing director. It is important to mention that since 1997 the Mitka and several other projects in the product service system had been carried out within the Kathalys team, like the sustainable office project (Brezet et al., 2001b).

The 1:1 model

The design team focused on building a working model and a mock-up model. The former was aimed at understanding the technical feasibility of the trike. The latter was intended to be shown as a "concept car" to be compared with other vehicles and to get feedback from the public.

THE WORKING MODEL

The challenge faced by the team was to build a three-wheeled vehicle where an upright position, entailing a high center of gravity, was combined with the tilting and steering mechanism of the two wheels in front. With the help of computer simulations, computer modeling and biomechanical models, the project team decided to install two separate mechanisms for steering and tilting, adopting a parallelogram construction, that is, the short beams of the parallelogram represented by the wheels were able to bend (Van Gemert, 2001). With this construction the pedal system needed to be positioned between the wheels in the centre of the parallelogram. A couple of problems, however, arose with this configuration, namely stability and maneuverability. First, the width had to be around 85 cm to ensure good maneuverability, which needed to be seriously improved. Second, a block system was required to moderate the tilting effect of the all-body vehicle. At low speeds the tilting effect was dangerously strong, the vehicle might just bend over due to the high center of gravity. After several parallelogram constructions, the tilting problem still existed and the project team was confident and committed to resolve it in the second part of the project despite the limited technical support from Gazelle where *"there is neither the know-how on 3 wheels configuration nor on the electric assistance."*[63] Concerns about the combination of a high center of gravity and a three-wheeled configuration were expressed by recumbent bike and velomobile producers, like Flevobike.

Besides technical problems, the width necessary for the tilting/steering mechanism works soon presented a practical problem: vehicles wider than 80 cm were unlikely to be able to pass through doors (as emphasized by the market research).[64]

THE MOCK-UP MODEL

According to the plan, the design team was able to build a mock-up of the Mitka vehicle for February 2001. It was built by Freewiel on the basis of the TNO model, although many technical details had still to be discussed. Meanwhile, Vd Veer designers worked on the weather protection and the styling of the Mitka. Finally, the mock-up was presented at FIETSRAI, the largest bicycle fair in the Netherlands, in the Gazelle showroom. The reason for showing the Mitka concept in public was twofold: (1) soliciting user feedback both on the vehicles and the design services (through a questionnaire) and (2) generating publicity to attract investors and partners.

The market research

Meanwhile the market research operated by the TUDelft group moved in four directions (Joore, 2001; Silvester, Knot, Berchicci, & Luiten, 2000):

1   Secondary analysis of the Nike intranet questionnaire to distinguish different target groups because in the first report the characteristics of the respondents had been described without going thoroughly into relationships between the different items of the questionnaire.
2   Group discussions with nine Nike employees in February 2001. The goal was twofold: first, to get insights and personal opinions about the Mitka model (1:3) and service around it; second, to generate ideas for valuable services.
3   Questionnaire at the FIETSRAI (N=142). The visitors were asked to express their opinion about the presented system consisting of the model, a video impression of the prototype and a graphic presentation of some of the service arrangements that had been proposed by the Nike employees in the group discussion.
4   In-depth interviews with 12 Nike employees. The aim was to get feedback on the Mitka system (product and services).

The results of the market research were rather blurry (Table 6.4). The secondary analysis did not find any significant differences between people in favor of the two- or three-wheeled version of the Mitka concerning their socio-demographics, situational characteristics, need for services or patterns of mobility. However, it suggested that those among the car drivers who chose the two-wheeled versions were "latent cyclists" – people using the car because of

Table 6.4 Results from the market research (February–May 2001)

Time	Event	Result
February 2001	Visioning exercise with nine Nike employees	• Potential users have difficulty envisioning daily life with the new artifact • The three-wheeled vehicle is seen to have a problem maneuvering and passing through doors • Mixed reaction to the radical design • Strong preference for leasing over ownership
March 2001	Interviews with bicyclists at FIETSRAI 2001	• Mixed reactions towards Mitka • Mitka system as appropriate for their situation for 57% of the car drivers • 61% of car drivers show willingness to buy it • Concerns about the infrastructure – technical service and parking • Not appropriate for transporting children • Services not particularly important
April and May 2001	In-depth interviews with 12 Nike employees	• Hesitance about the radicality of the design • Strong preference for non-ownership • Mixed reactions to rain protection • Preference for two-wheeled version • Potential users have difficulty envisioning daily life with Mitka

certain circumstances, but who would actually rather use the bike. This could create an unwanted rebound effect as explained in the consumer analysis:

> From a sustainability point of view, people traveling by pooling a car or by bus are not [the target group]. The danger of a so-called rebound effect of employees traveling presently rather sustainable changing mode by choosing the Mitka is realistic. During the development of the product service system around the Mitka concept attention should be paid to this rebound effect.
>
> (Silvester et al., 2000)

From the group discussion it emerged that:

> The three-wheel design was not so much appreciated, mainly because problems were expected concerning the maneuverability, which was, according to them, one of the most important advantages of a bike above the car. Many group-members were quite enthusiastic about the design, but also a relevant part thought it would be "too new" for them.
>
> (Luiten, Knot, & Silvester, 2001b)

On the other hand, a bunch of services such as foldable but fixed rain protection, financial support, no ownership (leasing), and maintenance and reparation arrangements were suggested as important conditions for adoption of the Mitka.

The results from the bicycle fair questionnaire appeared to be more optimistic than those from the discussion group (Luiten et al., 2001b).

> The results of the questionnaire revealed a fairly high [level of] enthusiasm: 46% of all respondents (N = 142) and even 57% of the target group (car-users between 5 and 20 km) evaluate the Mitka system as appropriate for their situation, ca[.] 48% of the target group stated they definitely will use the Mitka, and even 61% of the target group answered positively on the question whether they would consider to buy a Mitka. However, also 33% of the target group found the Mitka system not appropriate for their situation, and a rather large part of the target group did not have clear opinions about the Mitka-system.
>
> (Luiten et al., 2001b)

The respondents were also asked if and how much they were ready to pay for such a vehicle: 50% confirmed their willingness to buy the Mitka and among them 35% would spend roughly €1,350, 22% about €1,800, 22% ca. €2,250 and 7% ca. €3,400. On the contrary, the services developed for and around the Mitka were considered unimportant if not in place yet. As a result, "testing the acceptance and needs of new product-service system is difficult" (Luiten et al., 2001b).

The business development

While the design and the market research team were working on technical development of the vehicle and user acceptance, respectively, the Mitka coalition brought in a new actor, a consulting firm whose assignment was to develop a strategy for the commercialization of the new vehicle, establishing a new organization, the Mitka company.

The main idea for the business plan was to sell the attractive package of a "mobility solution" to employers of large and medium corporations. Consequently, the employees would have another transport option to choose from in addition to the car and public transport.

The Mitka company should entail a small, entrepreneurial management, with one director responsible for marketing and sales and three trustworthy managers for technological development, design and logistics and distribution respectively. As a first step, the Mitka needed to be intellectually protected.

The first evaluation of the production units and costs based on benchmarking was also drawn. The Mitka should take 1% of the market, that is 10,000 units per year. This estimation was made taking into account the number of electric bikes sold per year, between 8,000 and 10,000. In other words, the Mitka was going to double the number of electric bikes. The price should be fixed around €2,700, the same as the average electric bike. These figures, however, referred to the full production, while for the first year, it was estimated that the number of Mitka produced would be between 1,000 and 5,000.

The business plan also recommended and urged the design team to finish the first prototype in order to have a real-life test and to indicate the cost of it, to enable a more realistic financial assessment.[65]

Meanwhile, the DfS director became aware of another case of transport problems and searches for solutions. On the island of Texel, the tension between the desire to promote tourism while holding back the number of cars on the island reached a climax. An idea emerged that Mitka might be part of the solution to Texel's problem (Brown et al., 2003). As a result, a series of students' projects started to analyze the Texel mobility system (Boelens, 2002; Heijnen, 2001; Steenbergen, 2002).

6.2.4 Late development period: the prototype

When the MOVE I program finished, the team had great hopes of introducing the Mitka to the market. As the project manager said: "[the MOVE I] resulted in a mockup of the Mitka vehicle, which doesn't function but looks perfect."[66] There were encouraging signs to support their enthusiasm. First of all, the MOVE committee confirmed a willingness to deliver subsidies for the following project, but stressed that the service aspect of the Mitka required much more attention.[67] While the design team was working hard during summer 2001 to get the first electric prototype on the scene, the consulting firm was actively looking for business partners and adjusting the business plan. Finally, the publicity-generating activities for the Mitka project included photo opportunities with the Dutch crown prince and his wife sitting in the Mitka.

One could observe that this was a turning point for the project. After a long period of only taking low risks and keeping the social context secondary to the engineering and the product design, the high level of publicity and the perceived increasing value of the Mitka concept raised the stakes for all the participants. This created a sense of urgency within the coalition. The general feeling was clearly expressed by the business developer: *"the world stands still without the Mitka."*[68]

First, the rapidly approaching pilot stage had elevated the Mitka project to a higher level of corporate attention. In a meeting in September 2001, before the final MOVE II proposal was submitted, the Gazelle director was willing to invest significantly in the project for the next three years (not only money from the PR budget) if clear figures on the costs, time and market potential of the vehicle were disclosed. In the same meeting, the Nike delegate pointed out the increasing interest expressed by Nike at the corporate level with regard to the commercialization of the Mitka.

At the beginning the participation of Nike was more like a game – a new project to get fun from that. The parking problem was there, but it was not enough to be really committed. When the Mitka was presented [to the public] the reactions were enthusiastic. In that moment the Mitka project, from a funny experiment, started to be more serious for us. Now the project is very important for Nike. Also the vice-president is getting enthusiastic about it.[69]

Second, new actors became interested in the project: Brabant Development Corporation (BOM) and a major Dutch insurance company. The former is a semi-public development agency for the Brabant region in the Netherlands that had been pushing hard for innovation in transportation services. Brabant was planning to build a 13 kilometer demonstration route that was intended to serve as a testing ground for innovative ideas in transportation including fast, no-stopping bicycle lanes. The latter is currently in the process of expanding its core business to provide employers with complete mobility solutions for their employees. It became interested in including the Mitka in its range of trans-portation alternatives.

Therefore, the goal of MOVE II was actually to further develop the vehicle and the services and to test a number of prototypes in real-life experiments. Three main objectives were announced:

1   develop the vehicle to a prototype level with services;
2   implement and test ten prototypes with relative services in the Nike head-quarters and gauge user acceptance;
3   develop the market and establish the Mitka consortium.

The cost of MOVE II was estimated around €616,000, 50% to be covered by subsidies.

The plan was indeed simple. First build one prototype that was intellectually protected; then build a series of them to be technically tested with dedicated services by Nike employees; and finally, show the Mitka to the media to attract potential investors. It was observed that confidence and optimism were shared by all of the participants and all expectations concentrated on the technical development. In the same meeting in September 2001 and in the MOVE II project proposal, the Mitka consortium planned the first prototype by the end of the year, and the first series in spring 2002.

The prototype phase

Looking more closely, the project was not without challenges. Building the first prototype required the project team to carry out several working packages:

1   concept development of the new steering and tilting system;
2   concept development of the new roof;
3   concept development of the new sitting position;
4   development of the luggage unit and child seat;

5   development of the propulsion system, the choice of the battery technology and the power control;
6   concept development of the frame and suspension;
7   elaboration of the storage services.

Except for point 5, all the working packages entailed completely new design and development techniques. There were very few standard parts, so that everything needed to be made by the project team, which had little specific experience. The concept for the storage service was worked out by a student designer (Dekker, 2002).

Even the choice of the propulsion system, battery and power control was challenging. According to the speed and electric motor power, the Mitka could have been registered as an electric bike (2.5 kW, max. 25 km/h), a moped (4 kW, max. 25 km/h) or a scooter (4 kW, max. 40 km/h, with compulsory use of a helmet). The project team also decided to drop the child seat because it was perceived as an accessory to the design, which could be incorporated at a later stage.

Unfortunately, the first finished working Mitka was far from ready by the end of the year or the beginning of 2002. Significant technical problems emerged at the end of 2001. For example, the new tilting/steering system, designed ex novo, did not function properly because the vibrations of the fork created serious problems for the stability of the vehicle at high speed. These technical drawbacks meant a longer development time and shifted resources. Therefore, the budget allocated for service and market development was partially diverted to the technical development of the prototype and recruiting also to experts from TNO Automotive.[70]

The unexpected technical problems did not undermine the confidence of the project leader, although in a memo to the management meeting in February 2002, he admitted that the cost of developing the first prototype was higher than expected. Therefore, the decision to build a series of ten Mitkas had to be carefully evaluated after the prototype test, although many among the partners wanted to have at least one vehicle. Moreover, the electric motor was not functioning properly and the weather protection was not yet ready. A decision on power for the propulsion system had not been made, although Gazelle stated that it was only interested in the commercialization of the new vehicle if the Mitka could be registered as an electric bicycle rather than as a moped.

THE NEW ORGANIZATION

The organization chart[71] also changed (see Figure 6.4). Two teams were officially created: the strategy and the commercialization teams. The former encompassed the traditional partners plus BOM and the insurance company. Its function was not defined in detail; however, it entailed management support for the Mitka project. Besides the strategy team, a commercialization team was

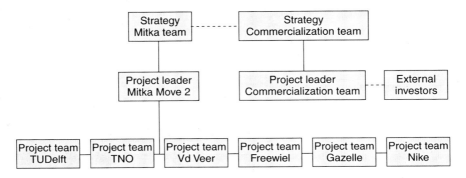

Figure 6.4 The organizational chart for the Mitka project (February, 2002).

established, led by the consulting firm director. Its function was to prepare a business plan, find potential financial partners and manage the public relationship.

Meanwhile the project team was working hard to solve the many technical problems. TUD researchers were preparing the testing, encompassing both practical arrangements such as installation and transport of the vehicles, and recruiting test persons among Nike employees. Everyone was waiting for the prototype.

THE PROTOTYPE

The occasion came on May 2, 2002, when all of the partners (which included the TNO director and one Nike CEO) gathered together to see the first Mitka prototype and decide what to do next. Their high expectations turned into disillusionment. Although the prototype was ready, the electric engine was not working properly and the roof was not in place; more time was needed. Financially, a significant part of the budget was already spent and the cost for building three to five vehicles was estimated at around €100,000. One completed and finished vehicle would only cost around €40,000. The day before the meeting, however, the cost of one vehicle in the pre-industrial series was set at €20,000 according to the business developer.

Two scenarios were presented: the first, and most optimistic one, contemplated finishing the current model in a couple of months and focusing on the construction of three to five vehicles that would be ready for September 2002 and then the testing. The second scenario entailed the completion of the first vehicle in a month and testing with lead users during the summer. Everyone chose the second scenario because they wanted to see the "perfect" vehicle on the road before thinking of investing significant resources.

The prototype created anxiety among the partners. The Gazelle manager, talking about the state of the project, said:

The negative aspect is based on the absence of a product after two years....

Now it is time to make a product that is working and functioning properly. No more promoting because it is already two years that the Mitka model is shown and the public can lose interest in something which never ends in a product.[72]

On the other hand, some members of the project team felt frustrated. They felt that their efforts were not fully recognized by the team management and that the process was too bureaucratic and slow with endless discussions.[73]

Given this concern, new surprising developments occurred within the coalition. TUDelft proposed looking for other partners within the car industry. It was felt that, if the Mitka targeted car drivers, car companies were more suited to producing and distributing such a vehicle than bike producers. They looked for car companies without success. Nevertheless, the TNO team felt confident of the chance to have the Mitka produced by Gazelle. In the following meeting in July, while the management group stressed the need to finish the prototype and find commercial partners, one of the main partners, Gazelle, decided to stop investing in the three-wheeled version because the Mitka, although still a better alternative to a car than a bike, was too expensive and outside the core business of the organization.[74] In light of this, the Gazelle director decided to develop a two-wheeled version of the Mitka, stating that the new project was independent from the current MOVE II project.

A second issue arose: *Who owns the Mitka?* According to TNO, the answer was easy, TNO owned 40% of the rights to the three-wheeled Mitka; Vd Veer Designers/Gazelle owned 40% and the rest was owned by Freewiel Techniek. Eventually, any two-wheeled concept was going to be owned by Gazelle/Veer. The problem was the position of TUD. They were out of the deal and so opposed it. Tension inevitably arose among the participants until a compromise was reached: 20% to TUDelft of the 40% owned by TNO, which was 8.2% of the total. In spite of the increasing diverging opinions within the coalition, the project leader bet on the test, which could turn the Mitka three-wheeled version into a profitable business case potentially able to attract new investing partners.

While the test preparation was shaping up (selecting test drivers, writing the test manual, fine-tuning services and building up logistics), the Mitka vehicle was still lagging behind schedule. Although the roof was completed, the battery system and the battery recharger were not working properly. Moreover, the distance range of the Mitka was not clear. It appeared to be around 25 kilometers based on one test. There was also a legal issue – the 4 kW engine allowed speeds up to 40 km/h, which requires the user to wear a helmet according to safety regulations. Helmets are required for vehicles with a speed of more than 25 km/h.

The propulsion system issue highlighted the different visions within the coalition. According to the Nike manager, the Mitka should be fast, aggressive and sportive to fit the organization's image. Therefore, the propulsion system needed to push the Mitka to 40 km/h at least, without a helmet. On the contrary, the Gazelle director wanted a Mitka limited to 25 km/h, which could be registered as a bike.

The Mitka should be very attractive and fun to ride (and it is). The speed should be around 40 km/h without helmet: this is important because the image of Nike is sportive, fast, cool, fancy and trendy. If the Mitka needs to be on the car street for that reason, it is acceptable, but not with the helmet, please.[75]

Therefore, the project team faced a technical and political dilemma, more speed meant more power, which in turn required the user to wear a helmet. The problem was solved by introducing a two-speed mode under the dashboard – a bicycle mode and a moped mode. This solution was seen as a compromise between the need to address the legal issue and Gazelle's insistence on a bike-registered vehicle on the one hand and the willingness of the project team to have a fast, appealing vehicle for car drivers on the other.

These problems created repeated delays of the test, which was postponed many times, sometimes just a couple of days before it was due to start. The project manager was so eager to let Nike employees test the Mitka that there were only a couple of pre-tests focused solely on the battery recharge cycle. Finally, on October 22 the test of the new Mitka vehicle began.

The test

The real-life test was different from that planned. The number of Mitka available for testing was neither five nor ten as expected, but only one vehicle. Due to the problems mentioned, the test had been postponed from spring to autumn. The preliminary technical tests were not carried out as expected; therefore a great deal of uncertainty existed as to the actual functionality of the concept.

Besides the vehicle, test drivers benefited from a raft of related services: maintenance, a parking lot in the Nike Building, battery rechargers at home and at the office, a manual on how to use the Mitka and a travel diary.

Although more than 13 people signed up for the test, only two were selected plus the DfS director. The reason related to the selection criteria for this special testing. The potential test drivers needed:

*   to commute over a distance of between 10 and 15 km;
*   to have shelter for the Mitka and a power supply;
*   to ride for at least two weeks to test the Mitka in different settings (weather conditions, shopping or recreational use, etc.);
*   to be preferably car drivers; and
*   to be enthusiastic about driving the Mitka.

After the initial screening, two enthusiastic American Nike managers were chosen; they lived just 12 km from the office and had a suitable storage place for the Mitka.

The first driver, a product marketer, commuted just a couple of days with the Mitka, driving early in the morning and returning around 10 pm. He stopped riding after that because he thought it was too dangerous to drive the Mitka. The insufficient lighting, poor visibility and poor maneuverability forced him to drive during off-peak hours to avoid other bikes along the path. He reported precisely the following critical factors:[76]

1   Insufficient lighting – driving in the dark was dangerous because the lights did not provide enough illumination on the road (in that period of the season it was dark in the early morning and in the afternoon).
2   Poor visibility – the windshield provided protection from the wind and the rain but it was difficult to see out of it, especially when it was raining: "Without wipers it is very hard to see and the little wing on the top doesn't help the visibility also. Moreover, it reflects the lights of the cars making the visibility worse."
3   Poor maneuverability – "it is not easy to pass other bikes. It is heavy to steer and the steering is not precise, it was fighting all the way home!". When riding a normal bike, the weight of the body goes to the bar and helps you to steer, but on the Mitka the weight was on the seat and made it difficult to maneuver. It was also heavy on the front and very light on the back. There was no precision in the steering. Moreover, "it is not easy to steer with one hand while signaling the direction with the other one out or ringing the bell".
4   Speed limit – max 28 km/h and then you could not go any faster with the human power.
5   Pilot – when you switched off the Mitka the pilot also switched off, thus losing the data.
6   No shock absorption system – "All the bumps you can feel on your spine! Moreover you cannot lift your body like on the normal bike. It is unpleasant."

He also proposed some solutions: replacing the windshield and lighting. On October 25, the third day of the test, the project manager decided to halt the pilot test and fix the urgent problems.

After two weeks, the project team worked on the vehicle, changing the lighting system but not the windshield. This was because the change would require the complete substitution of the windshield system, an operation thought to be too complex and time-consuming. The only recommendation given to testers was not to use the windshield in the rain and in the dark. The test started again on November 12, but this time the DfS director drove the Mitka from the university building in Delft to his house 13 kilometers to the south and back the next morning. The first evening, he did not recharge the battery, feeling confident that the Mitka would be able to cover the trip back the next day. Unfortunately, the power assistance stopped after approximately 19 kilometers. He described his impressions in this way:

As long as the power assistance was working, I was pleasantly surprised for the extraordinary speed (28 km max) the Mitka could reach. However, once the battery went off, I felt as a loser who was not able to pay for a real good vehicle for disabled people. I was as fast as a snail and on little hills I had to step down and push it.[77]

The overall evaluation was in line with the first Mitka driver: poor visibility in rainy conditions, poor maneuverability and danger in passing other vehicles. On the contrary, the sleek appearance was highly appreciated by neighbors and relatives. However, he also decided to stop the test.

After maintenance, without substantial changes, the test started again with the first test driver, who was able to ride it for three days. However, his evaluation did not change. On November 29, 2002 the second and the last "official" test driver started the Mitka test, which lasted one week. Interestingly, his evaluation was more positive than that of the previous driver. On the one hand, he made similar comments about the effort to maneuver, yet on the other hand, he felt that it was fun to ride in this way, although he never drove in rainy conditions. He particularly appreciated the sitting position with the back support, a feature similar to that in the new Giant bike: the EZB Revive.

The two Nike drivers also had mixed feelings about the organization, which appeared "rather disjointed and opaque, although the project team members individually seem very pleasant, eager, and committed[78] (first driver). Moreover, it looks like there is a phase of reorganization, no clear procedure[79] (second driver).

On December 5, 2002, the test was over and serious questions regarding the safety issue remained unanswered. Meanwhile, at the management level, there was hope that, with an effective public presentation of the Mitka, they would be able to raise the capital needed to produce 50 Mitka vehicles, especially with the help of BOM. However, when the partial results of the test were presented to the management group on December 12, BOM avoided dealing with the issue. Intriguingly, only the most optimistic test driver was formally invited. The occasion for the press conference and the search for potential partners and business people occurred on the same day, where everyone could test the three-wheeled Mitka on Nike's sport track in Hilversum. This event also created a great deal of publicity, with TV reports and newspaper articles praising the new vehicle as an alternative to the car.[80] As a big surprise the two-wheeled Mitka version created by Vd Veer for Gazelle was also presented to the press, the Easy Glider.

6.2.5 The termination of the three-wheeled Mitka development and the implementation of the spin-off: the two-wheeled Mitka

In July 2002 Gazelle decided to bet on a two-wheeled version of the Mitka, and use the three-wheeled version as a PR tool. The two-wheeled version would respond to Giant's EZB, a new, slightly recumbent bike with a back support. Vd Veer designers started to work on the two-wheeled version and in October 2002 the first pictures were in the newspapers: "the little brother of the Mitka."[81]

After a trial with the three-wheeled Mitka, the Gazelle director decided that it was too innovative, too expensive, too heavy and too far from Gazelle's target group, cyclists.[82] Moreover, the power assistance and roof were too complex, creating never-ending problems. In addition, Gazelle wanted a bicycle and not a scooter or a moped, which included any bike with 4 kW as power assistance, according to the regulations. According to the designer, the three-wheeled Mitka was a brand new kind of bike with a frame and sitting position between a regular bike and a recumbent one. Adding the power assistance and roof, it was a unique vehicle. After working for more than two years on the three-wheeled Mitka, the task of designing and developing a two-wheeled bicycle with similar ergonomics was not difficult. Consequently, it took only three months to come up with the first prototype with electric assistance. The knowledge gained about the body and sitting position of the three-wheeled Mitka were transferred to the two-wheeled vehicle. The first prototype also had the same engine and set of batteries, allowing a speed of 40 km/h. This new electric bike was still considered out of the core business of Gazelle because electric bikes featured in its product portfolio. Nevertheless, it was a big step in the right direction because, according to Gazelle, "this gives you a lot more bicycle as it's lighter, more maneuverable and sportier [than the three-wheeled Mitka]."[83] This prototype was shown during a press conference in December 2002, but the development did not stop there. The designers took two directions. First, making a two-wheeled Mitka without electric power assistance and weather protection for production and distribution in 2003 to compete with the Giant Revive EZB already in the market. to The second direction was further developing the version with the electric engine.

The "regular" bike, called Easy Glider, was presented to the FIETSRAI in March 2003 and it was nominated, together with the Giant EZB Revive DX8, for the "Best Bicycle of the Year 2003" award, for innovative design and a revolutionary relaxing sitting position. It got also a second nomination in 2004 (Figure 6.5). Its name stems from the ease with which the user can regulate the sitting position along the diagonal frame. The price for such a bike was about €1,095 in 2004 and there were about 2,000 Easy Gliders on the street in May of that year.

It is a different story for the Easy E-Glider with power assistance. The main problems were the price, speed and Gazelle's skepticism about entering the new electric bike market. While the power/speed ratio and the problems related to street regulations were well recognized, price remained an issue. How much should such a bike cost? The price was linked to the Mitka development. The same engine and battery construction was extremely expensive and heavy; therefore, the second prototype was given a different, much smaller engine, but in the same position between the rear wheel and pedal system. It was presented at the same bicycle fair in 2003 and later tested on Texel Island (on April 9, 2003) where bike rental companies were encouraged by a local non-profit organization, the Sustainable Texel Foundation[84] to adopt innovative bicycle concepts.

The second prototype, however, was still too expensive, estimated at around €3,500. Finally, the designers decided to set up a standard 400 W engine, easy to assemble on the front wheel with the necessary kit. With this less complex

Figure 6.5 Two-wheeled versions of the Mitka, the Easy E-Glider.

and cheaper configuration, the cost of the Easy E-Glider dropped to around €2,000. Nevertheless, Gazelle seems to be reluctant to produce the Easy E-Glider.

With the end of the Move II program at the end of 2002, the three-wheeled Mitka project suddenly lost impetus. Although a functioning prototype was developed and to some extent tested as expected, the promised 50 pre-series vehicles and the pledged creation of services were not delivered. Moreover, the lack of business partners forced premature termination of the three-wheeled Mitka. After three years of product and service development and about €1,150,000 of investment, the Mitka project ended with two power-assisted prototypes, one three-wheeled and one two-wheeled, and one two-wheeled spin-off on the market, taking into account both the generated publicity for the participants in the consortium and the learning process.

Comments from key actors

After the termination of the Mitka project, some of the key actors were asked to reflect on it and to check the accuracy of the descriptions in this chapter. From this reflective task, two interrelated issues clearly emerged: the goal and the outcome of the project.

As emerged during the discussion on February 22, 2005, the original goal of TUDelft in the Mitka project had been narrower than TNO's goals. The Mitka project was seen mainly as a demonstration project for sustainable mobility by some members of the TUDelft team, although the project soon came to represent a market opportunity. Contrary to this view, the former project leader confirmed that the TNO team had been strongly committed to introducing the Mitka to the market as an alternative to the car since the beginning of the project, having always considered it an attempt to achieve system innovation.

The Gazelle director's motivation has been a matter of discussion in the final part of the project. According to the former project leader, the goal of Gazelle was clear: developing an innovative three-wheeled concept. During the interview on March 25, 2002, when asked about his goal for the project, the Gazelle director confirmed that fact, although he added that the Mitka also acted as a marketing tool, providing publicity for the company. According to the business developers interviewed on January 7, 2005, Gazelle might have had a double agenda, with the main intention being to generate publicity. This interpretation seems to have been partially confirmed by the designer in a phone conversation on February 22, 2005, who suggested that Gazelle achieved one of its goals with the great deal of publicity generated by the Mitka project. In an email received on February 15, 2005, the Gazelle director suggested that the Mitka project had turned out to be a successful project primarily for Gazelle only, for marketing reasons and for the opportunity it engendered in developing the Easy Glider. It is important to emphasize that the above-mentioned interpretations are *post factum.*

With regard to the outcome of the Mitka project, the Vd Veer director said:

It is not a success. When everyone was super excited with the first model we were not successful to reap the moment and finding a solution for the bending system. We didn't succeed to define the next step and the Mitka became heavy, poorly maneuverable. Maybe we should take a step back and make it simple for leisure purpose and for a niche market and not for a large one. Maybe the first target group should be elderly people, although it may kill the project! However, our society is becoming older and they have the money to effort such a thing.

Back to your question: I think it is not a success but there are some successful elements in It ... We learnt a lot, with a good network. In the future we are going to make more things with TNO or TUD. We learnt also how to get subsidies. Finally, the spin-off of the Easy Glider! If we were not involved with the Mitka the Easy Glider could not reach the catalogue of Gazelle. So that's a very positive outcome![85]

Addressed with the same question, the Gazelle director responded:

The development of the Mitka was a difficult process with never-ending discussions, with continuously different people and organizations and, with never-ending product development. Conclusion: the whole project was too complex and too expensive. Result: never a perfect prototype … What is worth for Gazelle? Yes, for public relations … [and] it was relatively easy to develop the Easy Glider.[86]

The business developer pointed out that the Mitka project had failed from a business perspective, because it had been mainly technologically driven while the business development had been understated, with no strong commercial partner from the outset of the project.

However, the former project leader defined the Mitka project as "a great success with little money", because it created an innovative and important step towards a sustainable society while increasing the public and policy makers' awareness.[87]

Who knows whether the two prototypes will sleep forever or, sooner or later, awake again.

6.3 The Mango case

A velomobile is a very good bike, but a bad car.

Ymte Sijbrandij[88]

This section constitutes an in-depth case study of the Mango development based on 18 hours of interviews with the two founders and others involved in the project, carried out between December 2003 and October 2004 (five interviews in total), supported by magazine articles such as "Velo Vision" and internet sources concerning velomobiles. Moreover, an email survey of Velomobiel's clients was performed. The main events of the Mango history are reviewed in Box 6.4.

Unlike the Mitka case study, retrospective data collection was the main source for this case, requiring the interviewer to recall events, facts and decisions that had occurred in the past. Given the entrepreneurial and young character of the firm, the number of interviews is unsurprisingly low. The interview will cover the two levels of analysis: the entrepreneurial level and the NPD process level. At entrepreneurial level, motivation, prior experience and opportunities are analyzed. At project level, the focus is on decisions resulting in the Mango development process.

6.3.1 Velomobiel, the firm and the products

Not to be confused with the type of vehicle illustrated in section 6.1.2, the firm under study is called *Velomobiel* (Dutch translation of velomobile). The company was founded by Allert Jacob and Ymte Sijbrandij in 1999 under the name of J&S Fietsdiensten (J&S bicycle service). In it changed its name to Velomobiel, to raise its visibility, with the arrival of a new partner, Theo van Andel. The company comprises three individuals: Allert Jacob is the designer and developer of Velomobiel's two vehicles, while Ymte Sijbrandij is the market developer and Theo van Andel is in charge of the assembly line, with all three working on the production line.

Box 6.3 The Mitka history

Event time	Who[89]	What	Why
Initiation period			
1996	TNO + Batavus	Developing a new bike concept for longer distance than the current one	To apply ecodesign To create space for sustainability Need in the market
1997	TUDelft	Projects on sustainable solutions for substituting the car over short distances	High environmental impact of car use To design and develop sustainable product innovations
1997	TNO + TUDelft	Kathalys established	Technical development (over braking, gears, etc.)
1997	Stork + Poliform	As new partners	Too innovative for them
1997	Batavus	Refuse the third proposal and jump out of the project	Out of the core business
1998	TNO	Looking for partners Change of the project leader	To develop the "Bike plus" concept
1999	NIKE	As a new partner Consumer research within Nike employees	Nike perspective: Sustainable manager enthusiastic about the idea Imminent parking problem in the headquarter TNO perspective: Good image
1999	Gazelle	As a new partner The P. Van der Veer Designer as head designer (Gazelle's subcontract)	Lead users client Gazelle perspective: Potential business opportunity Nike part of the coalition (image) Public relations TNO perspective: Need for bike company
Early development period			
1999	TNO + Nike + Gazelle	Fourth proposal for EET-KIEM: accepted cost: €216,000 Change of the project leader	To develop a family-friendly compact vehicle, more comfortable and functional than the bicycle

Box 6.3 continued

Event time	Who[89]	What	Why
2000	Stork	Leave the coalition	R&D committed but management disagreed (Their role started to be irrelevant for TNO)
Jan. 2000	TNO + Nike	Test with several bike concepts for two weeks	To get feedback and ideas about bikes' features and characteristics
Mar. 2000	TNO + Nike	Internet survey for Nike employees	To understand mobility behaviors
May 2000	TNO + Gazelle + Nike	Development of the three-wheeled version only, although two of the respondents preferred the two-wheeled version. Decision strongly supported by Gazelle.	To let them to create the own bike concept: a two-wheeled or a three-wheeled version. It is more innovative and attractive No real opposition to the Gazelle decision It is better for the environment (car driver as target group)
May 2000	TNO + Gazelle	Technical characteristics for the new concept: Two wheels in front and one on the back Weather protection Power assistance	To combine the car and bike advantages
May 2000	Freewiel Techniek	Join the coalition	Engineering company specialized in three-wheeled configuration
July 2000 Sept. 2000	TNO TNO + Gazelle + Nike	First Mitka (on scale 1:3) presented at Nike symposium Presented the Mitka in a symposium at Nike head office	Looking for partners and publicity also inside TNO Result: press and new entrepreneurs interested
Oct. 2000	TUDelft	New partner	To perform consumer research and environmental life cycle analysis To develop the Kathalys method
Oct. 2000	Coalition	MOVE I program Cost: €300,000	Technical feasibility of the Mitka vehicle To build a full scale mock-up To develop a market and a coalition for the Mitka
Oct. 2000	Project team (F+V+TNO)	Tilting and steering mechanisms as independent system: the parallelogram construction	To curve and bend simultaneously Width: 85cm, in spite of street regulations

Date	Actor	Event	Notes
Jan. 2001	Consulting firm	New partner	Business and economic development
Oct. 2000–Feb 2001	Coalition	Project team (F + V + TNO)	Mock-up model finished
Mar. 2001		The mock-up model of the Mitka presented on the FIETSRAI	Publicity and feedback
Feb.–May 2001	TUDelft	Consumer research	Looking for partners
		Group discussions	To generate ideas and get feedback on the Mitka
		A FIETSRAI questionnaire on the product and the designed services	Contrasting results
		In-depth interviews	
May 2001	Consulting firm + TNO	First business model	
Summer 2001	Project team	Working on the tilting steering mechanisms	
		Electric power assistance	
		Roof	
Sept. 2001	TNO + Gazelle	Presentation Mitka on TNO symposium: photo with the future queen	Publicity
			Looking for partners
Sept. 2001	Coalition	Enthusiasm and more commitments	
Late development period			
Oct. 2001	Coalition	MOVE II	Development of the Mitka product and relative services
		Cost: €616,000	Testing of ten prototypes
			Market development
Nov. 2001	Insurance company	New partner	Big company with a vast range of services like insurance and call centre
Nov. 2001	BOM	Big sale force B2B directly with employer (company's mobility policy)	A new road project with the Mitka as a perfect vehicle for it
		New partner	Division of the business development from the technical development
Feb. 2002	Coalition	Change in the organizational chart	Unfit steering tilting mechanism
Nov. 2001–May 2002	Project team	First prototype delayed several times	Power assistance failure
			Roof not ready

Box 6.3 continued

Event time	Who[89]	What	Why
May 2002	Coalition meeting	Price of one Mitka: €25,000 Urgent need for capital to build five to ten Mitka vehicles	The coalition decided to have just one Mitka but in "perfect" state
July 2002	Gazelle	Stop investing on the Mitka Focusing on a two-wheeled version only	Out of the core business Too expensive Car driver no real target group for the company Respond to Giant
Sept.–Oct.2002	Coalition	Irritability among partners	Never ending Mitka vehicle the intellectual property issues the test continually postponed
Oct. 2002 Oct.–Dec.2002	Project team Nike employees	Mitka ready Testing the artifact and the service in a real-life test	Contrasting results: fun to drive but also dangerous and poor maneuverability
Dec. 2002	Coalition	Presentation and testing of the 3 w Mitka and the 2 w Mitka by Gazelle	Publicity Looking for partners
Feb. 2003	Mitka	Coalition loosened Three-wheeled Mitka interrupted	No funds (No interests)
Implementation Mar. 2003	Gazelle	Presentation of the Easy Glider and Easy E-Glider on the FIETSRAI	
Mar. 2003	Gazelle	Production and distribution of the Easy Glider	

The Quest and the Mango are the two Velomobiles produced by Velomobiel. The first project was the Quest introduced to the market in 2000 costing €5,672 with the Mango appearing two years later at €4,500. The Quest is longer and faster while the Mango is cheaper and has a smaller turning cycle to improve maneuverability (Figure 6.6).

a)

b)

Figure 6.6 a) The Quest, b) the Mango.

In a way similar to the history of the Mitka, the Velomobiel development is related according to a timeline of events following van de Ven's scheme (Van de Ven et al., 1999). The events are described according to four phases: initiation period, early and late development period and implementation. The emphasis here is given to the Mango development, considered the synthesis of previous concept developments. Therefore, the Mango is positioned in the late development period whereas the first Velomobiel's product, the Quest, is positioned in the early development period.

6.3.2 Initiation period: the Alleweder experience

To fully understand the Velomobiel story, a step back in time is required, stopping the clock somewhere in 1993 when a special event was being prepared. In the occasion of the 365-days-fiets-prize organized by the Netherlands' magazine *Fiets* (translated "Bicycle"), Allert Jacob was asked to act as the driver of the *Alleweder*, a semi-covered recumbent bike produced by the *Flevobike* Company.[90] Allert Jacob was one of the racing champions of NVHPV (Dutch, human-powered vehicle association) and already a client of Flevobike, owning one of their recumbent models.

The Alleweder (literally translated from the Dutch as "*the all weather conditions*") was not designed by Flevobike, but by a civil engineering student, Bart Verhees, who for his final project, constructed a recumbent three-wheeler. After his graduation, he decided to build a canopy with aluminum sheets around the frame leaving open the front side (or the "nose"). The reason for building such a vehicle was to find a solution to the drawbacks of cycling, which was his passion: first, the lack of protection from severe weather conditions and second, the lack of comfort. His hobby was building small airplanes, so he had the skills to build a light canopy from sheets of aluminum. After the canopy, he wanted to make a self-carrying fairing (with no frame), like an airplane's fuselage but with the addition of wheel casing. To improve comfort, very soft suspension was added. This was the first Alleweder in the mid-1980s, which drove more than 50,000 km.

He wanted to start production but never succeeded. He tried to set up a list of potential clients willing to buy it, but the number of subscribers was too low to start a business case. In 1993, Bart Verhees decided to take the vehicle to Flevobike's owner, Johan Vrielink, a well-known producer of recumbent bikes, to get feedback and advice. Johan Vrielink saw a business opportunity in the Alleweder and made an immediate decision to take it to the 365-days-fiets competition. He wanted to test the concept's functionality and see how the public might react to the sleek, innovative vehicle.[91]

There were four basic requirements for participation. The bicycle should be able:

1   to drive 35 km in one hour (without electric help);
2   to carry 15 kg of luggage in a space of at least 80 liters;

3   to provide protection from extreme weather conditions; and
4   to only warrant low maintenance.

Alleweder won the competition with Allard as the driver. Thanks to the publicity advertising this event and the subsequent press coverage of it, the name Alleweder started to spread in the bike world. Potential customers started to contact Flevobike. They wanted to ride an Alleweder or even buy one. Consequently, Flevobike decided to produce the Alleweder. However, because the number of employees available was limited (at that time three family members) it could not cope with this unexpected success. Therefore, Flevobike asked Allert Jacob to work for the firm and he accepted. He explained his motivation in this way: "I studied to be a craftsman teacher, because I like to work with my hands. Bikes were my passion and in the beginning the work in Flevobike was about production: both two-wheelers and Alleweders."[92]

Allert Jacob's work took place in the workshop, building and modeling different metal parts of the Alleweder. As a tireless driver of the vehicle, Allert Jacob made additional improvements based on this extensive usage. "Being users of the Alleweder we encountered many little problems which were later addressed. In some way we anticipated customers' problems."[93]

The main changes were under the canopy. For example, the suspension, brakes and the chain guiding were redesigned and improved. These changes were introduced in a subsequent series of the Alleweder. Looking closer, the first series of 25 Alleweders were different from the others in the way that they were produced. The production of the first series involved labor-intensive work, where the aluminum sheets were cut with scissors and bent almost manually.[94] The rest of the production was done by the Fokker company, who had the right machines for cutting and modeling the different parts needed for construction. However, continuous improvements became a regular procedure during the development. "During that period you got skilled in design, production, materials and construction and experience with the customer and bike market."[95]

The first 25 Alleweders were sold for €1,132, later for €1,359 and finally for €1,586. The price increase was due to a miscalculation of the effective production costs, such as the labor hours. When production stabilized and the cost had been correctly calculated, the price increase was necessary. Between 1993 and 1998, Flevobike sold about 500 Alleweder, plus recumbent bikes. In the beginning, the demand was higher than in the late 1990s, when the market for such novelties stabilized and saturated. In the first year, around 120 Alleweder were sold, but in 1999, only 50 units were sold.

The bikes were sold to order. The customer ordered the vehicle, which was then built. The customers were provided with a kit including all the parts of the Alleweder and the tools needed to put it together themselves. The reason for providing the client with a kit instead of a ready-to-drive vehicle was mainly to keep the price low. Outsourcing the assembly meant fewer labor hours. Working on demand required an average development time of five months, whereas the assembly time was around 40–80 hours. Another advantage of the kit was that few clients required maintenance service. They were able to do it themselves. On the other hand, the market segment for such a kit was limited and quickly saturated.[96]

In 1995, Ymte Sijbrandij started to work at Flevobike as a book-keeper and shortly afterwards, he decided with Allert Jacob to become co-owner of the company. They had numerous ideas and they decided to invest in Flevobike. In the same period, Allert Jacob (after building 200 Alleweder and 400 recumbent bikes) decided to work only three to four days a week and spend the remaining time working on his own projects in the workshop, such as two-wheelers and a redesigned Alleweder.

The C-Alleweder

The Alleweder was one of the fastest bikes on the road, with comfort, weather protection, speed and luggage unit the main product characteristics. However, according to Allert Jacob, improvements were desirable and achievable. First, the speed. The Alleweder could become even faster by reducing the weight and improving the aerodynamics. Second, maintenance of the vehicle required time. For example, cleaning the chain, which would get dirty easily, was a cumbersome task.

Having a lighter and faster Alleweder required changing not only the shape but also the complete canopy, the fairing's material and consequently the production system. The current canopy's material, aluminum sheets, was not suited to fine bending because:

> Aluminum sheets can be bent only in one direction and not on two directions. This limitation affects any improvement in aerodynamics. You can only do it if you are capable of pressing, like in car production, but it is too expensive, and it makes it feasible only when you have a large number of parts to produce.[97]

It was decided that carbon fiber-glass could replace the aluminum sheets, which proved to be an optimal solution in case "you want to improve the weight and aerodynamics. Any shape can be done with fiber-glass."[98] Therefore the new product requirements were in place for a new version of the Alleweder: a faster and lighter Alleweder in carbon and fiber-glass, with better aerodynamics in a monocoque design. To improve the aerodynamics, drawings and small models were the tools utilized; however, some of the fundamental rules from the Alleweder vehicle, like the driver's position, were retained. "Rather than planning, it was a process of estimating, assuming and guessing."[99]

However, the monocoque design with carbon and fiber-glass was a real challenge for a designer inexperienced in working with fiber-glass. An opportunity for cooperation came along with the one-man concern, Mr Tempelman. This company specialized in fiber-glass/epoxy work, and at that time was producing the seats and nose cones for the Alleweder. After creating a first model in polyester, molds were ready for making the body of the *C-Alleweder*.

The first C-Alleweder (named "C" because of the carbon element in the body) was finally ready at the end of 1996. The body was carbon and fiber-glass, with no frame inside, only the gears and pedals were made of metal. The chain was inside the fairing meaning that no chain maintenance was required. The new C-Alleweder was indeed faster and lighter than the regular version. It had 15% more speed and weighed 8 kg less. Moreover, the luggage space almost doubled to 120 liters.[100] The design was also much smoother and linear than the previous version.

These visible improvements did not prevent other problems from emerging. First, it was time-consuming. The production time was around 40 hours. This was because of "the lack of experience in working with fiber-glass."[101] The second drawback was strongly related to the first one: it was very expensive to build one. The design did not take into account the production process because the C-Alleweder was not meant to be sold. Nevertheless, a small-scale production process was put in place to address increasing demand from new clients. Between 1997 and 1998 20 C-Alleweder were built. The price of the C-Alleweder changed three times. Going from €3,400 to €7,000, it became far too expensive, especially compared to the aluminum Alleweder.

In 1998, C-Alleweder production stopped and the molds were sold to Mr Tempelman, who built around 12 *Limits*, a copy of the C-Alleweder. Besides the cost and the high production time, two other factors influenced the decision to terminate production of the vehicles. To begin with, the speed of the C-Alleweder and its production process could be further improved according to the designer. Therefore a new project was on the horizon. On the other hand, the Flevobike founder did not fully support the development of the C-Alleweder. First, he had concerns regarding the production techniques. He preferred the metal manufacture to the fiber-glass. Second, even more crucially, the Vrielink family intended to stop producing recumbent bikes and the Alleweder all together and to focus on R&D alone. On the one hand, the 50-plus models were too many for a market whose size was not increasing as much as it had in the past. Therefore downsizing was necessary. On the other, Johan Vrielink thought that the bicycle industry needed more R&D to improve the obsolete production system. Consequently, "I sold everything and I invested in the future working in R&D only. If we compare the bike with the car we are still driving the T-ford model. The bike is more than 100 years old and nothing changed!"[102]

This decision had a major impact on the relationship among the partners.

We were co-owners and in total there were five family members: on one hand the founder Johan Vrielink, the wife and the three sons. On the other hand, Ymte and I. So if you have a discussion on the future of the company it is very difficult to get your way with the family united against your ideas. We wanted to build our machines, because we liked and we saw the possibility for ourselves to make it happen. And Johan [the founder] didn't want anymore; he wanted to change the company and do only prototyping.[103]

With the C-Alleweder was already out of production, in spring 1999 Allert Jacob and Ymte Sijbrandij left Flevobike with a clear idea for a new project that was taking shape, a 1:1 scale model made of foam.

6.3.3 Early development period: the firm and the Quest

The new project was based on the C-Alleweder with potential improvements both in the aerodynamics and in the production process. The main product requirements were higher speed and ease of production. This time, nothing was left to approximations. Based on studies about wings, the first drawings recalled a "Darius windmill" wing that is not turned toward the wind, but stays still.[104] Similarly, riding a bike means confronting different wind directions.[105] "The shape of the wing section was a nice shape for a bike. The side wind might create a problem to the bike with this shape, but on the other hand a bike reacts very well with an in-front wind."[106]

From these drawings two small models were created, which were different in length and center of gravity. To see the differences in aerodynamics, the two models' contours were compared in a wind tunnel. A clear winner came out of the tunnel – the longer model was much better than the other one. The aerodynamics improved about 30% with a 10% increase in terms of speed. The next step was to cut the foam and shape it in such a way as to obtain a 1:1 scale model.

At the same time, after driving about 250,000 km with the aluminum and carbon fiber-glass Alleweder, Allert Jacob and Ymte Sijbrandij founded a new company, J&S, to be able to build a new vehicle with a lower air drag for practical use.

> Because I wanted to ride one, I wanted to have one! This was the first motivation to make it. It was the same for the C-Alleweder, I made it because I wanted to ride something like that. And we knew, thanks to the experience in Flevobike, it was possible to have a small company and to build and sell special bikes. If we didn't work in Flevobike, probably we would never have started a company. It is not easy to leave a job and start a new one, if you don't know anything about it. But we knew that it could be done, even better![107]

Starting a new company with the ambition to develop a new concept vehicle is not an easy task without financial resources. To cope with that, both of them started to do different jobs.

> Ymte became a truck driver for a furniture import–export company but kept his job as book-keeper for Flevobike, while I started in my garage a workshop with different machines and tools for machining. I had different assignments, for example I worked for Cab-bike [www.cab-bike.de] doing suspensions.[108]

If the model was clear, the molds were not. The opportunity to make the molds came when a friend of theirs, who was enthusiastic about the project and worked for a company specializing in bath fiber-glass construction, offered to help.

The designer identified two ways of reducing the production and assembly time for the new concept. First, they could reintroduce the metal frame so that the fiber-glass fairing could contain the metal frame with the enclosed chain. Second, they could avoid the painting process. From the molds, the fairing should be ready without additional steps such as plastering and painting. The new fairing had two striking advantages compared with the old C-Alleweder's fairing. First, the C-Alleweder's monocoque was difficult and time-consuming to produce because many of the vehicle's parts, such as chains, bottom brackets and derailleur, are inside the "fuselage". The pedals and the cranes were the only parts outside the "fuselage". Moreover, after the molding process, the C-Alleweder needed to be plastered to make it smooth and then it had to be painted; positioning all the parts inside plus the production and the painting process required time.

The Quest

Given his experience in machining, Allert Jacob was able to build the metal frame and suspension by integrating standard parts into the frame such as drum brakes, the chain, derailleur wheels and tires. However, given the limited experience and the complexity in working with fiber-glass, J&S decided to out-source the production of the canopy. The main requirement for the fairing was lightness without compromising the stoutness of the structure. Few companies were able to combine lightness and stiffness, especially for a small production series. The German *Go-One* was asked to do the job thanks to its experience building very light, model fiber-glass planes and proven capability producing such a high-quality canopy. Moreover, Go-One could cope with small-scale production. By taking the fairing out of the molds, it was already painted and ready to be assembled with a coating of polyester. Moreover, being just beyond the Dutch border, the transport cost was not an issue.

In February 2000, one year after building the 1:1 scale model, J&S shipped their first product: the Quest.

The Quest had an aluminum frame with two steering front wheels and a drive rear wheel, all covered by the aerodynamic fiber-glass/epoxy resin fairing and full independent suspension. The fairing protected the body from weather conditions and incorporated an enclosed drive train. Although the driver's head is outside, the fairing provided a headrest for protection in case the vehicle turned over and to reduce the air drag. The cover of the Quest was made of heat-formed foam, which is meant to be used in extreme weather conditions. The extended shape yielded a luggage space of more than 120 liters. The width was 76.5 cm. According to the designer, the width should be more than 75 cm and less than 80 cm. The Quest should be wider than 75 cm to be able to ride both on the bicycle paths and the car roads (as the street regulations set forth). On the other hand, the Quest needed to be able to go through regular-sized doorways, which are 80 cm across.

The first three Quest velomobiles were made for the designer, the future designer's partner and the friend who made the molds.[109] The first three vehicles were considered experiments rather than finished products because the designer wanted to test the thickness of the fiber-glass. The first one was considered too thick, the second one too thin, while finally, the third one had the right thickness according to the designer. Another advantage of the Quest was the production time, stabilized at 20 hours for the metal frame, taking into account the out-sourced fairing production. When the first Quest vehicles were on the road, the news spread rapidly through magazine covers and dedicated internet sites. This resulted in widespread interest and potential customers.

In a few months the J&S company received about ten orders. As in the case of Alleweder, the firm adopted the same method of constructing to order, with a waiting time of six months. Thanks to the experience with the C-Alleweder, the firm could comfortably calculate the cost of making the Quest, fixing its price at €5,672:25 (NLG 12,000). It was a pleasant surprise for potential users, because they compared the Quest price with that of the C-Alleweder and found it 23% cheaper. Despite inflation, the price of the Quest has remained unchanged since 2000 (as of 2005). Keeping the same price was possible because of improvements in the frame production. Accordingly, the efficiency in production came from an increase in the stock of metal parts and a faster and easier way to make them thanks to improved skills.

6.3.4 Late development period: the Mango

The two Quest producers could not cope with the increasing demand for the Quest, so decided to ask Theo van Andel to join the company and in March 2001 J&S changed its name to Velomobiel. After a meeting with the IHPVA, it was decided to spread the word "velomobile" for fairing recumbent bikes. Changing the name to Velomobiel was seen as a natural step. Production stabilized at three-quarters of a Quest per month. Although the Velomobiel partners were busy making the new Quest, they had time to test and ride it in different competition events and tours around Europe. They traveled thousands of kilometers, from which they obtained positive results. First, testing the Quest in real-life situations in all kinds of weather conditions demonstrated the good quality of the concept (see for example Sijbrandij, 2002). Second, the Quest got a lot of attention from cyclists and potential users, partly because of the ease with which it won races. Ymte Sijbrandij was the Dutch champion of recumbent cycle racing several times.

The entry of Quest in the bicycle world was welcomed as the fastest bike within the recumbent bike and velomobile category for practical use (excluding bikes designed for racing only). Thanks to its aerodynamics, the power from the cyclist needed to keep up a certain speed is less driving the Quest than other bikes on the market. Thus far (October 2004), the Quest is still the fastest bike on the street (Eland, 2004).

With the development of the Quest we searched for a bike with the best specification for speed and daily use. Speed is an important aspect of comfort, even if you are not interested in riding fast. Riding a fast bike means that you can ride at "normal" speeds with little effort which means you can cover a longer distance in a relaxed way.[110]

Compared to the already fast C-Alleweder, the Quest is 10% faster. This means 30% less effort to reach the same speed, which increases the comfort.

The Quest however was not without drawbacks. Maneuverability was somewhat sacrificed for comfort and speed. For example, the front wheels were covered to decrease the air drag, which reduced the ability to steer. Consequently, potential users were concerned with the large turning cycle (10.7 m) and the limited maneuverability in cities or in situations where a narrow turning was required.

The Mango

This problem represented an opportunity to contemplate the development of another vehicle with the same design characteristics but that was easier to maneuver and simpler to produce.

We want to make something less extreme than the Quest, which is focused on the best aerodynamics. So the idea behind the Mango was to build a less extreme vehicle, cheaper and affordable for people, easier to maneuver in the city, fitting in the shed, and easier to produce also. The speed is lower, but still quite fast for a bike.[111]

Early in 2002, a new project was started at Velomobiel: the Mango. The requirements for the new vehicle were better maneuverability and a cheaper price than the Quest. The body length was shortened by about 40 cm and the fairing did not cover the front wheels so as to reduce the turning cycle. The rear sides of the shells were made narrower than Quest's without losing stiffness in the fairing. The weight of the Mango needed to be similar to the Quest to provide more stability. For the Mango vehicle, the designer decided to use a larger number of standard parts inside the fairing than in the Quest vehicle. For example, unlike the Quest, the drive chain integrated in the Mango was a standard 8-speed derailleur transmission (27 derailleur gears) as well as a standard rear axle. More sophisticated and expensive parts were offered as optional. A simpler and faster production process of the aluminum frames also helped to keep the price low.

In June 2002 the first Mango was produced and it was tested during the summer (Eland, 2002a). In September 2002, the first Mango was introduced in the market for €4,500, 20% less expensive than a Quest, with a turning cycle of 7.8 m.

While the Mango had improved stability and maneuverability and was cheaper than the Quest, it was also slower and had less luggage space. The reduction in terms of speed is around 8% (Bakker, Hoge, & Laan van der, 2004), while the luggage space was reduced by 30%.

> A bike is always a compromise between demands. This compromise does not have to end in the same bike for everyone. The Quest is the fastest, but some people are willing to trade off a little bit [of] speed for a more compact bike like the Mango....
>   Nothing in life is for free; the price [to pay for the tradeoff] is some loss [in] luggage room and speed.[112]

As with the Quest, the Mango attracted the curiosity of many people in the bike world through well-known information channels. Orders started to pile up on Ymte Sijbrandij's desk, which indicated that they had made the right direction.

6.3.5 *Implementation: the market*

In the last few years the Quest and the Mango have received a great deal of attention from specialized magazines. For example, *Velo Vision* magazine, based in the UK, reported a test among four major velomobiles: Versatile by Flevo-bike, Cab bike by German Cab Bike Company, the Mango and the Quest. In terms of speed, comfort and energy efficiency, the Quest was assessed as the best bike; while the Mango was the cheapest and the most stable (van der Laan, 2004). Based on the velomobiles' energy efficiency tests (Eland, 2004), the Velomobiel vehicles seemed to be among the most efficient bikes for commuting within 40 km as illustrated in Table 6.5.[113]

The Velomobiel company not only produces the Mango and the Quest, but also metal parts for other recumbent and velomobile producers in the Netherlands and abroad.

From March 2000 until October 2004 around 170 velomobiles had been sold, 40 had been ordered for an 11-month long waiting list. Figure 6.7 illustrates how Velomobiel's production output has increased from an average of two vehicles per month in late 2000 to four per month since 2003. The increase in production output is explained both by the entry of Theo van Andel in 2001 and the small, yet continuous, improvements made in the production process. The current priority of Velomobiel is to reduce the production time and consequently the labor cost (Figure 6.7). In this way the price may also decrease.

Currently the Velomobiel has one of the highest production outputs in the velomobile world, as illustrated in Table 6.6.

According to Velomobiel, owners making profits in this very small market sector is more of an exception than the rule.

> In the IHPVA[114] scene, there are a lot of people who are dreamers. And there are many appealing vehicles and many people who give always advice on how to do better and so on. And they seem to know everything about it,

Table 6.5 Differences in speed and power of various velomobiles in comparison with a regular bike

	Year	Speed at 250 W	Speed difference compared to the Quest	Difference in power provided by the cyclist, compared to the Alleweder at the same speed
Regular bike		29 km/h	40% slower	174% more power (685 W required)
Alleweder	1993	42 km/h	15% slower	0
C-Alleweder	1996	45 km/h	8% slower	16.4 % less power (209 W required)
Quest	2000	49 km/h	0	33.6 less power (166 W required)
Mango	2002	45 km/h	8% slower	16.4 % less power (209 W required)
Versatile	2004	41 km/h	17% slower	6.4% more power (266 W required)

Table 6.6 Production output: comparison among the velomobiles

	Total number of vehicles sold	In production since	Number of vehicle sold on average per year
Leitra	250	1980	10
Cab-bike	66	1998	10
Quest	120	2000	25
Mango	50	2002	17

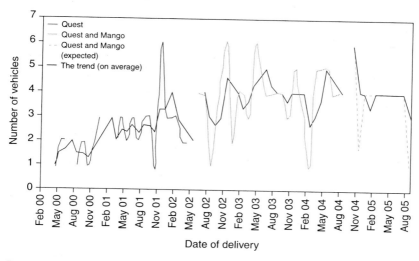

Figure 6.7 The Velomobiel's production output in terms of vehicles delivered.

but there are few people who make something like that, and there are fewer people who have founded a company and make a living with that. I think we are the only one.[115]

After driving 120,000 km with their velomobiles, Velomobiel is looking forward to producing, improving and cycling their creatures in the future.

Box 6.4 The Mango story

Event time	Who	What	Why
Initiation period			
Late 1980s	Bart Verhees	Design and development of a fully aluminum fairing recumbent bike provided also with suspensions: the Alleweder	Comfort, weather protection
1993	Bart Verhees	Alleweder to Flevobike	Failing in producing alone Flevobike well-known recumbent bikes producers
1993	Flevobike	Joining the 365-days-fiets competition	To test the Alleweder concept
1993	Allert Jacob	Driver of the Alleweder	As NVHPV champion racing
1993	Allert Jacob	Competition winner	
1993	Flevobike	Start of the Alleweder production	Public positive toward the Alleweder
1993	Flevobike	The family company owner asked Allert Jacob to join the firm	Too few people able to cope with increasing orders for the Alleweder
1993	Allert Jacob	Start to work with Flevobike	Passion for cycling and making bikes
1993	Ymte Sijbrandij	Start to work with Flevobike	Passion for cycling
1993	Flevobike	Alleweder production only, assembly by the user	Cheaper
1993–1995	Flevobike	200 Alleweder produced and sold	
1995	Allert Jacob and Ymte Sijbrandij	Flevobike co-owners	To be fully part of the decision process
1995	Allert Jacob	Start to work in the spare time on a new version of Alleweder	Improving the speed and maintenance
1996	Allert Jacob	Fairing with fiber-glass and carbon without metal frame: the C-Alleweder	Faster and enclosed drive train
1997	Flevobike	Start producing the C-Alleweder	Increasing orders from clients
1998	Flevobike	Stop producing the C-Alleweder (after 25 units delivered)	Production cost and time too high Not willing to work with fiber-glass Few experienced with fiber-glass production
Early development period			
1998	Allert Jacob	Designing improvements for the C-Alleweder	Requirements: Less production time Faster

Date	Actor	Event	Remarks
1998	Flevobike	The family firm decided to stop producing both Alleweder and recumbent bike, R&D only	Market considered suited for special bikes
1998, early 1999	Allert Jacob	Building of 1:1 foam model, shaped in the wind tunnel	Improvements needed in production techniques; Increase of 30% (10% in speed) in aerodynamics
Early 1999	Allert Jacob and Ymte Sijbrandij	They left the company	Disagreement over the firm's strategy
Spring 1999	Allert Jacob and Ymte Sijbrandij	They founded a new company: the J&S Fietsdiensten	To build a new vehicle
1999	Allert Jacob and Ymte Sijbrandij	Performing different jobs	To be able to finance the new vehicle production
1999	Allert Jacob	Design of the fiber-glass fairing production	Better production process, requirements: After the molding process ready to use
Late 1999	Allert Jacob	Metal frame production	Reintegrating the metal frame (simpler); Experience in machining metal frames and suspensions; Less experience in fiber-glass
2000	Go-One	Fairing outsourced	
Early 2000	J&S	Molds ready	
Spring 2000	J&S	Test of the Quest	
2000	J&S	Introduction of the Quest: the fastest bike in the market; 15 Quest delivered	
Late development period			
2001	Theo van Andel	Join the J&S	To be fully part of the decision process
2001	J&S	Change of the name to Velomobiel	
Late 2001	Allert Jacob	Design requirements for a new vehicle given the feedback of potential and current customers	More maneuverable, simpler to produce and cheaper
Implementation period			
Spring 2002	Velomobiel	Introduction of the Mango	40 cm shorter; 20% cheaper
September 2004	Velomobiel	109 Quest and 58 Mango produced and delivered	

7   Analysis of the Mitka and Mango cases

The previous chapter described the innovation journey of both the Mitka and Mango actors, highlighting their motivations and objectives and illustrating the design and development decisions that were made. This chapter will take a step further and analyze these cases. Sections 7.1 and 7.2 illustrate the analysis of the Mitka and the Mango cases respectively, while section 7.3 presents a cross-case analysis. The goal of within-case analyses differs from the goal of cross-case analysis. For the Mitka case, the objective of the analysis is to understand how and under what circumstances environmental ambition and project innovativeness influenced decision making and subsequently affected the product concept. The Mango case analysis is instrumental to the analysis of the first case, which is characterized by a low level of environmental ambition. The purpose is to verify whether the Mango case can be distinguished from the Mitka case in the way the innovation process was undertaken. Therefore a comparative case study analysis will reveal similarities and differences in the innovation processes.

7.1 The Mitka case

7.1.1 Introduction

Was environmental ambition a determining factor in shaping the innovation process? How did project newness influence decisions? This section will cast light on the innovation journey of the Mitka coalition. The analysis of the case follows the same chronological timeline adopted in the description chapter, when four periods were identified. Nevertheless, the analysis focuses mainly on two development periods when the crucial decisions were taken. Those development periods are analyzed at the management level and at the project team level respectively. This section evaluates the extent to which environmental ambition and the radical undertaking affected the support process, the attitude, the commitment of the coalition of the management and the project teams. Finally, this chapter also discusses the conditions under which the coalition's decisions influenced product complexity.

The management team encompasses the TNO team and the project leader, the Gazelle director, the business developer, the DfS group and the Nike manager.

The project team involves the Vd Veer designer, the TNO team, Freewiel Techniek and the TUDelft team. Although many decisions were made with the support of all of the partners, strictly technical decisions were made by the project team while the management team focused mainly on business and market development.

The following subsections, 7.1.2 and 7.1.3, illustrate why the Mitka project should be considered a radical undertaking with a very high level of environmental ambition. Subsections 7.1.4, 7.1.5 and 7.1.6 explain how these two constructs are related to the management support process, to project team commitments and to product complexity in the early and late development periods respectively. Subsection 7.1.7 discusses the implementation period and reflects on the Mitka outcome from different perspectives.

7.1.2 Environmental ambition

In the initiation period, the four scattered events had something in common: the idea to develop a new concept as an attractive alternative to car use was driven by the strong concern that the current mobility system, heavily reliant on the car, was having a negative impact on the natural environment. Air pollution due to NO_x and CO_2 emissions depleting the ozone layer, the increase of congestion, noise and uncovered infrastructure costs were considered the main problems of the car mobility system. For short distances in particular (5–20 km), the Kathalys group saw the alternative vehicles to the car as unsuitable for the growing individual mobility needs of commuters. Regular bikes, well suited for trips of up to 5 km, were considered uncomfortable for longer distances. On the other hand, public transport was unable to meet efficiently the needs of suburban commuters.

Therefore, a new mobility concept could provide the flexibility and the accessibility of the bike with the protection and comfort of the car. The justification for starting such a project was based on the win-win paradigm: contributing to alleviating the depletion of the natural environment and simultaneously exploiting business opportunities for mobility needs that had previously been poorly addressed. Moreover, the policy agenda at national and European level at supported projects related transport issues.

The environmental ambition of the TNO team was the driving force behind the teams' efforts to find partners in the bike industry and other organizations to act as clients, such as the Nike company. Within the coalition it may be naïve to state that the environmental ambition was shared uniformly by all of the participants. The TNO team and the TUDelft team were the most ambitious (as demonstrated by the establishment of the Kathalys program), while the designer and the Gazelle director were driven mainly by the innovative opportunities. However, decisions were taken jointly.

Environmental ambition also manifested itself in the decision to submit applications for two subsidy programs where the environmental dimension was clearly expressed in the subsidy program mission.

The high level of environmental ambition was also reinforced by embracing and further developing the PSS conceptual framework. Unmistakably, the PSS philosophy dictated that only through a new product-service combination, often developed and implemented beyond the boundaries of a single organization, could a real environmental improvement be achieved.

The concern for the natural environment was not only restricted to the idea itself, but also manifested itself during the process. It was repeatedly stated, mentioned and openly expressed during discussions, public presentations, conference papers and official documents, such as reports or submission proposals. *How did this ambition influence the project?*

7.1.3 The project innovativeness

The Mitka constituted a radical project for several reasons.

The PSS concept. The brand new, human-powered, weather-protected vehicle, with power assistance for a 40 km range, original design and unique sitting position, was seen by most of the participants as neither a bike nor an electric car, but rather as a one-of-a-kind means of transport. It was not only the vehicle that made the Mitka unique, but also the specially designed services around it. The maintenance, the call-a-car, and the leasing services were considered an integral part of the Mitka and made it a completely new mobility solution. The exceptionality of the Mitka concept was again reinforced by the PSS conceptual framework, which states that the combination of new products and services together with new organizational settings is likely to lead to a radical improvement for the natural environment (Luiten et al., 2001a).

The high degree of uncertainty for the organization. In Chapter 2, the undertaking of radical innovation processes for an organization has been defined as the conditions under which *the organization copes with a new and unfamiliar domain, where different technical and business skills are required.* The decision to develop a trike instead of a bike, in spite of the users' preference, increased the level of uncertainty in the innovation process because the team was facing a new dramatic challenge. Many tasks were completely new for the project team. For example, the Gazelle company's capabilities, while well suited for creating and developing a bike, were untested for a luxury trike. Moreover, unlike other bike manufacturers, Gazelle had never integrated electric assistance in the pedal system. On the other hand, the TNO team had never built a steering/tilting system, while Freewiel Techniek's core business was vehicles for disabled people. The nature of the challenges was not restricted to the technicalities, but also encompassed business and market development. In spite of significant experience in product development, the small consulting firm and the TNO manager had limited experience in developing a business plan or finding potential partners for this specific product. Therefore, the entire team was facing, to a certain extent, an unfamiliar domain with limited skills.

New market. The Mitka was meant to be a radical product for a new market. The former project leader used to warn everyone not to confound the Mitka with any other human-powered vehicle, such as a recumbent bike, because the design, the technology and the objectives were of a completely different nature. Therefore, it was felt that the Mitka had no real competitors with regard to vehicles resembling bikes. A new market also meant that potential users were not completely aware of it; therefore interactive group discussions, interviews, surveys and public presentations were carried out, not only to get feedback on the concept, but also to let people get acquainted with the Mitka.

A new organizational setting. Mitka development was carried out by a heterogeneous coalition rather than a single established organization. As the PSS framework suggests, an interorganizational setting is better equipped for developing PSS concepts than a single one because of the broader changes needed in the system (Luiten et al., 2001a). However, this coalition had strong innovative characteristics due to the high number and heterogeneity of the partners. The individual actors were part of up to seven organizations, ranging from an insurance company to research institutes, with different interests and missions.

7.1.4 Initiation period choices

The TNO team motivation to start such a project was driven by the strong belief that, to reduce environmental problems caused by the current mobility system, new solutions in terms of products and services were necessary. The initiation period, which lasted more than three years, was by definition a phase of searching for opportunities. Given the scattered initiatives and the strong commitment of the TNO team to address environmental issues, the team was able to create the conditions for obtaining initial resources and partners. It turned a broad vision of a societal problem into a specific project: a human-powered vehicle. The TNO team was the triggering entity able to form the network through a "hub-and-spoke" approach, typical of engineering processes.

Within the coalition, reflection, self-assessment and consideration of the actors' roles took place. The general attitude toward the Mitka project was mainly supportive (see Table 7.1). The commitment of Gazelle and Nike was limited to genuine interest in participating in an innovative environmental project that could generate publicity and provide a business opportunity.

7.1.5 Early development period choices

Management team: attitude, commitment and support

The high level of environmental ambition was not only translated into an attribute of the product, but also influenced some of the key decisions. The assumption that a greater environmental benefit related to the radicality of the project was strongly held and supported during the whole process. Therefore the choices did not moderate the radicality of the concept. In fact, they accrued the radicality and the complexity of it.

One of the major critical decisions faced by the project and the management

Table 7.1 Changes in the Mitka development process

	Issues	Initiation period	Early development	Late development	Implementation
Management team	Attitude	Fun, green innovative	Enthusiastic, free publicity	From enthusiastic to wait and see	Opportunistic behavior
	Commitment	Low	High, increasing	Low, decreasing	Very low
	Support	Supportive	Highly supportive	From supportive to wait and see	Low
Project team	Attitude	Enthusiastic, fun, learning	Enthusiastic, fun, learning	Enthusiastic, fun, learning	
	Commitment	High	Escalating	Escalating	
	Required capabilities	Limited	Limited	Limited	
Setting rules	Management	Leading	Leading	Waiting results	
	Project team	Executing	Leading, executing	Leading, executing high	Leading, executing
Product/service system	Degree of complexity	High	Going beyond	High	High for the three-wheeled development Low for the two-wheeled development
	Infrastructure and regulations boundaries		Going beyond	Going beyond	
Market research	User preference and feedback	Largely dismissed	Largely dismissed	Testing; largely dismissed	

team in March 2000 was the wheel configuration of the Mitka. The innovative survey on Nike's intranet resulted in a consistent preference for the two-wheeled over the three-wheeled version. Up to 66% preferred the two-wheeled bike. Nevertheless, the management team chose the three-wheeled version. *Why did the coalition choose a direction contradicting consumer preference?* The explanations listed in chapter 6 denote how the decision was influenced by the search for a higher degree of innovation and significant concern for the environment.

Both the management and project team were keen to develop a new mobility solution. They were interested in something very different from the current bike, which would be so attractive to car drivers (their target group) that they would be convinced to leave their car at home or not even buy a second one. In particular, Gazelle's participation in such a project meant free publicity, which reinforced its image as an innovator that takes care of the natural environment. Therefore, the more radical the project the better. Along the same lines, Nike was willing to explore new means of mobility.

Besides the innovativeness of the three-wheeled version, the TNO team was also concerned about the overall impact of such a concept on the natural environment. Since the car is responsible for the depletion of the environment, any decision in the Mitka process should clearly focus on a specific target group: car drivers only. Therefore, the new PSS needed to be attractive to car drivers and exclude cyclists. Consequently, a Mitka resembling the bike might involuntarily target the cyclists, the most environmentally friendly commuters. To avoid this rebound effect, the Mitka design needed to be unique and closely resemble the comfort of a car.

The coalition, especially the Kathalys group, felt that the two-wheeled configuration would not address the main objective of the project: a new concept able to meet consumers' need while drastically reducing the environmental impact of the current mobility system. Another two-wheeled bike would not constitute a system innovation. Environmental ambition influenced the decision to choose the three-wheeled vehicle.

The management team dismissed the user preference for the two-wheeled version. The TNO team justified the 66% preference for the two-wheeled version in two ways: the consumers' conservative attitude towards something new and many car drivers' preference for the three-wheeled version. Given the uniqueness of the trike, they argued, lead users may not fully understand the potential of such a concept because it is demanding and sometime prohibitive for them to detach themselves from the current transport system. In other words, lead users may not be not able to identify the futuristic trike as a solution to their commuting needs. In the same way, the team preferred to see and focus on the 35% of car drivers, who saw the Mitka as a moderate alternative to the car.

On the other hand, they supported the thesis that the majority of the car drivers preferred the three-wheeled version, although the results showed a different picture. Some 60% of the total number of car drivers ($N = 33$) and 50% of the car drivers commuting between 5 and 30 km ($N = 24$) chose the bike version (see Table 6.3).

Again, the combination of the willingness to pursue a radical undertaking with the belief that only a major change in car drivers' behavior (switching modes of transport) could stimulate a leap-frog toward a better natural environment may explain such an interpretation of the data and the following decisions. The prospect and the high expectations of having a radical and environmental concept in the market may explain their strong commitment to this wheel configuration.

After the public presentation of the Mitka 1:3 scale model and due to the positive public reaction and the press releases, the enthusiasm among the participants rose and increased their willingness to proceed in exploring the promising Mitka trajectory. This was a dramatic change in attitude and commitment, and it occurred throughout the coalition (see Table 7.1).

This proactive attitude was translated into a new set of objectives for the MOVE I and II projects, a new means of transport with dedicated services for a consistent market. The "go" decision to invest €316,000 in examining the technical feasibility of the vehicle was an expression of the combination of the partners' heterogeneous rationales.

These motivations may be differentiated in two components: rational and non-rational. The rational motivations may encompass the publicity that resulted from participation in the project and the relatively small financial investment each partner had to make. In addition to that, the opportunity to develop a new vehicle meant acquiring and mastering new technical capabilities. More subtly, the non-rational motivations are related to the euphoria of undertaking a radical project giving birth to a sleek, innovative vehicle, which looks good and everyone likes, despite few performance judgments being in place. Everyone was affected by this enthusiasm, which resulted in the project being pushed through. Furthermore, there was the feeling among the TNO team that they had finally developed a real PSS with a significant environmental benefit. The environmental ambition manifested itself in public presentations and meeting discussions where the environmental dimension of the project was emphasized. The management team was emotionally involved in the project, engaged both by its innovativeness and the feeling of "doing the right thing" for the natural environment. The psychological rewards derived from this environmental concern and the innovativeness of the project might have been one of the non-rational factors why it garnered such enthusiastic support.

Given the radicality and the environmental ambition of the team, the coalition was unable to foresee the technical problems derived from the current assets and the project manager seemed to overlook the different "souls" of the coalition. As a result, it seems that the advocacy process was strongly influenced by both rational and non-rational components, allowing the Mitka project to progress through the first important go/no-go decision stage.

Project team

The project team had no doubts that choosing the three-wheeled concept meant exploring new frontiers of design and having the opportunity "to play" with the

Mitka concept. The choice of the three-wheeled version meant combining the willingness to engage in a new and radical undertaking with the ambition to create a sustainable product service system that minimized any rebound effects.

The project team lost Stork company but was reinforced by Freewiel Techniek, who specialized in three-wheeled vehicles for disabled people. However, the Mitka project was also a new and challenging task for Freewiel despite its knowledge of the three-wheeled configuration. In fact, its expertise concerned the configuration with two wheels in the back and one in the front, which is typical of vehicles for disabled people and of some recumbent trikes. This configuration is technically simpler because the steering mechanism involves only the wheel in the front. Therefore, the new participant's expertise did not significantly improve the team's abilities to cope with the development of the Mitka.

The Mitka model presentation's success, combined with the highly ambitious targets set in the MOVE I program, forced the team to adopt all of the previously chosen product attributes of the "ideal" alternative vehicle to the car. They were happy to do so. Consider the great challenge: to develop a new human-powered concept with great novel technical features, such as a new roof, a new tilting steering mechanism with a new sitting position, electrically powered, with the growing expectation from the management team and the public (see Table 7.1).

The escalation of commitments locked the project team within the boundaries of this ideal means of transport. The project team did not challenge the requirements of the Mitka. On the contrary, it tried to accomplish all of them, inspired by the Mitka "muse". Consider for example the combination of the high sitting position with the three-wheel configuration. According to various designers and experts, this combination creates stability problems because the center of gravity is too high. The driver could easily lose balance, especially at moderate speed and in windy conditions. The center of gravity, as they argued, needs to be low, for instance, by making the vehicle longer as with the recumbent bikes. This problem did not prevent the project team from renouncing and changing the product requirements.

Intriguingly, it seems that these commitments, not only let the team stick with the original ideas, but even pushed it to opt for the most complex and radical solutions among different technical choices. For example, the team would choose the superior ideal solution rather than the simpler and more elegant one. Consider some of the technical dilemmas presented in Table 7.2, such as the wheel configuration or the propulsion system. With regard to the latter, the team opted for a new and costly battery system and a complex engine rather than looking for a more standard and affordable propulsion.

Moreover, there was the tendency to dismiss current, known technical configurations. For example, many recumbent bike producers faced similar problems with the wheel configuration and the sitting position. Nevertheless, the team was keen to work on its own.

The search for superior solutions and the overconfident attitude in combination with the lock-in effect of the original requirements pushed the Mitka concept beyond the current street regulations, infrastructure and sometimes against one of the partner's interests. Again, consider the vehicle width and the propulsion system (see the Table 7.2). The Mitka's width was 85 centimeters, five centimeters too wide to pass through most regular doorways. This requirement was explicitly mentioned by most of the market research respondents. On the other hand, the chosen propulsion system was too powerful, allowing speeds of 40 km/h, which then required the use of a helmet, to the great dismay of the Gazelle director. Nevertheless, the project team insisted on keeping the Mitka on this track, dismissing the legal issue.

Another justification for this behavior was clearly expressed by the project leader, which may give an idea as to how environmental ambition dictated the development process. The PSS philosophy indicated that only through dramatic changes in the current system could significant environmental benefits be achieved. Therefore, the development of the Mitka should not necessarily be constrained by the current regulations and infrastructure; on the contrary, it might provoke a desirable change in the system, shaping it and making it more sustainable.

The high level of environmental ambition and the radicality of the project facilitated the escalation of the team commitments to decide on a course of action that resulted in a high degree of product complexity. The stringent question of how to align short-term goals, such as market expectation and technical feasibility, with long-term ambitions, such as system innovation, was not addressed.

Product attributes and product complexity

The decision to develop a new PSS with a new three-wheeled configuration, a new sitting position, a brand new roof with power assistance and a new set of services presented both technical challenges for the team and business and market risks for the entire coalition. For example, the designers and the TNO team did not have the necessary experience and specific capabilities with a three-wheeled configuration vehicle to enable informed decisions. Moreover, the concept was perceived to be complex by the lead users within Nike. This approach fostered by the high ambition level and by the radical undertaking increased the complexity of the PSS and specifically of the product. The large number of new components created an unstable and poorly defined set of interactions. The team had difficulty coordinating single developments and the whole product architecture. The team's limited experience with some of the new components and the lack of priority among the product components and their developments increased the complexity of the concept.

Table 7.2 Technical dilemmas during the development of the Mitka

Dilemma	Issues	Management	Project team	Product	How solved
Wheel configuration: 2 or 3 wheels?	Users preferred 2 wheels	3 more innovative and radical; car drivers as focus group; big change in the system; 2 less innovative; bikers' preference; no change in the system; no rebound effects; conservative users (too innovative for them)	3 innovative and challenging less experience: "never did before"; 2 less innovative, no fun, experienced	3 radical, more complex 2 easier, less complex	3-wheeled chosen
Wheel configuration: 2 wheels forward or backward?		2 in front = better image	2 in front = more innovative	2 in front = highly complex	Bending system
Tilting and steering: which configuration?	Legal problem: >80 cm not allowed on the bike road	—	The best system: Independent tilting-steering system with the pedal system between the wheels	Independent tilting-steering system: highly complex	Independent tilting-steering system, Width = 85 cm
Power assistance: <25 km/h or 40 km/h?	Legal problem: >25 km/h = helmet (scooter)	Gazelle = no scooter Nike = high speed	Fast without the helmet	<25 km/h	Power control switch 25–40 km/h (illegal without the helmet)
What kind of propulsion?	Standard or new assembled one		New assembled propulsion	Standard = cheaper and easier to install and function New assembled = costly, time-consuming, complex	New assembled
Which kind of roof?	Rain protection, visibility, safety		Light modular Plexiglas, or textile	Light modular Plexiglas	

7.1.6 Late development period choices

Management attitude, commitment and support

This phase started just as the previous stage began, with great enthusiasm after another public presentation of the Mitka mock-up, when the future King of the Netherlands sat on it next to his wife. Marketers affirmed that everything displayed with the Princess would sell. This proverb, combined with high expectations created the conditions under which Gazelle and Nike were prepared to invest in the Mitka. Rather than performance criteria, prospects and expectations of the coalition acted as the main mechanisms for project support. Before any real commitment could be made, the vehicle needed to be ready. Therefore, another project, MOVE II, was set up, and €600,000 invested to fulfill the ambitious objectives. These objectives included having the final Mitka prototype

Table 7.3 Technical inconveniences illustrated by the disharmony between the objectives' announcements and their effective delivery

Announcements	"The Mitka prototype ready for"
Meeting on September 23, 2001 MOVE II proposal (November 2001)	First Mitka on November 2001 "3 Mitka for Nike in the beginning of the year 2003" March 2002 first series of prototype ready
Email on December 6, 2001	First prototype delayed, probably only one in early 2002
January 30, 2002 Memo from the project leader in preparation for the management meeting	March 2002 the prototype April 2002 the test The decision in May 2002 whether to build 10 Mitka between June and September 2002 or not
Management meeting February 2, 2002	Early April 2002 3 or 5 vehicles for the testing
Management meeting March 13, 2002	Late April 2002 Few vehicle for the testing, probably 3 Price unknown, but "quite expensive"
Management meeting with all the partners May 2, 2002	One prototype ready, but motor ill functioning and without roof. Cost: €25,000 each Test in June 2002 with only one (roofed)
End of May 2002	Test in September–November 2002
July 3, 2002 (confirmed in August)	Test starting on September 1, 2002
End of august 2002	Test starting on September 17, 2002
Halfway through September 2002	Test starting on October 3, 2002
End of September 2002	Test starting in the second half of October 2002
Beginning of October 2002	Test started on October 22, 2002

ready, tested and finally produced. Unfortunately, it took eight more months, 16 months in total before anyone could ride the first Mitka. Expectations based on emails or meeting announcements of the coming prototype and testing were regularly dashed (see Table 7.3). One of the effects of this procrastination of the project was the relocation of resources. Resources previously allocated to market research activities were transferred to strictly technical product development activities.

The long waiting time had a huge impact on management's spirits, with the enthusiasm turning into disillusion. Nevertheless, managers let the project team work on the Mitka, adopting a "wait-and-see" attitude. Therefore, the project team was actually leading the project while the management team awaited the results.

This new coalition mind-set uncovered some fundamental differences in problem definitions and expected solutions among the participants. These problems had been set aside for too long and were largely internalized by the project manager, only to emerge at this stage. Table 7.4 summarizes the differences among the individual actors.

The presence in the coalition of many influential actors exacerbated difficulty of managing different interests and goals – the greater the number of participants, the greater the probability that their goals will not be congruent with each other. Here the liabilities of the heterogeneous organizational setting manifested itself. This included the long decision-making process to arrive at agreement while the members' interests were mostly implicit. Consider for example the discussion on the intellectual property of the Mitka or the debate on the propulsion system, or even more illustratively, the decision of the Gazelle director to develop the Easy Glider alone. The poor communication among the management members emphasized the skeptical view of some. Consider the confusion about the cost of the Mitka. The wait-and-see attitude, combined with the revelation of different actors' interests and poor communication, jeopardized any real commitments and postponed any reflections, self-assessment and critical evaluation of goals and objectives. Moreover, the fact that management failed to fully comprehend the technical development reinforced this attitude.

Project team

The "wait-and-see" attitude of the management clashed with the great efforts of the project team to have a perfect riding model ready by summer 2002. The project team was completely in charge of the project by this time and the team members' commitments strongly escalated, allowing them to work extra hours and sometimes on the weekends. The team was determined to finish the Mitka vehicle despite management's indolence.

The strikingly different attitude of the project team toward the Mitka led to the deterioration of communication and coordination with the management team. Given this situation, it is not surprising that the Mitka organization appeared opaque and disorganized to the two test drivers.

Table 7.4 Roles and interests within the coalition

Roles of actors	Problem definition	Solution to problem	Risks taken	Contribution and attitude
TNO Project leader	People drive cars for short distances because bicycles are slow, involve too much effort, and are weather-dependent. People reject Bike Pluses because of image, poor marketing, conservatism	New vehicle: faster, power-assisted, weather protective. New vehicle: sleek, bicycle-lookalike. Partner: high marketing potential	Medium: reputation, prestige	Active in finding financial support, assembling project team, visioning, design, networking and publicity
Nike Client	Insufficient environmental image. Insufficient parking for employees. Protect company image	Participate in the project while using Nike logo on new vehicle. Offer new vehicle to employees. New vehicle: fast, attractive, innovative, sleek	Low: financial	Wait and see. Surveyed attitudes
Gazelle Business developer	Bicycle market saturated. New features needed	New vehicle: bicycle with extra features. Avoid radical changes. Chance to join Nike in a project	None	Wait and see. Passive participant. Brought product designer and engineering designer into coalition
DfS Knowledge keeper, strong project supporter	Current trends in car use for home-work commuting not sustainable. Alternative product-service needed in mobility	New product service system combination for sustainability transition	Medium: reputation, prestige	Involved in all stages. Students involved. Networking and publicity seeking
Government program Financial support	Niches needed for development of radical ideas into sustainable mobility solutions	Promoting experiments in development and testing of new product service	Medium: financial (diffused), reputation, prestige	Long-term support without interference

Although the coordination was inadequate, the project team strongly focused on the Mitka's development. The team narrowed down the design options rather rapidly, thus limiting the flexibility of the concept to respond to future surprises in technical design. Notably, there had been numerous opportunities during the preceding two years to foresee these problem areas. As the project was approaching the pilot stage, several unresolved issues loomed large. The most acute are summarized in Table 7.5. The table shows that many of the unresolved issues are related to the three-wheel design, the radically different, sleek appearance and the practicalities of daily life with the Mitka.

In spite of these problems, the project team did not reconsider or re-evaluate some of their choices; on the contrary the team seemed to be locked in with the original ideas to maintain the same development track.

Furthermore, it is surprising that the market research (see for example the Table 6.4 in Chapter 6) was often dismissed. This research clearly indicated that the Mitka was highly appreciated, but remained unsuitable for most people because of its radical appearance, that the fact it was perceived as highly expensive and hard to use and store. Moreover, the testing unmistakably denoted the limitations of the concept.

This was a kind of paradox. The decision to start such a project was based on the assumption of combining user need, an ideal mobility concept, with more general societal needs, the preservation of the natural environment. However, crucial decisions during the process were not influenced by the users' preferences. The team's escalation of commitments and the high level of environmental ambition in combination with a lack of firm coordination by the management team, precluded any self-assessment or reflection on the ideal means of transport with regard to technical problems, infrastructure barriers or potential users' perceptions.

Another paradox lay in the fact that the Kathalys method was created to assess both the innovation process and the environmental performance, yet never fully implemented or adopted. Despite the project leaders' strong belief in the Kathalys method, it was not followed thoroughly. Instead the team focused almost entirely on the "product service system" and the "sustainable" tracks, overlooking, for example, the "economical feasibility" or the "organization" track (for a complete description of the Kathalys method, see Box 6.2). Having said that, the method was undeveloped and still under construction, consequently it was not completely reliable. Nevertheless, the method was not improved and it was only partially tested in other domains. A systematic evaluation or self-assessment of the Kathalys method was not performed.

Intriguingly, despite the high level of environmental ambition and the great deal of experience in environmental assessment tools, such as life cycle analysis (see Chapter 4 for a review), no specific quantitative environmental assessment was performed at this stage of the process, only qualitative ones.

Table 7.5 Unresolved barriers to Mitka development

Technical design	• Propulsion system not functioning well, battery recharger out of order • Bending mechanism needs improvement • Roof not ready yet
Infrastructure	• In "walking" cities (i.e. Amsterdam) and in narrow bicycle roads (i.e. the island of Texel) Mitka can be perceived as too wide for the small roads • Residential storage difficult, too wide to pass through regular doors = an obstacle to widespread adoption • Facilities for battery recharging and technical assistance for maintenance and repairs problematic
Regulations	• Speed limit for electric vehicles (25 km/h) unless helmets are used but human-powered vehicles do not require helmets
User acceptance	• Sleek form attractive to some potential users, but a liability for others, for whom Mitka departs radically from their accepted meanings and routines of daily life
Market factors	• Price a deterrent to individual users, although alternatives to private ownership exist • Nike liked sleek and innovative design, including three wheels, while Gazelle sought to avoid radical departure from a bicycle

Product complexity

Working hard and strong commitment did not prevent the technical problems from emerging. The testing demonstrated the limits of the prototype, while the services, except for maintenance, were not yet in place. Moreover, serious concerns arose during the test. The test drivers perceived the prototype as complex, not "easy-to-handle" and occasionally even dangerous. The longer-than-expected development time for single components and the difficulty integrating these components testify to the growing complexity of the project. The project team was keen to carry out the development of all components almost simultaneously, although some needed more development time than others. For example, the development of the sitting position (similar to the Giant EZB Revive) required less effort and time than the development of the new cover or the new tilting-steering mechanism. This failure to assign priorities might have resulted in a greater level of complexity.

7.1.7 *Implementation period*

The reported discussion on the goal and outcome of the project at the end of the description chapter reflects a mix of different interpretations, interests and some making sense of things after the fact.

The formalized goal, as noted in the project proposals and business plan, clearly suggested the intention to introduce a new environmentally friendly vehicle into a new market, with some details as to how to achieve this. Given the heterogeneous setting, next to this explicit goal, other implicit goals might have coexisted, such as publicity generation or raising awareness of mobility problems. However, the actors' justifications and attempts to make sense of things after the project's termination may have understated the formalized goals and emphasized the "secondary" goals. The network setting highlights these different interpretation's schemes.

Consider, for instance, the different interpretations of the project's outcome held by the Gazelle director and the TNO former project leader. To understand the interpretations' nuances an analysis of the broader context is required. These individuals work in different organizations where missions as well as business models are different. Gazelle's revenues come from selling bicycles in the mass market, targeting only a small segment at the high end of the market. Therefore, it is not surprising that the director considered the Mitka an expensive, complex and never-ending product. On the other hand, TNO's revenues stem from subsidized projects and consultancy with a large turnover. From this perspective, it is unsurprising that the former project leader considered the expenditure rate of the project low. The question is then how money is used in a NPD project. Consider, for instance, how an entrepreneurial firm like Velomobiel would invest it. Moreover, due to the significant environmental ambition of the project leader, the Mitka project was, and still is, perceived as a real attempt at system innovation.

The Mitka was a fascinating project, in which several people worked for several years towards achieving an ideal mobility concept. This did not happen. The formalized goal was not achieved and the project was prematurely terminated despite many actors' desires, the project team's determination, generous business plans and more than €1 million investment in the three-year project. The poor performance of the expensive product, together with the lack of potential investors, signalled the end for the Mitka project. Paradoxically, if the development of the three-wheeled Mitka has died a death, the development of its "little brother", the Easy Glider, is tremendously alive. The spin-off, developed by Vd Veer, has been perceived by the coalition members as a success.[116]

What emerges as another dimension of success is the learning experience, which encompasses technical capability as well as capabilities in working as part of a team for some team members. The dominant mode of learning was technical and came at later stages only. The successful spin-off is the result of the technical learning experience as clearly stated by the designer in chapter 6. However, the learning experience did not help the team as a whole to reflect on, assess and continue the project together. Besides the technical learning, the publicity generated by the project positively influenced all of the actors in the coalition, lending the companies they represented the image of innovators and environmentally conscious organizations.

7.2 The Mango case

7.2.1 Introduction

How did Velomobiel's start-up cope with a radical project? This section will analyze the innovation journey of the Velomobiel entrepreneurs. The objective of the analysis is to understand how Velomobiel's founders made decisions and the consequences their actions had on the product concepts. As in the description, the analysis follows the same chronological timeline. While the Mitka case was analyzed at two levels, the management and the project team levels, in the Velomobiel case such a distinction is superfluous since the decisions were taken only by the two Velomobiel founders. However, their decisions concerned both the development of new product concepts and the creation and survival of the new firm. Unlike the Mitka case, the development of the Mango can be seen as the last of a series of innovative concepts. This section starts by explaining Velomobiel's innovation path from the project innovativeness perspective. This is followed by three sub-sections that analyze the decisions made during the initiation, development and implementation periods. First, environmental ambition is analyzed.

7.2.2 Environmental ambition

Unlike the Mitka case, Velomobiel's founders had no ambition to develop and implement innovative concepts for the sake of the natural environment. Their passion for new and fast HPVs drove them to create a business out of it. They were interested in building new velomobiles for people like themselves. Intriguingly, Velomobiel's vehicles are seen by several actors in the environmental field as environmentally friendly or sustainable products because their use may substitute car use. As the survey among Velomobiel's clients illustrates, almost one commuter out of three uses a velomobile as a substitute for the car (see Table 6.2). Although the Quest and the Mango are considered green products, environmental concern was neither the driving force nor the goal for Velomobiel's founders.

7.2.3 The project's innovativeness

Velomobiel's project, the first product as well as the newly born company, were radical for several reasons.

The new product. The creation of a series of velomobiles such as the Alleweder, the C-Alleweder and the Quest had a certain level of novelty. The Alleweder with its aluminum fairing and full suspension constituted a radical vehicle. It was the first bicycle with these characteristics in the market. Bart Verhees was not the inventor of a new kind of vehicle, but of a new way of building bikes with a self-carrying canopy made of aluminum sheets. At that time, the American *Windcheetah* was already on the market, although its canopy was much smaller and not aluminum. There was also another company, the Dutch *M5*, which was making three-wheeled bikes although they then changed to produce only two-wheelers. Flevobike was the innovator of the Alleweder because it was able to produce and introduce it to market. The C-Alleweder, designed by Allert Jacob, was a radical concept due to the adoption of a new material, carbon fiber-glass, and the absence of a metal frame inside the fairing. These were great novelties for a commercial, human-powered vehicle. The Quest is not as radical as the two previous versions of the Alleweder. In fact, it is a combination of both models' advantages and the use of modern instruments such as, for example, the wind tunnel. Nevertheless it is the fastest, human-propelled vehicle for practical use in the market. The Mango represents an incremental step from the Quest concept, but it can be seen as the last of a series of innovative concepts, the most market-driven vehicle.

The high degree of uncertainty. The design, the development and the production of the C-Alleweder and the Quest were radical undertakings for the designer and his partner because they represented a serious challenge that had never been attempted before. First, Allert Jacob was not a designer, in spite of his passion for cycling. His experience was limited to machining production and craftsmanship. Second, besides the design, he also needed to get acquainted with production processes. Consider, for example, the learning experience in making a scale model, building molds or working with new materials.

New organizational setting. Besides the technical aspects, the start of the new company also required new capabilities and resources in developing the business model, coordinating suppliers, marketing the new product and communicating with potential clients. Therefore, the learning process also included learning new skills regarding the organizational functions required by a newborn company.

A new market. The term velomobile, which refers to faired, human-propelled vehicles, was introduced in 2000. At the same time the company J&S changed its name to Velomobiel. Velomobile was not just a neologism but it signalled the birth of a new market segment in the bike market. Therefore the Alleweder and the Quest became the first products in this special niche market. Since then, the term velomobile has been officially recognized by the IHPVA.

7.2.4 Initiation period choices

The decision by Johan Vrielink to produce the handmade Alleweder allowed Allert Jacob to start new work and be part of a new phase of the Alleweder's development. From cutting the aluminum sheets with scissors to machining the suspensions or fixing the derailleur, Allert Jacob built his technical skills and competences learning how to produce and assemble this special vehicle. Besides these competences, the extensive use of the bicycle, both for leisure and for competition purposes, created the conditions for him to be able to identify the strong and weak points of the vehicle and identify areas for improvement. Thus acquired knowledge and expertise not only about the production phase but also about the usage phase. Moreover, feedback from the Alleweder users matched his impressions (see Table 7.6. for an overview of the Velomobiel development process).

This learning experience and Jacob's passion for cycling enabled him conditions to envision a superior bicycle not yet in the market: a fast, comfortable, light and weather-protected, human-propelled vehicle. He soon came up with a shortlist of product requirements for a new version of the Alleweder. Although he was not a designer, he managed to design from scratch and develop the C-Alleweder prototype. The search for the fastest, lightest, maintenance-free vehicle influenced his decisions to develop a radical new vehicle characterized by a new monocoque fairing with less air resistance and composed of a lighter material, carbon fiber-glass.

Although these choices made the vehicle faster, lighter, more comfortable and maintenance-free, they produced the undesirable effects of making the product expensive and difficult to build. There were additional steps in the production process, such as plastering, painting and the assembly line. Moreover, the limited experience in working with new materials such as fiber-glass and the related production process increased the complexity of the product, the production time and consequently, the cost. The unfamiliarity with the new production process and the labor-intensive nature of the process made it difficult to set a definitive price for the C-Alleweder. Consider not only the frequency of the change (three times in the first year), but also the extent to which the price changed, from €3,400 to €7,000. The C-Alleweder experiment was a learning experience for the designer as well as for Flevobike, but it had little impact on the financial assets of Flevobike, thanks to the product differentiation strategy.

Table 7.6 Changes during Velomobiel's development process

	Factors	Initiation period	Early and late development periods	Implementation
Velomobiel founders	Attitude	Enthusiastic, fun, learning	Adaptive, reflective, resourceful	Adaptive, receptive to users, resourceful
	Commitment	High	High	High
	Required capabilities (technical/managerial)	Limited	Building up	Developed
Product concept	Degree of complexity	High	Decreasing	Low
	Infrastructure boundaries	Within	Within	Within
	Production time/cost	High	Decreasing	Decreasing
Market research	User preference and feedback	Largely accepted	Largely accepted	Largely accepted

The high price and the production complexity were the main reasons why the C-Alleweder was withdrawn from the market despite being the fastest and most innovative, human-propelled vehicle for practical use that was maintenance-free.

7.2.5 *Early development period choices*

The C-Alleweder represented an important lesson for the designer. He realized that the design and use of new materials for a completely new monocoque fairing could not be done without thinking about the production and assembly process. To present a vehicle in the market in a short period of time, the design needed to be functional to the production process. Therefore, the next project's design should also take into account the production phase, without compromising the product requirements of the C-Alleweder.

Before proceeding with the new design, Allert Jacob decided to build new capabilities with regard to fairing shapes to improve the C-Alleweder's air drag flow. Consequently, the Quest's design was the result of accurate studies rather than intuition or improvisation. The designer's idea was to create a faster vehicle but a less complex concept, by adapting sophisticated aerodynamic solutions to a much simpler vehicle body. Consider, for example, the reintroduction of the new metal frame about which he had specific knowledge or the removal of the carbon fiber in the fairing. Table 7.7 illustrates some of the technical dilemmas faced by the product developer during the development process.

The production process also needed to be simpler. Given the designer's inexperience with fiber-glass and the relative high production time of the fiber-glass fairing, Jacob decided to outsource the production of the fairing. Thanks to the network of recumbent and velomobile producers, he was able to find a firm that was able to produce high quality fiber-glass ready to assemble, without plastering and painting. Therefore, the simpler metal frame production and the outsourcing of the fiber-glass created the conditions for a simpler production system with a decreased production time.

Besides the production, there was also concern about the assembly phase. The market for the "do-it-yourself" clients with the Alleweder's kit system was perceived as saturated. Therefore, the assembly phase was considered part of the company tasks rather than a user task. This provided an opportunity to enlarge the market.

Besides the technical struggles experienced during the development of the Quest, the developer also faced a new challenge. The change in Flevobike's strategy forced Allert Jacob and Ymte Sijbrandij to leave the company and start one of their own in order to develop the Quest. Thanks to their adaptiveness and the experiences they had accumulated at Flevobike, they were able to establish new functions for the technical, business and market development of the new firm. As for the development of the Quest, they showed adaptiveness to the evolving situation by carefully using their limited resources to achieve their goal.

Table 7.7 Technical dilemmas during the Velomobiel's development process

Improvements for	Requirements	Dilemmas	Choices/how it was solved	Results	
				Achievements	Drawbacks
Alleweder	Higher speed/ better design	Aluminum vs new material (carbon/ fiber-glass)	Carbon carbon/ fiber-glass	C-Alleweder	High production time (plus painting and plastering process)
	Higher comfort	Metal frame vs monocoque	Monocoque	New aerodynamic fairing/high speed Enclosed drive train	No experience with fiber-glass molding
	Better maintenance				High cost
C-Alleweder	Higher speed/ better design	Carbon/fiber-glass vs. fiber-glass	Fiber-glass	Quest Less production time and cost: no painting and plastering process	Users' concerns on maneuverability (too long, high turning cycle)
	Lower production time	Metal frame vs monocoque	Metal frame	Outsourced fairing production Experience in metal frame	Cost
	Lower cost				
Quest	Smaller turning cycle		Shorter	Mango	Slower
	Lower cost		Box wheels open	More comfortable More maneuverable	50% reduction of luggage space
	Lower production time		Use of standard parts	Cheaper	

7.2.6 Late development period choices

Thanks to the choices made during the design and development stages and after a prolonged test, J&S was able to present the new Quest to potential clients as a new vehicle that was faster and cheaper than other velomobiles in the market, taking into account the withdrawal of the Alleweder. More than the extensive use, tests and contests, it was the user feedback and first impressions of potential clients that were the driving forces for Velomobiel's founders to rethink the Quest concept. Consider, for example, that the length and turning circle were the main concerns of the potential users because they were concerned with having good maneuverability. Moreover, the price was perceived as being too high. Intriguingly, Velomobiel decided to develop a new vehicle, the Mango, to respond to this potential target group. This decision suggests that Velomobiel's founders considered not only the consumers feedback very important, but also the potential users' opinions. Production costs and time are still important issues, however their adaptiveness and accumulating experience in producing both the Quest and the Mango helped boost their productivity output (see Figure 6.7 in the previous chapter).

7.2.7 Implementation period

The choices taken during the development of the Mango denote a shift in the learning curve. While the initiation period coincided with the acquisition of knowledge and experience in developing a vehicle, and choices were based on a trial-and-error approach, the early development period corresponded to a phase of adaptiveness and resourcefulness. The choices made were elegant and efficient solutions rather than superior and more complex ones, as occurred during the development of the C-Alleweder. In the late development period the choices were influenced by the experience accumulated by Flevobike, which created the conditions to launch and sell its product. Moreover, the Mango was Velomobiel's response to potential consumers' complaints about the Quest's limited maneuverability and high price.

What the choices in this innovation journey have in common is that they were based on feedback from users and potential clients, which were then reinforced by Velomobiel's founders experience with the vehicle.

7.3 Cross-analysis

While the two previous sections have analyzed the two cases separately, this section turns to a comparative analysis of the cases. The goal is to compare the two innovation processes and highlight the contrasting features. This section seeks to answer the question illustrated in Chapter 1:

> What are the differences in the decision-making process between high and low environmental ambition level projects?

As a matter of fact, the decisions taken along the two project development processes reveal different approaches to product development. Before that, one must remember why the researcher decided to compare the Mango case with the Mitka case. The projects had similar objectives but contrasting motivations and they occurred in different organizational settings. The technical objectives of Velomobiel's founders were similar to those of the Mitka actors. They wanted to develop a new, human-powered vehicle for practical use with specific character- istics, such as weather protection, comfort and speed. The motivation for the two projects were however different. In the Mitka case, the goal was to replace the car, for travel within a 25-kilometer range, with a new concept. This goal was driven by the teams' high level of environmental ambition and a perceived busi- ness opportunity. The environmental ambition acted as a design imperative. In the Mango case, the opportunity to build the fastest and most comfortable bike (and make a living out of it) was the main motivation. The organizational settings in each case were new, yet they were different. One was a start-up while the other was a coalition of heterogeneous actors. The cases are compared in their design and development choices, the way the users' feedback was employed and finally, how technical and market knowledge was built up (see Table 7.8).

7.3.1 Design choices

There are key differences in the ways the two concepts were designed and developed. Although the two project teams started with a similar complex design problem, given their limited experience and similar product attributes, they took two different approaches to finalize the concept. In the Mitka case, the project team's choices made the concept even more complex due to the number of new attributes and interactions. Furthermore, the team did not compromise on the original attributes and avoided trading off some attributes even in cases of apparent conflict. Consider, for example, the choice to have the speed switch in the Mitka: having no fixed speed limit (25 km/h and 40 km/h) could cause prob- lems for street regulation (for the registration of the vehicle and the need for a helmet) (see Figure 7.1). Moreover, they seemed to be locked into the search for the perfect vehicle so that they went for the most impressive engineering solu- tions. In contrast, Velomobiel's designer decided to decrease the concept's degree of complexity, combining innovative technical solutions with well- established practices. The design process was continuously adapted in the way that some attributes were compromised at the expense of others in search of a balance among the diverse requirements. Consider, for example, the tradeoff between maneuverability and speed in the development of the Quest and the Mango (see Figure 7.1 and Table 7.9). Furthermore, Table 7.9 illustrates a qualitative comparison among velomobiles and Mitka concepts according to some attributes, taking the Alleweder as a reference. To optimize the design, the designer opted for simple, yet elegant solutions. This is visible in the smooth price trend of Velomobiel's vehicles' development compared with that of the Mitka, except for the C-Alleweder (see Figure 7.2).

Table 7.8 Similarities and differences in the Mango and Mitka case innovation process

		Mitka development	Mango development
Objectives	Technical	Development of a new human-powered vehicle for commuting in the 25 km range	Development of a new human-powered vehicle for practical use
	Market/ target group	Mass market/ car drivers, -commuters	Niche market/commuters
Product requirements		Weather-protected / Comfortable / Fast / Replacing the car in the 25 km range	Weather protected / Comfortable / Fast / Chain maintenance free
Motivations		Concern for the natural environment / Business opportunity	The search for fastest and most comfortable bike for practical use / Low concern for the natural environment
Organizational setting		New coalition of heterogeneous actors	From a small firm to a start-up
Decision making		Slow/consensus seeking	Fast/ two individuals
Management team	Attitude	From enthusiastic to Wait and see	Adaptive/resourceful
	Commitment	Mixed	High
	Advocacy	Supportive	Supportive
Project team	Attitude	Uncompromising / Lock-in effect / No product attributes trading off / Looking for the superior solution	Compromising / Trading product attributes off / Looking for the superior solution but adopting elegant solution
	Commitment	Escalating	High
	Required capabilities	Limited	Building up
	Degree of complexity	Increasing	Decreasing
	Degree of uncertainty	High	From high to low
	Series of innovations	None (one spin-off)	3
	Infrastructure boundaries	Going beyond	Within
Market research	User preference and feedback	Searched but largely dismissed	Largely accepted

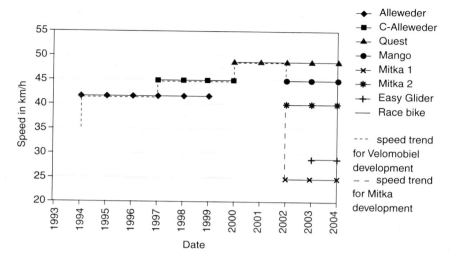

Figure 7.1 Speed changes during the Velomobiel and Mitka processes.

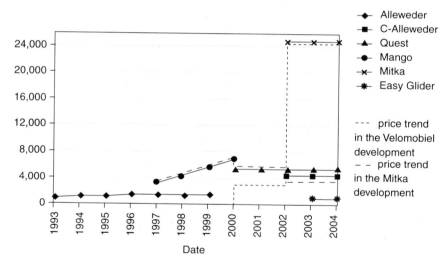

Figure 7.2 Price changes during the Mitka and the Velomobiel's vehicles development processes.

Another difference was the approach to the final concept. The Mitka team chose to take a large step in the design scale-up without engaging in-between, simpler prototypes but going for the best solution. Alternatively, Velomobiel's founders decided to take smaller steps in the design scale-up, and developed an in-between innovative vehicle, the C-Alleweder, to build technical experience and procure helpful feedback.

The two innovation processes also differ with regard to the current infrastructure and regulation boundaries. In the case of Velomobiel, the design choices were based on consumer's daily use. Their vehicles were developed to function within the boundaries of the current infrastructure. Consider, for example, that the Quest's width was deliberately designed to allow the Quest to fit through doorways and make use of both roads and bicycle lanes. In contrast, choices for the Mitka took the current infrastructure only partially into account. Potential consumers' concerns about the width of the Mitka were dismissed and the annoying legal issue of the helmet was set aside.

The two projects also illustrate how the decision-making processes were shaped by the organizational forms. In the Mitka case, the heterogeneous organizational setting required consensus seeking, which resulted in a slow and sometimes cumbersome decision-making process. Alternatively, the two-person company in the Mango case allowed for fast decision making. Moreover, their proximity to velomobile customers permitted rapid information exchange.

Finally, engagement with external actors was also undertaken differently in each case. The Mitka actors were seeking publicity and potential financial partners rather than expertise and technical knowledge. In fact, they were reluctant to engage in and be associated with existing networks of skilled workers and practical technicians who had been developing similar vehicles. On the other hand, Velomobiel's founders were engaged in a small, yet resourceful, network where technical problems were shared. These considerable interactions helped the Velomobiel actors with limited resources strengthen their expertise and be able to outsource part of the production to trustworthy partners.

7.3.2 Market research, test and feedback

Velomobiel's founders and the Mitka coalition considered the role of potential users very important during the innovation process. Potential users were asked to give comments, express opinions and, in the case of the Mitka's development, they also had the opportunity to create and envision their own concept vehicle. Despite the continuous quest for user involvement, the two development

Table 7.9 Qualitative comparison among the vehicles based on some product attributes, taking the Alleweder as the reference

Product attributes	C-Alleweder	Quest	Mango	Mitka electric-powered	Mitka human-powered only	Easy Glider
Less effort	+	+ +	+	++	− −	+/−
Weather protection	+	+	+	−	−	− −
Maneuverability	+/−	+/−	+	+/−	− −	+ +
Luggage space[2]	+ +	+ +	+	− −	− −	− −
Maintenance free	+ +	+ +	+ +	+/−	+/−	+/−

processes differed with regard to the application of the user feedback in the actual product development phase. In Velomobiel's case, the actors paid a great deal of attention to the feedback obtained through their extensive use of the products and that of the lead users. The continuous interactions with the clients of the Alleweder, the C-Alleweder and the Quest created the conditions to exchange opinions and critical observations, which were coded as possible improvements. Moreover, through competitions and recreational activities, Velomobiel's founders were able to grasp the perceptions and reactions of potential users towards velomobiles. Consequently, these exchanges created strong ties between the Velomobiel founders and the velomobiles' users, which increased the very legitimacy of Velomobiel's action. They asked for feedback, which was translated into product attributes for new concepts, happened during the development of the Mango. In the Mitka case, more sophisticated market research was conducted at several stages of the process through surveys, group discussions, interviews and testing. Nevertheless, the users' preference and perceptions toward the Mitka did not entirely influence and shape its design and development. The lock-in effect of the design choices and the team's perception of doing something unique created conditions whereby user preferences were dismissed if they contrasted with the main development path, while favorable user preferences were highlighted but, unfortunately, proven to be minority views. Consider, for example, the moderate preference of Nike car drivers for the Mitka concept, the choice of the three-wheeled configuration rather than the two-wheeled one (see Table 6.3) or the emphasis put on the positive impressions of only one test driver dismissing the negative perceptions of the other two drivers. Moreover, the absence of testing prototypes in between development stages also delayed user feedback. The coalition asked for feedback on several occasions, which were generally not translated into product attributes.

7.3.3 Technical and market knowledge

The ability to build expertise and knowledge in the two cases also differed. The Velomobiel founders were able to acquire technical skills and knowledge and market experience through adaptiveness and user feedback. In contrast, the Mitka project team, while coping with technicalities and slowly gaining the specific competences, was not able to build a market for the vehicle. Moreover, the diverse motivations, the mixed commitments and the limited experience within the coalition did not allow the management team to build the necessary organizational functions to permit exploitation of the Mitka concept.

7.3.4 New proposition and conclusion

Table 7.8 illustrates the similarities and differences between the two innovation journeys. From this comparison, it is evident that there is a striking difference in the attitudes towards the innovation journey. Remarkably, the difference in attitude recalls the conceptual framework of Garud and Karnoe (2003) concerning the approach to complex technological projects explained in Chapter 2, the breakthrough vs the bricolage approach. It was explained that the very attitude taken toward the radical undertaking influences its process and likely its outcome (Garud et al., 2003). Applying this conceptual framework to the Mitka and Velomobiel cases, the role of environmental ambition is revealed to have played a crucial role in the innovation approach.

In the Mitka case, the search for the ultimate solution to mobility problems and the high ambition targets combined with the dismissal of user preferences and existing knowledge outside the team evoke a breakthrough approach (see Chapter 2). In contrast, in the Mango case, the accumulation of knowledge through a sequence of product innovations, the constant search for feedback and the attitude to adaptation and tradeoff recalls a bricolage approach.

From the Mitka case analysis, the high level of environmental ambition has emerged as a mechanism behind the search for the most impressive engineering solutions to alleviate environmental problems. It seems that the high level of environmental ambition may also have influenced the approach to the radical undertaking. As a result, the iterative process between empirical data and the conceptual framework is instrumental in formulating a new proposition.

P4 A development team with a high level of environmental ambition performing a radical undertaking is likely to adopt a breakthrough rather than a bricolage approach.

In the next chapter this proposition will be discussed together with the others.

8 Discussions, conclusions and recommendations

8.1 Introduction

This book examines the relationship between environmental ambition and the innovation process. Environmental ambition has been defined as the specific intention to design and develop new products and services that have a significantly lower environmental impact than the products and services that they aim to substitute. Therefore, how and to what extent environmental ambition influences the way new products and services are developed is the main research question of this thesis. The empirical domain has been the mobility system, in particular the human-powered vehicle sector. This domain is seen simultaneously as a source of environmental problems and as the locus of innovative opportunities. The rationale for this explorative study is to better understand and explain why efforts to develop environmental products do not always translate into the effective implementation and adoption of these products.

To be able to answer the main research, question both the environmental product and innovation literature have been reviewed. This provides an opportunity to develop a conceptual model of the role of environmental ambition on product performance (looking specifically at management support, project team commitment and product attributes) by formulating a set of propositions. Consequently, an empirical examination has been performed where two sequential case studies have been described, in Chapters 6 and 7, and analyzed, first individually and then jointly.

This chapter has a number of purposes. First, it presents the main findings. It then reformulates and discusses the implications of the emergent propositions for the environmental and innovation literature. Afterwards, a fine-tuned conceptual model is presented. Additionally, the results make room for further implications beyond the propositions formulated. Second, it illustrates the scope and limitations of this research study. Finally, it suggests recommendations for scholars, practitioners and policy makers.

8.2 Main research findings

The research question formulated in Chapter 1 was:

> How does the environmental ambition of managers and product developers influence their decision making during the product innovation process?

This research shows that environmental ambition influences the innovation process in various ways. Environmental ambition is one of the reasons why a firm may engage in NPD and it is likely to have an impact when objectives are established, resources mobilized and performance criteria evaluated. A high level of environmental ambition increases the complexity of the product innovation process. Concern for the natural environment encourages the search for innovation opportunities; however, the actual exploitation of these opportunities may be difficult because of the non-rational nature of environmental ambition.

Environmental ambition may reinforce beliefs that managers hold about "what is feasible", which leads them to pursue a radical path. Because of the high degree of uncertainty involved, it may not be possible to evaluate fully the outcome of any radical paths and their performance.

With unclear performance criteria, the individual evaluation of events may represent the manifestation of one's own beliefs. Data inconsistent with this individual evaluation may either be ignored or appear as noise (as suggested by Garud & Rappa, 1994). Data consistent with this individual evaluation may be perceived as information and rearranged in a manner to reinforce an individual's beliefs. This perception occurs because individuals may be more interested in confirming their beliefs than in actively trying to disprove them (Weick, 1979).

Therefore, environmental ambition may be a non-rational factor that justifies and reinforces the belief that one is "doing the right thing" for the natural environment, which results in psychological rewards, and the belief one holds about "what is feasible or what is worth attempting".

The influence of environmental ambition as a non-rational factor in complex projects may result in:

- support for projects regardless of how well the project unfolds over time;
- an escalation of commitments; and
- a difficult tradeoff among product attributes.

The results from the Mitka case highlight the complexity of performing and supporting radical projects that are strongly driven by environmental ambition. The high level of environmental ambition was a strong motivation to start the project, yet it was not restricted to this mission. It also manifested itself in the making of key decisions during the development of the Mitka, for example, the choice between the three-wheeled and two-wheeled versions. Environmental ambition also influenced the way general, yet different, needs were addressed. In the Mitka case, a tension emerged between addressing social needs and market needs simultaneously, which do not necessary coincide or overlap with one another because of the difference in goals and in the time horizon.

It seems that a dichotomy existed between short-term and long-term goals, which was not fully understood by the management and the project team. The team saw a number of new product attributes in a single concept, the changes required in infrastructure and the prospect of making the Mitka a blockbuster in the market as possible short-term goals rather than long-term ones. The short-term goal to introduce the Mitka to the market clashed with the time required to develop the Mitka product service system in light of the infrastructure changes. Environmental ambition seems to have made the distinction between long-term and short-term goals unclear. Radical projects driven by environmental concerns may imply higher risks due to a higher degree of complexity, given the ill-defined nature of the concept of greening. In the next section, the main findings are explained through a reformulation of the propositions and discussions.

8.2.1 Reformulating and discussing the propositions

After describing the Mitka case in Chapter 6 and analyzing it in Chapter 7, this section goes a step further and sharpens the propositions put forward in Chapter 5. In this section, the propositions are recapped, reformulated and discussed.

The first proposition

This proposition addresses the implications for the management team in supporting radical projects that carry a high level of environmental ambition. The tentative proposition was:

> P1 Decision makers with a high level of environmental ambition will support environmental projects and thus lower the performance-judgment threshold.

The management team supported the Mitka project, investing time, human and financial resources, despite the mixed commitments. The psychological rewards of doing something positive for the natural environment influenced decisions to prolong support for the Mitka project on various occasions, even when faced with poor or unclear performance. Environmental ambition is confirmed to be a non-rational component in the advocacy process. Nevertheless, environmental ambition alone may not be sufficient to lessen performance-judgment thresholds. The network members were willing to support such a project despite the moderate risk involved for each of them, especially at the start of the project. On the other hand, there was a great deal of uncertainty within the management team regarding the uniqueness of the project. The high level of environmental ambition, in combination with the individually perceived moderate risk and unclear performance indicators, reduce the performance-judgment threshold. Therefore, this proposition is partially confirmed. The first proposition is rearticulated here:

RP1 A high level of environmental ambition is likely to influence the managers' support process, which will result in a lower performance-judgment threshold when the individual risk is low and unclear performance indicators exist.

The results from the Mitka case highlight the complexity of performing and supporting radical projects that involve shared responsibility and are strongly driven by environmental ambition. Consequently, this study finds that supporting radical projects that address societal needs may increase, rather than decrease, the uncertainty of the innovation journey. Moreover, addressing society's needs may not be sufficient for meeting market needs and reaping profits. In situations with a high level of uncertainty and unclear performance indicators, environmental ambition may influence the go/no-go decision. A radical project with high potential environmental gains may be enthusiastically supported by the management team, which implies that the threshold for the performance indicators may be lowered. This results in a greater degree of management support, regardless of how well the project performs. Similarly, radical and environmentally driven projects may also garner support from management because of regulatory or social pressure and publicity. This support involves lowering unobserved performance thresholds. As a result, managers may support an environmentally driven project regardless of its performance. This is in line with Abrahamson's model in which companies may adopt tools and pursue the innovation in an inefficient way, especially when the level of uncertainty regarding the innovation is high (Abrahamson, 1991).

This proposition is also consistent with a small, yet increasing, body of environmental literature, which outlines the difficulties management faces in clearly defining environmental issues and measuring environmental performance (Banerjee et al., 2003; Chen, 2001; Walley et al., 1994). The Mitka management's difficulty in checking performance judgments is inconsistent with the assumption of many scholars that radical innovations driven by environmental concern lead to better economic performance (Hall & Vredenburg, 2003b; Hart et al., 1999; Senge et al., 2001). For example, Hart and Milstein state that "*Future economic growth will be driven by those firms that are able to develop innovations that leapfrog standard routines and knowledge, and address society's needs.*" (Hart et al., 2003: 63). However, they do not seem to be concerned with the higher degree of uncertainty involved in adopting a radical approach to NPD projects and the difficulty in dealing with environmental performance.

With regard to the innovation literature, this proposition is consistent with studies on support for projects persisting despite poor performance (Gimeno et al., 1997; Green et al., 2003; Schmidt et al., 1998). This research extends the literature on NPD proposing that environmental ambition is a non-rational component of the support process for innovative projects. Furthermore, it is in line with studies that illustrate technology evolution as a socio-cognitive process (Garud et al., 1994).

The second proposition

This proposition addresses the implications for the project team's commitments when dealing with radical projects driven by a high level of environmental ambition. The tentative proposition was:

> P2 In a radical undertaking, decision takers with a high level of environmental ambition are likely to escalate their commitments.

The high level of environmental ambition of the team emphasized the search for the ideal means of transport for a more sustainable mobility system. The high level of environmental ambition and the radicality of the project locked the project team into a course of action. This course of action entailed a limited reassessment of design choices, which occasionally challenged the current infrastructure system, avoiding trading off and dismissing signals from potential users. The high level of environmental ambition and the radicality of the project reinforced each other in a positive feedback loop. Moreover, the supportive management team, which was waiting for the concept to materialize, did not moderate the escalation of commitments by the project team. The second proposition is rearticulated here:

> RP2 In a radical undertaking a high level of environmental ambition is likely to influence the commitments of project team members, as decision takers, resulting in an escalation of commitments.

In the Mitka case, the combination of a high level of environmental ambition and the radical undertaking facilitated the escalation of commitments by the project team. This proposition is strongly related to the previous one. It emphasizes how the commitment of the project team, which is actually responsible for the design and development of the innovative and environmentally friendly concept, is likely to escalate when the management is supportive.

The environmental literature does not specifically address the effect of environmental ambition on project team commitment during project development, although it gives some clues to the way that coordination and communication within the team may be affected when undertaking environmental projects (Handfield et al., 2001; Lenox et al., 1997). For example, Handfield et al. (2001) found a difference in expectations and perceptions within the team between the supporters of environmentally responsible manufacturing tools and the users of those tools, the designers. Given the lack of empirical data and conceptual frameworks within the environmental literature, the results from the Mitka case should be considered a welcome, yet small, step towards understanding how a project team's environmental ambition can affect the innovation process.

This contribution also has implications for the innovation literature. Previous studies found that the escalation of commitments was likely to occur when the project team was performing radical undertakings (Green et al., 2003; Schmidt et al., 1998). The findings from the Mitka case confirm these from previous works, yet suggest that environmental ambition is an important factor in the escalation of commitments. The high level of environmental ambition not only triggered the search for radical solutions to mobility problems, but also reinforced the lock-in effect in the decision-making process. The explanation may lie in the psychological rewards of doing something new and beneficial for the natural environment. These findings are consistent with the work on entrepreneurial firms, where, despite poor financial performance, many businesses were kept alive due to psychological rewards (Gimeno et al., 1997).

Consequently, this study finds that supporting radical projects that address societal needs may increase rather than decrease the uncertainty of the innovation journey. This means that some projects have been continued despite their poor performance, which may explain why some green products have performed poorly.

The third proposition

This proposition addresses the implications of a team's environmental ambition for the product concept. The tentative preposition was:

> P3 A high level of environmental ambition will likely increase product complexity.

The high level of environmental ambition led environmental entrepreneurs to assume that only through the search and development of radical solutions is it possible to decrease the burden on the natural environment. The search for radical solutions and the integration of new attributes increased the complexity of the Mitka concept. Another effect of the high level of environmental ambition on the product concept emerged: the dilemma of trading off different product attributes while taking into consideration the environmental dimension. The team occasionally decided to avoid tradeoffs. The third proposition is here rearticulated:

> RP3 A high level of environmental ambition will likely result in a higher degree of product complexity.

The previous propositions suggest that, when the search for radical solutions is driven by a high level of environmental ambition and psychological rewards are obtained from doing something good for the natural environment, the uncertainties in undertaking innovative projects increase. Consequently, the complexity of the product concept is increased. On the other hand, incorporating environmental attributes that are ill defined (Chen, 2001) may intensify this complexity even more, which may in turn negatively affect product performance.

This proposition is consistent with the innovation and product design literature. It is argued that successful products are the result of product advantage, unique benefits and meeting market demands (Brown et al., 1995; Cooper et al., 1987, 1995a; Montoya-Weiss et al., 1994). In other words, commercial success depends on how well a product meets consumer requirements (Freeman, 1982; Rothwell et al., 1974). A successful product comprises a set of attributes that are by definition balanced. Incorporating new attributes into a product, such as environmental ones, should be carefully balanced with more traditional attributes. Thus, the integration of environmental attributes should not conflict with traditional product attributes or performances, such as safety and convenience. Giving a higher priority to environmental attributes at the expense of other parameters (like customer requirements) may affect product performance. Thus the tradeoff described above should reflect consumer requirements. Market information and market analysis are considered crucial stages in the development process when it comes to addressing existing needs. This is especially true when people's attitudes towards the environment are not translated into their purchasing behavior. It is argued that it is only by focusing on market information that the tradeoff between these two types of attributes may lead to superior performance by green products.

Market information, for example, a solid understanding of consumer preferences, may be of little help when it comes to developing radical innovations (Balachandra et al., 1997) because a radical product incorporates by definition parts that are unknown and uncertain. Although some specifications may be rational and based on objective decision making, others are more subjective. Indeterminate attributes can be judgmental, subjective or ideological, and they are difficult to translate into product attributes, as such a translation will be inherently political in nature. When designers try to integrate indeterminate attributes into the design of a product, the additional tradeoffs increase the complexity of a project. Designers face a dramatic dilemma: *How to incorporate environmental attributes into the design when they will be perceived differently by various stakeholders? How to incorporate specifications that are ideological without increasing the risk of market rejection?* This is a result of the complexity of greening.

This complexity may make product developers more reluctant to address environmental concerns. On the other hand, environmental concerns may be the main rationale for developing a new product, in which case environmental attributes may be overemphasized at the expense of market-driven product specifications. Testing assumptions during the development process may help identify and incorporate important market-driven requirements. Otherwise, the product may turn out to have an added value in social, technological and environmental terms, and respond to social needs and fundamental research priorities, while failing to address market demand. Veryzer (1998a) found that some aspects thought to be important by a development team are in fact occasionally not at all important to consumers. The role of feedback in radical undertakings needs more attentive investigation. With the discussion of the next proposition this issue is examined more extensively.

The fourth proposition

Another proposition emerged from the comparative analysis of the Mitka and the Velomobiel cases that specifically addresses the way actors approached the radical undertaking.

> P4 A development team with a high level of environmental ambition performing a radical undertaking is likely to adopt a breakthrough rather than a bricolage approach.

A striking difference was found between the approaches that recalled the typologies Garud and Karnoe (2003) described as bricolage and breakthrough approaches. They found that a bricolage approach rather than a breakthrough one was more effective in resolving complex technological projects, such as wind turbine development. The former denotes adaptiveness, trial-and-error experimentation, fast development and sequences of innovations, while the latter emphasizes the search for leap-frog achievement, for the best and superior radical solution (see Table 8.1).

The findings are compatible with this interpretation. In the Mitka case the avoidance of tradeoff, search for superior solutions, effects of locking-in and dismissal of feedback and knowledge from outside the team denoted a breakthrough approach. This implies that a causal relationship may exist between the high level of environmental ambition and the approach chosen. As explained earlier, the PSS philosophy and disruptive innovations supporters favor rapid and radical changes in society through new radical technologies, moving from products to services or redesigning existing infrastructures (e.g. Brezet et al., 2001b; Hall et al., 2003b; Hart et al., 2003; Luiten et al., 2001a; Tischner et al., 2002; Weaver et al., 2000). This approach, driven by a high level of environmental ambition, reflects a breakthrough rather than a bricolage approach. From the work of Garud and Karnoe (2003), the pursuit of a breakthrough approach may have caused their supporters to fail in delivering the promised technology because they may have stifled the learning process. Similarly, the Mitka actors may have failed *because* of their pursuit of a breakthrough. The bricolage approach, as emerged in the Mango case, emphasizes the role of feedback in trading off product attributes, while the breakthrough approach underestimates feedback, which is banished as an option to employ only in the later stage of the development process.

Some theoretical implications emerge. In contrast to the arguments in most of the environmental literature, a radical undertaking, while desirable, is beset with a great number of uncertainties. To reduce this intrinsic complexity, the adoption of a breakthrough approach with the search for dramatic outcomes to add value in environmental and social terms *in primis*, may not be advantageous. On the contrary, a bricolage approach, characterized by adaptiveness, continuous feedback and a series of innovations, may be effective in reducing uncertainties during a complex innovation process. An essential benefit of the bricolage

Table 8.1 Differences between the breakthrough and bricolage approaches

Elements	Breakthrough	The Mitka example	Bricolage	The Mango example
Goal/vision	Ambitious Strong commitment	A unique sustainable concept for commuters (fast and weather-protected)	Ambitious Flexibility	The fastest, weather-protected bike in the world
How to achieve	Leap-frog	One radical three-wheeled, roofed concept	Small-step	First, the C-Alleweder (the fastest, yet too expensive) Second, Quest (the fastest) Third, Mango (less fast but more maneuverable and cheaper)
Feedback	Postponed	Conservative users	Accommodating after a radical step	After the development of the Quest and feedback
Search for information	Inwards	Within the coalition	Outwards	Getting information from the recumbent bike world
Product concept	Unique	Three-wheeled Mitka	Series of innovations	Three concepts
Development cycle	Longer	Three year, one prototype (and spin-off)	Shorter	Five years, three concepts (average 1.6 years)
Expenditure rate	Higher	Around €1 million	Lower	Around €50,000
Attitude towards problems	Looking for superior solutions	Ex. new wheel configuration	Looking for simpler and elegant solutions	From the carbon fiber to the fiber-glass From the monocoque to metal frame and fiber-glass
Changing exogenous/endogenous conditions	Inertia, lock-in effect	No change in product requirements	Adaptiveness, resourcefulness	From highly technical to user-friendly concepts
Degree of complexity during the process	Steady/increasing	No change	Steady/decreasing	From the C-Alleweder to the Mango

approach lies in the importance of feedback in helping project developers trade off product attributes. Moreover, it may help to balance what is economically and ecologically sound. Another distinctive characteristic in the bricolage versus breakthrough approach is the different learning process involved. Although any radical undertaking is essentially explorative in nature (March, 1991), the brico-lage approach seems to be related to a higher degree of organizational learning compared with the breakthrough approach, given its intrinsic trial–error experi-mentation, self-assessment and adaptive character.

There are also important implications for innovation studies. First, the find-ings confirm that environmental ambition is likely one of the triggers to pursuing a breakthrough approach. In the Garud and Karnoe works (2001, 2003) this spe-cific construct has not been studied. Therefore, it is a significant contribution to their conceptual framework, which does not fully explain why one kind of approach is chosen at the expense of another one. The Mitka case may demon-strate how a high level of environmental ambition may be one of the mechan-isms influencing the choice of a breakthrough approach. Second, adapting this framework from the macro-level of the technological domain to the micro-level of radical product development may strengthen the conceptual framework and enrich its intrinsic value. In the Mitka case, despite requesting potential users' feedback, not all of it was translated into definite requirements for the concept. In the Mango case, the opposite is true. The extensive testing and user feedback shaped the Velomobiel products. Therefore, the extent to which feedback is incorporated into the actual concept's development seems to play an important role in the project team's learning process, in user acceptance and the overall performance of the innovative product. This is consistent with the social con-struction of technology theory, where the technology is shaped by relevant social groups (Bijker, 1995).

This reasoning, however, does not prevent the emergence of crucial counter-arguments and reflection upon such arguments. The radical innovation literature also suggests that new radical projects or technologies often emphasize perform-ance criteria, the value of which is poorly understood. Existing customers and established organizations may not understand these new criteria and thus misun-derstand the value of the new products. Therefore market information may be of little help with regard to the development of radical products and feedback based on this misunderstanding may even harm the radical development process. Incorporating this negative feedback may jeopardize the project by divesting it of the potential added value yielded by its radicality. As a result, negative feed-back may increase the performance-judgment thresholds. In the assessment of value based on expected returns or negative feedback, it is likely that such pro-jects would be assessed as unfavorable.[118]

For example, it took 3M's Post it® Notes development team 12 years to realize that "the glue which doesn't glue" was a unique product rather than a wrong chemical reaction (for an abstract of the story, see Garud et al., 2001; Nayak & Ketteringham, 1986). With a less committed inventor, this distinctive product would probably not be one of 3M's major successes. On the other hand, as discussed previously, actors willing to explore new radical concepts who have a strong commitment to reap future profits may get emotionally involved and dismiss feedback a priori while becoming get locked into a course of action that may result in a failure.

What emerges from this discussion is an innovators' dilemma: to what extent do actors need to diverge from the market and technology environment to be able to create successful new radical products in a new domain, when performance criteria are unclear? This involves a tension between commitments with future expectations and flexibility with current paradigms (Ghemawat, 1991). A helpful approach may be represented by the bricolage strategy. Innovative actors may undertake a radical step that pushes their innovative idea forward and only afterwards might they consider getting and accommodating feedback. It is an ongoing negotiating process with divergent, radical steps followed by adaptive, reflective phases, where a continuous tension between learning and creation exists. The adoption of a bricolage, rather than a breakthrough, approach provides the means for learning about the hurdles of innovation and reduces market uncertainty. Back to the previous famous example, the Post it® Note's inventor mindfully undertook a radical path, but only through negotiation with other colleagues and feedback accommodation was it possible to shape his invention into an innovative superior product.

In environmental radical undertakings, it appears even more complicated because environmental ambition implies a tension between social needs and market needs when they do not overlap with one another. The tension between commitments with future expectations and flexibility with the current paradigm may be resolved in favor of the former when they imply product development concepts for a more sustainable society. Creating demand for environmental new products requires balancing not only commitments with feedback, but also what is sound environmentally with what is sound economically. Again, the bricolage approach appears to be the valuable and suitable strategy for environmental radical undertakings.

Redefining radical innovation

It is interesting to observe that in the bricolage approach the series of innovations are incremental rather than radical from the organizational perspective. Looking back to the case of the Mango's development, we can say that only the C-Alleweder can be considered a radical step for the Velomobiel founders, while the development of the Quest and especially the Mango involved only minor changes. However, Velomobiel's end-products are still considered radical from a market perspective. As a result, the bricolage approach entails an innovation process that is incremental *internally*, from the firm's perspective. The outcome of this innovation process, however, may have radical characteristics *externally*, that is, it is new to the market. The ambition of developing a new radical concept is translated into careful procedures where experiments and continuous incremental improvements are the norm. The Mango case confirms how a bricolage strategy may result in superior products rather than "just good enough" products. Rephrasing the 3M director, the motto for bricolage may be "aiming high, starting small".

In contrast, the breakthrough approach has radical characteristics both internally and externally. The ambition of developing a new radical concept is translated into radical procedures to achieve a radical and dramatic outcome. The high level of ambition and the choices made during the Mitka project demonstrate the high degree of innovativeness in the process where the development of the Mitka was perceived to be radical by the coalition and by the market. In contrast with the bricolage motto, the motto for the breakthrough approach may be "aiming high, starting big".

Given these differences, is the definition of a radical innovation articulated in this book still valid? The discussion of the breakthrough and the bricolage approaches suggests that we should reconsider the definition of a radical innovation given in Chapter 2. The radical innovation process from a firm's perspective was defined as "a process in which the organization copes with a new and unfamiliar domain, where different technical and business skills are required." It seems, however, that this definition only applies completely to the breakthrough approach, as demonstrated by the Mitka case. Then to what extent does this definition fit with the bricolage concept? With regard to initial ambition, this definition is consistent with the bricolage approach when one focuses on the beginning of the process or the initiation period. Fast, incremental cycles of development and implementation reduce uncertainty in the technological and organizational learning due to the accumulation of knowledge and expertise and the accommodation of feedback. Building up experience seems to be crucial for entering and surviving in market niches (King & Tucci, 2002b). The final outcome of this process is incremental from the organizational perspective while it may be radical for the market. In light of this, the bricolage approach features elements of radical innovation in the initiation period, which gradually turn into characteristics typical of incremental innovation through experimentation, flexibility and the accumulation of knowledge.

8.2.2 *The revised model*

Three of the four propositions were derived from the conceptual model illustrated in Chapter 5. The conclusions of the discussion on the propositions also have implications for the model. The propositions address a causal relationship between environmental ambition and product performance in radical development projects. The Mitka and the Mango cases show that a high level of environmental ambition may increase management support for a radical undertaking despite mixed or poor performance and the project team's escalation of commitments. Moreover, it was found that management support and the team's commitments increase product complexity due to limited experience and the great deal of uncertainty in dealing with radical undertakings driven by environmental ambition. In addition to that, the ill-formulated nature of the concept of greening, intrinsic difficulties in measuring environmental performance and the challenge of maintaining the intricate balance between environmental and traditional attributes increase product complexity even further. These factors together may jeopardize product performance. Through the cross-analysis a new proposition was derived. In light of this, one new construct is introduced in two discrete forms: the breakthrough and the bricolage approach. Based on the empirical data, a high level of environmental ambition is likely to influence the adoption of the breakthrough approach, which reinforces the relationships of the previously mentioned constructs. This implies that adopting a bricolage approach may moderate the effect of a high level of environmental ambition and reduce the overall complexity of the product (see Figure 8.1). The qualitative nature of this research and the limited number of cases studied do not allow one to deduce a relationship, if any, between the type of organizational form, the type of approach to radical innovation and environmental ambition. Here it is suggested, however, that the interaction between environmental ambition and organizational forms influences that strategy choice.

This model illustrates how, among other factors, the environmental ambition may play an important role in influencing the new product development. It suggests that a high level of environmental ambition may dictate the innovation process, elevating greening to design imperative status. This may cause new projects to be managed suboptimally, emphasizing objectives that may conflict with market-oriented objectives. Summarizing, this research study proposes a new theoretical statement that attempts to explain and predict how environmental ambition influences new product development. This claim provides a theoretical contribution to existing NPD and ENPD research.

8.2.3 Beyond the propositions

Case study research offers the advantage of examining in depth the context of the phenomenon under study. In light of this, this section is reserved for

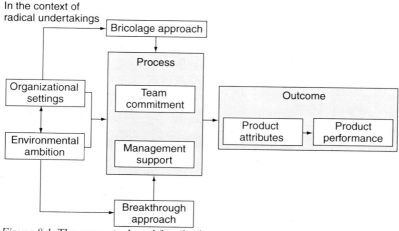

Figure 8.1 The conceptual model revised.

discussing emerging and relevant issues that go beyond the selected proposi-tions. This includes the organizational setting, expenditure rate, spin-offs exploitation, use of tools and the PSS concept.

Organizational setting: network vs. entrepreneurial start-ups

Chapter 3 discussed the advantages and disadvantages of different organi-zational settings in the struggle toward innovation. In light of the cases exam-ined, the formal network setting was compared with the entrepreneurial start-up setting. It was argued that, although in theory the network may provide the best locus for product innovation and overcoming the liabilities of newness and smallness that start-ups face, in practice managing networks successfully is extremely difficult, due to divergent opinions, hidden agendas, lack of trust, and intellectual property issues (e.g. Van de Ven et al., 1999). The findings from the Mitka case are consistent with this assertion. The mixed commitments, different interests, divergent opinions, low risk involved and serious discussions regard-ing the intellectual property did not create a conducive environment for product innovation. On the other hand, the Velomobiel start-up managed to overcome the liabilities typical of new companies. These findings are consistent with pre-vious works on successful start-ups, which are characterized as having func-tional expertise, making decisions quickly, being flexible, adaptive and allocating resources through an external network (Schoonhoven et al., 1990; Van de Ven et al., 1984). Remarkably, these characteristics recall the bricolage approach.

Expenditure rate for large and small projects

Another interesting issue is the relationship between expenditure, defined as the amount of cash that is invested during the development period and product implementation. In the Mitka case around €1 million was invested over the course of three years, which resulted in a working prototype. One explanation may be that greater expenditures signal more technically ambitious projects, which require more development time. Another interpretation is that great expenditures may be necessary but do not guarantee success. Therefore, just pouring money into a new highly ambitious project is not always a practical approach to getting a product into the market in the short term. This interpreta-tion is consistent with prior research. For example, Greiner (1970) found that a common feature of unsuccessful innovation implementation attempts is that they started highly ambitiously and on a large scale.

On the other hand, Velomobiel managed to develop, produce and sell their vehicles at a much lower expenditure rate than the Mitka consortium. The Velo-mobiel's expenditure was less than a tenth that of the Mitka consortium.[119] These findings are consistent with prior research on start-ups. For example, Schoonhoven et al. (1990) examined the product shipment of start-ups and found that, the greater the rate of spending, the longer it took to ship the first product. On the contrary, firms that spent less money got their product out faster. Similarly, Van de Ven et al. (1984) observed that new firms that reached a late stage of development were also able to spend much less than firms that were slower to develop.

As result, it seems that the greater the rate of spending, the higher the degree of project innovativeness and the longer it takes to develop.

Spin-off exploitation

Examining the Mitka case, one may state that at least a spin-off was developed and later introduced by one coalition member. In light of this, a question may be addressed: *Why did Gazelle first choose the trike configuration only to later abandon it and develop a bike?*

A possible lens of analysis to explain Gazelle's behavior is the absorptive capacity theoretical framework. Absorptive capacity is defined here as the firm's ability to acquire, assimilate, transform and apply new knowledge (Cohen et al., 1990; Zahra & George, 2002). The four organizational capabilities of knowledge acquisition, assimilation, transformation and exploitation are distinct, but complementary, and compose a firm's absorptive capacity. Acquisition is the capacity to identify and acquire externally generated knowledge, while assimilation refers to the firm's routines and processes that allow it to analyze, interpret and understand information obtained from external sources (Cohen et al., 1990). Discoveries and ideas that go beyond the firm's search area are neglected because the firm cannot easily comprehend and assimilate them. Transformation constitutes the firm's capability to refine routines that facilitate combining existing knowledge and newly acquired and assimilated knowledge (Cohen et al., 1990). Finally, exploitation represents the firm's ability to reap and incorporate knowledge into its operations (Van den Bosch, Volberda, & de Boer, 1999). Basically, the absorptive capacity helps us understanding both the search for new knowledge and its partial assimilation. The Mitka trike represented a great opportunity to acquire new knowledge, comprehend radically new concepts such as the three-wheel configuration, electric assistance and weather protection, and to share innovative ideas within a heterogeneous coalition. Due to the poor quality of the trike and, in general, the firm's difficulty comprehending the PSS philosophy, the firm did not have the ability to assimilate and further transform the new knowledge entirely. For example, the options of the three-wheeled configuration and the electric engine were abandoned. Then again, the company was able to assimilate part of the new knowledge and to codify this in its own routines. The new knowledge concerning the design and the sitting position was associated and exploited with the well-known frame of reference of the bike. Therefore, Gazelle was able to "absorb" the most familiar features of the Mitka leaving out those that were too radical and unfamiliar.

The use of tools

Another implication may be derived from the findings with regard to the creation and utility of tools and methods for developing new products and environmentally innovative concepts in particular. The Kathalys method was developed during the Mitka project "*for developing Sustainable Product Service Systems*" (Luiten et al., 2001a). Nevertheless, it apparently did not achieve its goal. One possible explanation lies in the nature of the method. It is too ambitious and too general to be effective. On the one hand, the unfinished method tried not only to design and develop the product according to a fixed sequence of activities, but also to set up services and the appropriate organizational setting, constantly measuring the environmental performance. This method aspires to achieve too many objectives without formally prioritizing them.

On the other hand, the method narrowly focused on the product track, where the effective product design takes place, and the sustainability track. This is understandable if most of the PSS methods are developed by people with a background in design and a concern for the natural environment (Beerepoot, 2004). Consequently, limited experience in organization, business and innovation itself, beyond the product design, might have diminished the effectiveness of the method.

Another subsequent explanation may lie in the degree of innovativeness underlined in the method. The change from basically designing products to providing functionalities increased the level of conceptualization and consequently the degree of complexity. This implies that, the greater the degree of innovativeness, the lower the effectiveness of any method aimed at innovation (e.g. Schon, 1967; Van de Ven et al., 1999). Moreover, the users of the new method, such as managers in established companies or in new coalitions, may perceive it as too unfamiliar, posing the risk that it will not be used.

PSS: products and services?

Although the Mitka started as a product service system concept, the services never materialized, they were only conceptualized. One simple explanation is that the services, meticulously studied, would have evolved if the product was ready to be introduced. Product development took priority over service development. This is confirmed by the "wait-and-see" attitude expressed by the Mitka management team. However, the idea of distributing new human-powered vehicles not only through regular retailers but also directly to companies for their employees' commuting needs represent a valuable business model (Horst, Luiten, Brezet, & Silvester, 2005).

One should also consider that PSS is still a young discipline that needs to be "nurtured", where trial and error is a crucial part of the learning process. Some scholars are contributing significantly to this research field. For example, Mont (2004: 69) proposed defining PSS in four elements: products, services, infrastructure and network, "*which should be designed concurrently and need to be continuously adjusted to each other aiming at system innovation"*. Although guidelines have been formulated to develop PSS, it seems that the intrinsic complexity in simultaneously designing the four elements (or even just one of them) has been overlooked. This is explained in the innovation literature and it is illustrated by the Mitka case. A clear example of this strategy is developing a new product with original services for a new infrastructure within a new network. Given the degree of uncertainty involved when any company innovates or changes just one of these four elements, it is desirable for the company's objective to have clear priorities. One may argue whether a radical product innovation is necessary for a new radical PSS. As explained earlier, a service innovation can be radical even with regard to existing products.

8.3 Scope and limitations

This study examines how the intention to develop radical environmental products and services influences the new product development process. The field research focuses on radical new product development processes in two different organizational settings in the human-powered mobility sector. They are similar in their design requirements expect for one element, the environmental dimension. Although both are considered sustainable concepts, in the Mitka case the "greening" attribute was afforded the highest priority while in the Velomobiel case it was not one of the product requirements. Thus the scope of this study concerns the development of human-powered mobility concepts whose relationship with environmental ambition was the phenomenon under study. The Mitka case presents evidence of an increasing phenomenon in which environmental ambition is one of the main motivations for starting a new business venture (Larson, 2000) or creating a complex technological project. Thus, to what extent can the model and the findings be generalized?

Yin (1994) affirms that a common criticism of case studies relates to the difficulty in generalizing from one case to another, no matter how large the set of cases concerned. In fact the findings need to be generalized to the theory rather than to other cases. This explorative study contributes to theories such as the escalation of commitments where non-rational factors may dictate innovation processes. By introducing environmental ambition as a new construct, this study demonstrates how a high level of environmental ambition affects the innovation process. In general, this research extends the work on radical undertakings, combining environmental issues with innovation theories. The conceptual framework and the relationships between environmental ambition and product performance in radical undertakings are proposed for theory building. The exploratory character of the case study enables us to understand under which conditions these relationships come to exist. Therefore the conceptual framework and the new relationships should be generalized and applied to the study of other cases. However, this research can only be generalized to the extent that the theoretical dimensions are captured in this study, that is, the relationship between environmental ambition and decisions taken in radical undertakings.

The results of this study are also likely to hold outside the human-powered mobility sectors. When environmental ambition is one of the key motivations for undertaking radical product development, there is the risk that its influence could increase the complexity of the project itself.

Nevertheless, the generalization is not automatic due to a number of limitations. First, these findings are based on a limited number of cases from one specific context. The main theoretical contributions result from an in-depth case (the Mitka) and a polar-type case (the Mango) where theoretical replication logic has been applied. The weakness is that building theory from cases may result in a narrow theory because the theory may describe an idiosyncratic phenomenon. Therefore, study of other cases with a high level of environmental ambition in different organizational settings would be welcomed to strengthen the results. Because of time limitations, literal replication to other similar cases was not possible.

Second, this research entailed an iterative design process between the empirical data and the theory. The strength of this approach is that it allows new relationships to emerge. The weakness is that the findings could not be tested because the new relationships were induced from the cases. Further research can improve the generalization of the results by translating the propositions into testable hypotheses based on a large sample of ENPD projects.

Third, this research study mainly made use of the organizational innovation literature. However, what has emerged from the cases is the important role of cognitive processes and social structures in undertaking new product development projects. Future research on product innovation may focus more explicitly on literature concerning behavioral and psychological theories in explaining managers' decisions under uncertain conditions.[120]

Fourth, the research was itself a learning process. The participation in the Mitka project helped to build and accumulate experience in conducting interviews and juggling empirical data and theoretical frameworks. As the study proceeded, procedures became more rigorous, increasing its reliability.

8.4 Rival explanations

This research attempts to explain how environmental ambition influences decisions in ENPD projects by theorizing based mainly on one case study. Therefore, one may propose other explanations as to why the project, for example, became too complex or too costly. For instance, limited or inadequate skills and expertise within the team or simply mismanagement may have caused the Mitka project to mismatch the desirable, yet too ambitious, objectives. Or the Mitka coalition may have represented a unique organizational setting where low shared risks and great publicity was expected. In a few words, the radicality of the project and environmental ambition might have had nothing to do with the project.

These rival explanations require an attentive discussion.

First, the project did not achieve the expected outcome because of mismanagement. In the innovation literature, as illustrated in Chapter 2 (see Table 2.3) lack of managerial skills (e.g. Cooper, 1975) and poor planning (e.g. Crawford, 1977), for example, are well-known factors resulting in project failure. Identifying mismanagement as the cause of failure may explain the phenomenon under study, although this explanation may appear too reductive. We should ask ourselves why a group of capable people, from well-known companies, made ineffective decisions or evaluated project performances poorly. What caused the mismanagement? As previously discussed, the radicality of the project may at least explain why the evaluation of performance criteria was overlooked or unrecognized, leaving room for additional explanatory non-rational factors like the environmental ambition. The latter may also explain why the project was extremely ambitious.

Second, the project team did not have the necessary technical skills to undertake such a project. As already explained in Chapter 2, the innovation literature may point to deficient resources and/or activities (Cooper, 1975) as the main cause resulting in a project's failure. Furthermore, by definition, in radical undertakings existing technical skills may not be adequate and only through a process of learning and unlearning is it possible to build the necessary skills. Therefore, it is not surprising that the lack of skills and resources in a radical undertaking may have created problems for the project's development. Again, we should go beyond a simple answer to better understanding the phenomenon under study. The question is why, during a two-year project, was the team not able to develop the appropriate skills? Why did the technical development become more, rather than less, complex? The search for the ideal and superior environmental vehicle in a product development process with few learning and evaluation phases, typical of the breakthrough approach, may explain why the team's expertise was never developed.

Third, another rival explanation may be very rational. The real motivation of some coalition members was free promotion with low risks involved. For some the project was just a means to commercially promote their brand, for others it was just an environmental showcase for policy makers and a means to get money for another project. If this is the case, two options emerge: (1) everyone had this double agenda; or (2) all but a few did not have it. This implies a dichotomy between, on the one hand, formalized and codified goals upon which everyone had agreed and, on the other hand, unofficial, obscure and surreptitious goals. Basically, some team members might have lied to the others. In this case, despite the triangulation of different sources of information, it may be difficult for a researcher to fully understand the "deep structure" of social behaviour, given the socially constructed "reality".

8.5 Recommendations

The findings, discussion of the propositions and the research's limitations allow some important points to emerge and to be reflected upon. These points are translated here into recommendations addressed to a heterogeneous audience, encompassing scholars, practitioners and policy makers.

8.5.1 To ENPD scholars

ENPD is a young and fast-growing research field aiming to address and foster innovation in new products, services and infrastructures within different organizational settings, which incorporates environmental issues. By enlarging the boundaries of the phenomenon under study some important implications emerge.

First, moving from redesigning products to designing whole systems entails exploration, knowledge and the use of different conceptual and theoretical frameworks due to the multidisciplinary nature of the research and the added level of uncertainty and complexity in understanding the phenomenon. Stronger integration with NPD literature will help us understand the risks and uncertainties involved in trying to introduce environmental concerns into product development. Furthermore, rather than trying to design new ENPD tools, it may be worthwhile turning to the existing NPD literature to see how environmental concerns, as a subset of market preferences, can be translated into product specifications. This book takes a small step in this direction by bridging existing theoretical frameworks for studying unexplored phenomena in ENPD with the results of introducing new relationships. In particular, stronger integration with the NPD literature is beneficial to ENPD for understanding the risks and uncertainties involved in incorporating environmental issues into product development. Adapting NPD theoretical models to the growing need to develop environmentally conscious products may help practitioners by giving them better research-based models.

Second, to advance ENPD theory and practice, explanatory studies seem, at least for the foreseeable future, to be needed as much as normative and prescriptive studies of ENPD. The focus of much research should give less emphasis to prescriptive questions such as "how does one successfully design ENPD's" and more prominence to understanding the ENPD phenomenon. For example, the main research findings of this study necessarily raise other questions regarding new product performance. Such questions include: *How do you evaluate new performance that is poorly understood by the market and which criteria are suitable for evaluating performance, especially environmental performance?*

Moreover, due to the level of uncertainty implicit in dealing with environmental issues, better definitions, constructs and variables of environmental issues are needed if we want to understand and communicate the assumed value of environmental concerns as market opportunities. The advocates for environmental issues have a new interpretative structure that is likely to increase the difficulties of communication. The differences in interpretation between the designers, marketers and people in favor of environmental issues may hamper communication. Different perceptions of environmental opportunities and possibilities within a multifunctional team, combined with organizational routines, may hinder the development of ENPD and explain the relatively modest performance of green products. Lenox et al. (1997) argue that merely improving communication channels is not enough if one wants to build capabilities for creating environmental products. It is only when one manages to bridge existing knowledge resources with interpretative structures through effective communication that one is able to create genuinely new environmental products. Moreover, the problem of communication between supporters of environmentally friendly products and designers may be caused by the hazy definition of greening. Although a common understanding of environmental information may exist, a team will still have to answer questions such as how environmental attributes contribute to product performance.

Third, scholars engaged in the constant race to feature better environmental innovation in products and processes seem to support the breakthrough strategy in radical undertakings. Here it is suggested that a bricolage, rather than a breakthrough, approach seems to be a better strategy for dealing with the intrinsic uncertainty of radical environmental undertakings, as it results in more learning and a better understanding of this phenomenon.

Fourth, occasionally in the environmental field there is the tendency to divide business companies into good guys and bad guys in accordance with their willingness to undertake more or less environmentally ambitious projects. The role of scholars is to investigate under which conditions companies are more or less inclined to respond to environmental opportunities and to help them search for or identify those opportunities, not to morally judge them. Finally, integrating the ENPD literature with the regular NPD literature would strengthen the legitimacy of the field because it would allow researchers to build on a wealth of valuable insights.

8.5.2 To innovation scholars

Drucker states that new opportunities for innovation stem from changes (Drucker, 1998). Changes are required by the public and government authorities who perceive an increase in the negative environmental effects of industrial processes. Consequently, businesses are pushed to search, develop, adopt and adapt solutions to respond to environmental problems and to address emerging markets. Here it is suggested that the way companies respond to the call of incorporating environmental concerns into product development may give NPD scholars an interesting research agenda. In particular, radical ENPD projects may allow researchers to study the way NPD teams in general balance paradoxical ambitions and demands. Moreover, assuming that resources will become scarcer and regulation more stringent, green entrepreneurs may create new niche markets and green entrepreneurship may evolve into an interesting research field. Therefore, a better integration of the environmental and innovation fields seems plausible and desirable.

8.5.3 To managers/practitioners

A number of recommendations are made for managers dealing with environmental issues. First, environmental ambition may be considered a non-rational component of decision making and it may influence the support process. If an organization is to develop products that address environmental concerns, its managers need a better understanding of both the support process and environmental ambition.

Second, in managers' struggle between commitment and flexibility and in their effort to balance environmental issues and market demands, it is suggested that they adopt a bricolage strategy. Such a strategy seems to be suitable to complex radical undertakings. This is particularly true when new performances in emerging markets are easily misunderstood.

8.5.4 To project team/designers

Designers should be aware of the danger in being too involved with their own creations and getting locked into a course of action. By strongly believing in their concept, designers can run the risk of escalating their commitments while dismissing feedback, especially when radical projects are concerned. Highly ambitious design projects entail greater complexity, longer development time, more resources and unclear performance criteria, where non-rational factors, like environmental ambition, may be influencing the decision-making process. Therefore, due to the uncertainties involved in radical developments, many assumptions are made concerning the benefits of new products. However, these assumptions need to be tested as soon as possible in the design process, especially with regard to market requirements. This would also apply to market requirements that refer to societal concerns as well as to the environmental impact of products. Such environmental requirements may be poorly formulated when they are based on ideology, in which case the level of complexity of the design process increases without there being a clear consensus with regard to the environmental goals. In light of this, as previously discussed, designers may adopt a bricolage strategy in complex technical projects, balancing their own ambitions with valuable feedback. The concept should be "flexible", where technical attributes are continuously balanced with market attributes in a co-evolution dynamic process. Designers need to carefully select new attributes that may be misunderstood, while environmental attributes need to be aligned with the market demand (see Box 2.2).

Second, besides design attributes and functionalities, designers should carefully envision to what extent the context will be affected. For example, in the mobility sector, the production system, the infrastructure, consumer behavior and regulation heavily influence and occasionally hamper the development of new vehicles. Any new concept will create its own market niche. Changing more than one element at a time is bound to increase the degree of uncertainty and jeopardize the project. On the contrary, by adopting a bricolage approach, designers envision their concept in a context whose elements do not need dramatic changes. One may argue that, in an era of continuous technological change, it is difficult to decrease the technological complexity of new products that also affect the system all around. The complexity of a product should lie within the product itself, not in the interface. Consider the evolution of the propulsion system in the car. The adoption of the "green" electric car in the mass market requires too many changes: new infrastructure for recharging, smaller kilometer range and users learning new skills. Similarly, the introduction and diffusion of fuel-cell cars requires costly infrastructure, new production systems and new safety regulations, which make it unlikely that we will see any of these cars in the near future (van den Hoed, 2004). On the other hand, the diffusion of hybrid cars in the United States market does not require any change in the infrastructure and user behavior because the complexity of this technology lies inside the product.

Finally, another recommendation deals with design education. Designers and design education institutions focus their efforts mainly on established organizations. They seem to overlook new business ventures as a source of inspiration and locus of design and business opportunities. Therefore, PSS entrepreneurship courses like those held at Industrial Design Engineering, Delft University of Technology are welcome steps in the right direction, because they aim to bridge different complementary disciplines: traditional product design education and service development integrated with entrepreneurship education, spiced with a flavour of greening.

8.5.5 To mobility policy makers

Subsidy programs such as those involved in the Mitka project represent the struggle policy makers face when attempting to promote sustainable innovative concepts within the mobility system. How can policy makers promote such innovative concepts more effectively? Although this study did not investigate the role of policy makers or the effects of particular policies, it acknowledges the importance of policy in stimulating technological changes in the mobility system. Consequently, some general recommendations can be made based on the findings.

First, this study shows that innovation is a dynamic process where the desirable outcome cannot be fully controlled by managers, designers or investors. Although subsidy programs require focused objectives and detailed plans to monitor innovative projects, they also need to lend innovators the flexibility to cope with unexpected events and complex problems with the option of changing the process. Fixed schedules and unchangeable objectives may even hamper the process of innovation.

Second, the development of any innovative mobility concept is constrained by a set of environmental conditions, such as fixed infrastructure and inflexible regulations. Given the degree of innovativeness, many concepts require more "room to maneuver" and they would benefit from more flexible regulations in the short term while they prove themselves. The German Velotaxi concept represents an example in which local policy makers changed regulations to allow the innovation to be tested, implemented and diffused first, followed by national policy makers.

Third, small entrepreneurial firms rather than established organizations seem to develop, produce and implement more radical innovative concepts in the mobility system. More focused and dedicated policy programs are necessary to stimulate and "nurture" entrepreneurs.

The fourth and last recommendation regards the importance of promoting bounded social-technical experiments in the mobility context to foster high-order learning (Brown et al., 2003). Moreover, assessing new technologies in large-scale programs and protected niches (Hoogma, 2000) seems to be necessary for addressing national policy agenda items, which are increasingly concerned with the concept of sustainability.

8.6 Lesson learned

8.6.1 Bricolage for green entrepreneurs: aim high, start and act small or vice versa

Perceived opportunities, vision and strong ambition are preconditions for setting up goals to create superior and environmental products; the question for practitioners is how to achieve these goals. There are thousands of books on the shelf describing strategies for superior performance for different organizations in different sectors. Nevertheless, there are no ready-to-use recipes nor one-for-all solution. Moreover, creating environmental products and/or services may increase the uncertainty of the innovation process. The bricolage approach is not necessarily better than others, like the breakthrough one, but it is basically an alternative approach that has demonstrated its validity in some cases such as the Mango and the development of the Danish wind turbine.

Therefore, from the literature and the empirical analysis, some lessons and practical suggestions may be drawn for bottom-up activities by green entrepreneurs.

The bricolage approach may be expressed with the motto "aiming high, acting small", which means that an ambitious goal may be achieved through small steps, spin-offs and continuous learning by doing. However, the opposite is also true. The process of trial–error and experimenting may also lead the entrepreneur to formulate ambitious goals. At this point, it is important to redefine the concept of bricolage, extending the discussion in Chapter 3.

In Chapter 3, the original definition of bricolage (Lévi-Strauss, 1966) was synonymous with tinkering, of making new forms from available tools and materials. This interpretation seems to stress the lack of an ambitious goal, missing the "aiming high" part of the above-mentioned motto and emphasizing the "acting small". However, the most recent definition of bricolage (Garud et al., 2003) suggests the existence of an ambitious goal in the process of innovation. These two perspectives of bricolage may complement one another. Both of them emphasize the role of experimentation, learning by doing or, in the words of Schrage the meaning of play (Schrage, 2000). It is through adapting, playing with the material at hand, designing and executing simultaneously and creating prototypes that the innovator learns and unlearns more quickly, communicates better and is increasingly confronted with tradeoffs. From an organizational perspective, Ciborra refers to the "learning by surprise" (1994) managerial skills of many firms, such as Olivetti, operating in a fast-changing industry, when the strategy is compounded of a mixture of ready-made arrangements, not-yet-made visions, subjective plans and interpretations, but is sufficiently responsive to the new.

This first stage of the bricolage approach may be completed by a second stage where new business ideas emerge, ambitious goals are formulated and new opportunities discovered. Therefore, the goal setting or the "aiming high" may emerge *after* a period of trial–error and play. The innovation of the mountain bike is a striking example of the two phases of the bricolage approach. The pioneers of the mountain bikes first adapted their bike for cycling downhill on unpaved mountain trails, with whatever suitable components were available (such as hubs and drum brakes from tandems) and only later were some of them able to create a market out of this recreational activity (Berto, 1999).

The different interpretations of the term bricolage[121] may confuse some so should it be called something else? Despite this apparent confusion, the term is well known in the literature of innovation technology. However, in the rest of the chapter the term "experimental approach" is used as synonymous with bricolage approach.

Green entrepreneurs are driven not only by profit but also by their environmental ambition. Therefore, the "aiming high" often *precedes* and justifies embarkation on the innovation journey. From this perspective, some distinctive aspects emerge in the two-stage bricolage or experimental approach.

1 Flexible rather than ideological and fixed vision

Aiming high and having a strong vision and mission is important when starting any innovative activity. However firm commitment and environmental ambition should not lock the environmental entrepreneur's vision into a fixed ideological frame. Moreover, as discussed before, clear goals may also emerge after experimentation. The environmental entrepreneurs should not constrain themselves with plans at the very beginning, when ignorance is at its peak. Although the greater the environmental gain the better, it may be rather naïve to afford the highest priority to the environmental dimension. It is not suggested that the entrepreneur should give away the environmental ambition; he/she should realize how environmental ambition may increase the level of uncertainty in the innovation process. Setting goals that are too ambitious, as environmental advocates claim, may endanger the project. Given the ill-formulated nature of the greening concept, flexibility and resourcefulness are necessary for the innovation journey. In spite of flexible vision, the goal and the stake of each participant in the project should be explicit. The detailed objectives of the project may change slightly over time only through open consultation among the project members.

2 Build up your capabilities and create value through ready-to-use experimentation

What resources do you need? What resources do you have? The best way to build up capabilities and at the same time decrease uncertainty and ignorance is by doing simple tests or pilots. Experimentation enables the entrepreneur to understand the value of the concept. Testers' and lead users' feedback is crucial for value creation. "Option thinking" may be useful here, where a map of assumed values for all the actors is drawn to evaluate the opportunities and risks of the venture and to illustrate different innovation paths (Janszen, 2000).

The Mango case and the development of the Danish wind turbine illustrate how the actors involved adopted a low-risk approach to their complex processes. The first important step in technological development was the experimentation with moderate new technologies and materials to create the conditions in which to acquire capabilities and skills. The second step was to convert the experiment into a feasible application, a product ready to be implemented in the market. The first users were able to understand the new concept and give feedback to improve it. In this way, the producers were able to evaluate the first concepts, which may be bulky and not highly efficient (as with the first wind turbines) or too costly and difficult to produce (as the C-Alleweder) and make a profit out of it. Therefore, the experimental product ends up in the market, creating value for the customers and for the entrepreneur, who builds up capabilities, learns fast and may sustain further developments.

3 Series of incremental innovations to create radical products

Creating something that is considered great and cool by designers may have no added value to consumers. You often hear people say: "This product is so cool that it must be valuable to someone." But it may not be, because being valuable to some vaguely defined someone is not good enough (Magretta & Stone, 2002).

First, fast development loops rather than one leap-frog development step; second, the search for elegant solutions rather than superior solutions may act as risk-reduction measures in the innovation process. Feedback from an initial development loop may open up new innovative opportunities for a second and a third loop. The fast development loops method is similar to a method developed for software engineering, called *eXtreme Programming* (Beck, 2000). This method is based on fast-engineered product release or prototype, which are further improved and developed based on feedback from customers. This continuous and evolving product development allows customers as well as developers to identify important requirements for new product innovations. The short development steps between one product-prototype and another create a highly effective learning cycle for the developers, entailing few risks.

8.6.2 Liabilities of the bricolage/experimental approach

From the perspective of a high level of environmental ambition, this approach may show some drawbacks. In spite of fast development loops and risk reduction, the total development time needed to reach the desirable goal may be protracted. Given the series of innovations, the experimental approach may entail a longer development time than that required in the breakthrough approach.

Moreover, the experimental approach may not guarantee achievement of the original goal. Given the degree of uncertainty in any innovation journey and evaluating the feedback received, the entrepreneur may reconsider his/her original objective and change it. A change in objective is not necessarily a liability when the goal may appear unattainable or too ambitious. However, it may seem a liability for many advocates of the breakthrough approach when results do not match the predefined objectives. Figure 8.2 attempts to illustrate graphically the differences between the bricolage and breakthrough approaches. More generally, the bricolage approach may not be able to protect effectively the innovative concept, given the fast development loops and the high level of interaction with actors in the market. In contrast, the breakthrough approach may prevent competitors from duplicating the innovative concept, thus lending it a competitive advantage.

8.6.3 Illustration: developing the Mitka on a shoestring

How do we develop new sustainable PSS? What if the Mitka project had adopted an experimental approach? The "What if" method is hardly a scientific exercise, but it is a useful illustration of an attempt "to do things otherwise". The "what if" method is used here to reconstruct the Mitka case in an alternative way to breakthrough approach, this time adopting a bricolage approach. The "what if" will encompass primarily the technical development and the business model.

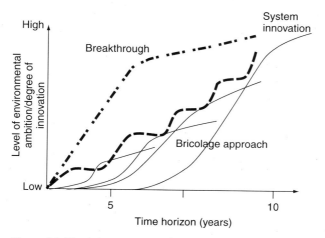

Figure 8.2 The bricolage and the breakthrough approaches.

The first "what if" regards the decision on wheel configuration: two or three wheels?

Choosing three-wheeled rather than the two-wheeled version meant innovativeness and greater environmental benefit. However, choosing three wheels also presented greater technical challenges, for the sitting position, the steering/tilting mechanism, the roof and the electric engine. An alternative way would have been to test both configurations: three and two wheels. The two-wheeled configuration might test the sitting position (the EZB) and the cover in a fast, cheap development loop without compromising the sleek appearance of the vehicle. A comprehensive test of the new vehicle (with or without the new cover) might give some insight into the technical feasibility and customer acceptance. The two-wheeled vehicles could be introduced into the market by Gazelle, with the intellectual property shared by the coalition. Although the new vehicle might not meet the original, environmentally ambitious goal, it might start an important step in that direction. The revenue could be invested in the challenging three-wheeled Mitka. Meanwhile, the three-wheeled configuration could be further developed and its progress carefully communicated to a large public for publicity purposes. The combination of a high center of gravity and three-wheeled configuration would need a fast technical test: the "experts" in the sector (the velomobile and recumbent developers) highlighted the technical challenges. With the knowledge accrued in developing the two-wheeled sitting position, a "quick and dirty", three-wheeled, light, human-powered vehicle (without electric engine, or cover) could have been realized and tested. Rather than searching for superior solutions, the team could have faced a few technical challenges at a time with a fast learning-by-doing process.

The added value of such development would stem from testing the technical feasibility and getting the first customer feedback. Again, it may not represent the "ideal" solution for the original goal but it might add just another step in the PSS innovation ladder. Adopting the bricolage approach, the technical complexity could have been reduced by prioritizing the technical challenges, by fast development loops with testing and implementation and accommodation of feedback. The development of a cluster of services for a newly materialized product is an important aspect for the overall success of a PSS. In the Mitka case, however, we found that, without a functioning artefact, the attached services may be conceptually valid yet incomplete. If the core of the PSS is a product, then it must be functioning and highly valued by potential customers.

From a business perspective, a clear idea of a business model should be in place. As Drucker (1954) once said, three simple questions managers and (environmental) entrepreneurs should ask themselves are: "What is our business?", "Who is the customer?" and "What does the customer value?". As has emerged from the description and analysis, these questions were clearly addressed in the Mango case, much less clearly in the Mitka case. According to Magretta and Stone (2002), a business model is a story of how an enterprise works, relying on the basics of character, motivation and plot. For a business, the plot describes how it will make money; for an environmental non-profit organization, the plot illustrates how it will change the world. Were the characters in the Mitka clearly delineated? Were their motivations plausible? Might the plot turn on creating value? If yes, value for whom?

The Mitka plot seems to have revolved around both of the goals: changing the world and making money. Using the "what if" method, a clearer idea of what the Mitka actually meant to the coalition might have emerged with a bricolage approach, because it forces adaptiveness, resourcefulness and accommodating feedback.

8.6.4 *Rethinking the system innovation thinking*

System innovation is a powerful concept for creativity. It forces one to think outside the box, destroying old concepts and relationships while reinventing new ones. However, the system innovation paradigm often lacks clear boundaries in both ambition and context. If we want to create a new sustainable mobility system, to what extent do we need to change it? What are the boundaries for the creative destruction process? In the Mitka case, the PSS concept of a new vehicle with dedicated services soon became a system itself. The services encompass not only maintenance service but also new infrastructures (such as a high-speed bike highway, electric rechargers in several places in the city, special shed etc.). In the literature on system innovation these aspects are barely discussed, especially from the business perspective. Moreover, given the poor definition of system innovation, how can we identify and evaluate a system innovation? How do we balance short-term goals with long-term ones? A stringent and clear definition of the boundaries of the system is needed.

Appendices

Appendix 1 Characteristics of the pre-selected cases

Projects

Sampling parameters	Mitka	Velomobiel	Velotaxi	Twike#	RoodRunner	Smarttrike
NPD	EHPV 3 wheels commuting Half-covered luggage unit	HPV 3 wheels commuting half-covered luggage unit	EHPV 3 wheels taxi sits 2 + driver half covered luggage unit	E(H)PV 3 wheels Sits 2 covered luggage unit	EHPV 3 wheels cargo	EHPV 3 wheels cargo
Innovation team	Several actors	2 entrepreneurs	2 entrepreneurs	3 entrepreneurs	Designers for the client	2 entrepreneurs
Organizational setting	Network of organizations	Start-up	Start-up	Start-up	Client: large and established company	Start-up
Environmental concern	High	Low	Low	Low	Low	Low
Year	1998–2003	1999–	1996–2000 2000–	1986–	2000–	2003 (?)
Performance/current status	Failure Abandoned when coalition split up	Success Private company funded by founders	Success Private company funded by founders	Success/failure Sold 600 then abandoned when market too small and not funded by venture capital	Success/failure Sold 400 to the client Stopped production (?)	Prototype Looking for venture capitalists
Spin-offs	Success/Easy Glider*					Smarttrike

Notes
EHPV: electric human-powered vehicle
HPV: human-powered vehicle
* Easy Glider bike was launched by one coalition actor in 2003
# Twike is a Swiss venture that had astonishing start but in the last 10 years the production has been irregular with changing ownership.

Appendix II Source of data

	Types	Number	Average length (min)	Year
Interviews	**Mobility sector**			
	Interviews with managers of leading bicycle companies*	8	60	2003
	Interviews with RoodRunner team (plus Smarttrike)	5	60	2002–2003
	Personal interviews with Velotaxi team	6	90	2003
	Personal interviews with experts on short-distance mobility*	15	90	2001–2004
	Personal interviews with Twike team	3	180	2003
	Personal interviews with CREE founder (the SAM project) by phone	1	60	2002
	Interviews* with project leaders: Greencab, Mixx, OV fiets	4	50	2003
	Interviews with managers of the leading Dutch bicycle industry manufacturers*	6	60	2004
Desk research	Organizational change within the bicycle industry in the last 15 years*	Database with 800 entries		2004
	Innovations within the bicycle industry in the last 15 years*			2004
	Catalogue of several personal transport vehicles*	Around 150 types		2003
Email Survey	Questionnaire sent to Quest and Mango's owners to know their mobility behavior.	50 mailed 23 received back		2005
Case study	Mitka project			
	Personal involvement in the process			2001–2003
	Formal interviews	25	90–180	2001–2003
	Discussions and answers by email	17		2001–2005
	Strategic meetings (with minutes)	4		
	Archival documents (emails, reports, newspaper articles)	>400		
	Velomobiel project			
	Interviews with the project team and founders	4	180	2003–2004
	Interview with persons considered important for the innovation process	2	120	2004

Note
*The research studies were performed with the help of a student team.

Contacts with the Mitka participants

Who	Company	When	note
Project leader 2000–2002	TNO	16 January	Int.
		October/December 2002	Dis.
		(during the test)	Em.
Project leader and initiator 1996–2002	TNO	September, October 2004	Dis./Em.
		November 16, 2001	Int.
		February 22, 2005	Int.
		March, 16 2005	Int.
Project leader 1999	TNO	December 16, 2000	Int.
Team	TNO	2001–2003	Dis.
Designer	Vd Veer Designers	January 18, 2002,	Int.
		June, 7 2002,	Int.
		February 11, 2004	Int.
		February 22, 2005	Int. p.
Director	Gazelle	March 25, 2002	Int.
Director	Freewiel, director	February 15, 2005	Em.
Facilities manager	Nike	January 25, 2002	Int.
		January 28, 2002	Em.
Researcher	TUDelft	April 22, 2002	Int.
		2000–2003	Dis., Em.
Researcher	TUDelft	February 22, 2005	Dis.
		2000–2004	Int.
			Dis.
DfS director	TUDelft	2000–2004	Em.
			Dis.
Manager	Move Program	May 7, 2002	Em.
			Int.

Contacts with the Mitka participants

Who	Company	When	note
Business developers	Consulting firm	January 23, 2002	Int.
		January 28, 2002	Dis.
		May 2, 2002	Dis.
		January 12, 2005	Int.
		February 7, 2005	Int.
Manager	Insurance company	May 2, 2002	Int.
Manager	BOM	8 May 2002	Int.
Meetings			
Strategy and project team		January 15, 2001	Rep.
		February 1, 2002	Rep.
		May 2, 2002	Rep.
		December 12, 2002	Rep.
Test			
First driver		October 23/24/25, 2002	Int. p.
		January 9 2003	Int.
			Em.
DfS director		November 14, 2002	Int.
		November 17, 2002	Em.
			Rep.
Second driver		December 5, 2002	Int. p.
		December 12, 2002	Int.
			Em.
			Rep.

Legend
Int. = interview
Int. p. = Interview by phone
Dis. = discussions
Em = emails
Rep. = report

Notes

1 For ease of communication, unless otherwise specified, the terms "environment", "environmental", "environmentally friendly" or "driven", and "sustainable" refer to the natural and physical environment.

2 An "issue" is a development, event, or trend perceived as potentially having an impact on the organization (Dutton, Fahey, & Narayanan, 1983) or on society. An environmental or ecological issue is related to the natural environment. Examples are recycling, energy and waste management, product stewardship, pollution prevention and sustainable development.

3 Individuals who pursue environmental policies and practices or address environmental issues in organizations are rarely defined in a unique way in literature, e.g. enviropreneurs (Menon & Menon, 1997), policy entrepreneurs (Drumwright, 1994), issue sellers (Bansal, 2003) ecopreneurs (Isaak, 2002) or environmental champions (Andersson & Bateman, 2000). Here the generic term "green entrepreneur" is used, stressing the search for and exploitation of opportunities related to environmental issues.

4 The term "product" is used as generically and stands for either a physical/manufactured good or a service. Thus, NPD stands for either/both new goods and/or service development (De Brentani, 2001).

5 The term "social" here refers to interaction between humanity and the natural environment.

6 As they put it, there are lots of $10 bills lying around waiting to be picked up.

7 The term environmental ambition is not new, having been used by Klassen and Angell (1998) to define the scope of environmental efforts by a firm's management. In this research study, this term refers specifically to the intention to design, develop and implement new environmental products and services.

8 One may ask whether NPD literature is appropriate to the study of product innovation within start-ups and network of organizations. Critics may argue that NPD literature focuses mainly on NPD processes, as a collection of activities that are systematically performed within established firms. The counterargument lies on the fact that new organizational forms generate new products with the adoption of general NPD processes in combination with new, ad hoc procedures. Therefore NPD literature encompasses, although only partially, product innovation in different organizational settings. Furthermore, although entrepreneurship research is growing at a fast rate, NPD literature is still extremely relevant to the study of product innovation in new organizational forms.

9 For example, "strategy" is a military term, introduced in the late 1970s in management and innovation literature.

10 Defined as a physically distinct portion of the product that embodies a core design concept and performs a well-defined function. The component is a physical implementation of the design concept.

11 For example, necessity, opportunity or dissatisfaction with existing conditions trigger people to search for improved conditions.

12 The term "environment" is used here to indicate the context in which an organization operates.

13 This table illustrates the dichotomy between radical and incremental in their extreme forms, attempting to explain the complexity of this definition of newness. The complexity of the phenomenon under study should not prevent the researcher from seeking simpler approximations of the reality with which to attempt to explain it.

14 Recently, environmentalists, ecology groups, consumer movements and a growing number of organizational scholars questioned the priorities of certain organizational decision makers regarding organizational objectives.

15 Values are defined, in this context, as the guidelines and beliefs that a person engages when confronted with a situation in which a choice must be taken (Gibson et al., 2003).

16 The term "non-rational factors" encompasses the social and psychological factors, such as bias in information processing or psychological benefits, that can cause one to misperceive and miscalculate losses and that induce errors in decision making.

17 How people think and act about innovation.

18 Although Dougherty does not explicitly refer to the radical products, the definition of radical innovation in this research study also encompasses new products for new markets due to similar levels of uncertainties during the innovation process.

19 Ritter and Weber introduced the "wicked problem" approach to overcome some weaknesses of the linear model approach. The linear model does not take into account, for example, the non-simple linearity of the design process.

20 For a review see Cohen, 1995.

21 "Organizational competence" refers to the capacity to generate innovation and "environmental fit" refers to the match between organizational competence and the state of the environment (Sorensen et al., 2000).

22 A product technology is an engineering diagram or prototype that demonstrates the product's functionality. To become a marketable product, it must undergo several stages of refinement and verification involving product architecture, parts assembly, aesthetics, and production feasibility (Wheelwright & Clark, 1992).

23 The term "environmental" is used here to indicate the context in which an organization operates.

24 In concentrated industries the marketing and manufacturing assets necessary to exploit a technology lie in the hands of a few large, established firms, which tend to acquire ownership of these assets (Teece, 1996). These firms also have a cost advantage and market power allowing them to drive out new competitors (Nerkar et al., 2003).

25 For a recent review of the organization and the natural environment literature see Berchicci and King (Berchicci et al., 2007), where both the "pays to be green" literature and the "self-regulation" literature are discussed.

26 Institutional theory specifies that firms are embedded in an institutional environment that constrains their action and drives organizational change (DiMaggio & Powell, 1983).

27 The two terms are synonymous; the former used mostly in Europe and the latter in the US.

28 Examples of system innovation are a hydrogen economy, industrial ecology and customized mobility (Kemp & Rotmans, 2004). For an extensive review of system innovation literature, refer to the edited book *System innovation and the transition to sustainability* (Elzen, Geels, & Green, 2004).

29 The term "tool" refers to a systematic means for dealing with environmental issues in the product development process.

30 However, the new types of handset consume a lot of energy and are referred to as

energy "eaters". For example, due to a larger set of functions, UMTS phones require more energy to operate than previous GSM handsets.

31 Environmental attributes do not necessarily have to be separate from traditional attributes, and may, on the contrary, overlap or coexist. Problems may occur when tradeoffs are required and environmental attributes are overemphasized at the expense of traditional attributes, regardless of consumer preferences, technological or financial risks.

32 It combines economic and environmental objectives. The concept of "eco-efficiency" was coined by representatives of industry as a response to society to show industry's willingness to contribute to the goal of sustainable development. The claim was to "produce more from less" by managing natural resources more sensibly (Cramer et al., 2001).

33 However, a combination of products and services in a system does not necessarily reduce negative environmental or social impacts.

34 Theory is defined here in the words of Bacharach: "a statement of relationships between observed (*variables*) and approximated (*constructs*) units in the empirical world" (Bacharach, 1989: 498).

35 Mitka is a Dutch abbreviation that, translated, stands for: "Mobility solution for individual transportation over short distances."

36 In his book, Bijker describes the evolution and development of bicycle technology as a social process. Bijker is one of the proponents of the Social Construction of Technology (SCOT) theory, which states that any technological development is shaped by "relevant" social groups. The way in which these groups perceive and interpret the technological artifact's meaning influences the artifact's evolution. To know more about the SCOT theory and how to identify relevant social groups see Bijker, 1995.

37 It is not surprising that the first car builders were indeed bicycle producers. For example, the Humber company was the first to develop a bicycle with the diamond frame (in 1990). This company was also one of the first pioneers to implement an internal combustion engine in tricycles and quadricycles (in 1903 with the *Humberette*), which are the archetypes of the modern car.

38 For example, in Amsterdam the percentage of bicycle use with respect to other modes of transport, such as a car, motorcycle and public transport, decreased from approximately 80% in the 1950s to around 30% in the 1970s (de la Bruhéze & Veraart, 1999).

39 Check the website www.rijwiel.net to learn more about the history of the Dutch bicycle industry.

40 Giant company, located in Taiwan, is one of the biggest bicycle manufacturers in the world, producing more than four million bikes per year. Giant's European headquarters and production facilities are based in the Netherlands.

41 At Delft University of Technology three complementary studies were conducted by a team of master students to illustrate the innovativeness of the Dutch bicycle manufacturing sector, screening a broad range of innovations adopted and developed between 1988 and 2003. Two methods were employed. The first entailed a database of new bike concepts and parts introduced by the Dutch manufacturing companies. To build the database, articles from the monthly magazine *Tweewieler* (translated two-wheeler) between 1988 and 2003 were catalogued and categorized in digital form. The database encompasses more than 800 entries.

The second method entailed a list of relevant innovations introduced in the same period. Their relevance was established by 11 experts. Afterwards, managers from the main bike manufacturers were asked to establish the time of adoption of those innovations by their company and their relative market importance.

42 The term "niche" is defined here as a specialized market.

43 Although the first recumbent bikes were developed in the 1920s, it was not until the 1980s that they started to diffuse, especially in the Netherlands.

44 For a review of different HPVs, see www.io.tudelft.nl/research/dfs/mobility/.

45 This description is based on two interviews with the Springtime designer, one interview with the Mail company director and one interview with the GranturismoMobility founder. In addition, internet sources were employed (www.granturismomobility.com and www.springtime.nl, last accessed on November 2005).

46 Monocoque (French for "single shell") or unibody is a construction technique that utilizes the external skinning of an object to form most of the structure. This is as opposed to using an internal framework that is then covered with a non-structural skinning. Monocoque construction was first widely used in aircraft, starting in the 1930s.

47 Not to be confused with the type of vehicle discussed in this section, Velomobiel is a firm that produces velomobiles and one of the firm's studied in this research project.

48 In the Netherlands, 1,200,000 bikes are sold every year. Some 5% of these fall in the category of "races", "electric bikes", "folding bikes" and "recumbent bikes" (Bovag-RAI, 2003). According to recumbent producers, 10,000 recumbent bikes are sold every year.

49 The tour gets its name from "oliebol", a fried cake traditionally eaten in Holland at the end of the year (Eland, 2002b).

50 The father of a leading professor at the Design for Sustainability program at Delft University of Technology, after seeing his son driving the Mitka.

51 During the Mitka project, two kinds of subsidy program had been submitted to Novem: the EET (Economy, Ecology and Technology) and the MOVE. The requirements of the MOVE program differ from those of EET. The latter is based on developing new technologies, for example the EET-KIEM funds are earmarked for front-end projects, while the former aims at stimulating chain mobility. In the MOVE program technological innovation is not the primary goal.

52 Definition given by the former TNO project leader in 1999, interview on December 16, 2000.

53 VIP stands for "vision in product innovation". This is a method designed for lead users to generate ideas.

54 The project manager, interview on November 16, 2001.

55 The Nike manager, interview on January 28, 2002.

56 TNO-Kathalys report, July 1999–April 2000.

57 Based upon these percentages, two scenarios were created to calculate the environmental gain in switching mode. The first scenario was called "real", where 2.2% of car drivers would switch from the car to the Mitka. The second scenario was called "optimistic" where the sum of car drivers (2.2% and 35%) who considered the Mitka a reasonable and good alternative, was used.

58 Vd Veer director, interview on February 12, 2004.

59 The Gazelle director's preference for the three-wheeled concept was perceived by some of the team members as Gazelle's intention to develop, produce and implement such a concept.

60 Former project leader, interview on February 22, 2005.

61 In www.Kathalys.com, accessed on September 2000.

62 Ibid.

63 Interview on March 4, 2002.

64 In the Netherlands, bicycles are often stored inside houses whose frontdoors are around 80 cm wide.

65 A business plan was distributed to the Mitka coalition by the consulting firm on May 2001.

66 Consumer research results in the MOVE I project, final report 2001.

67 The Move project manager, interview on May 7, 2002.

68 The business developer, interview on January 23, 2002.

69 The Nike facility manager, interview on January 24, 2002

70 In the email from the project leader to the TUDelft team on December 6, 2001.

71 The organizational chart was presented at the meeting on February 1, 2002.
72 Interview on March 4, 2002.
73 Interview with one of the project team members.
74 Meeting report on July 3, 2002.
75 Nike facility manager, interview on January 28, 2002.
76 Interview by phone on October 24, 2002.
77 DfS director, on November 19, 2002.
78 Interview on January 9, 2003.
79 Extracted from his test diary report.
80 For example, *De Telegraaf*, national newspaper on January 18, 2003.
81 *De Volkskrant*, national newspaper on October 5, 2002.
82 As explained by Vd Veer director on February 11, 2004.
83 On www.gazelle.nl, last accessed October 2003.
84 The organization's mission is to promote the economic growth of Texel through tourism while protecting its main cultural and environmental assets.
85 Interview on February 12, 2004.
86 Email on February 15, 2005.
87 Discussion on February 22, 2005.
88 Interview on October 13, 2004.
89 For ease of communication the actor's function is omitted. However, keep in mind that this list refers to individuals rather than to institutions.
90 The Flevobike company is a small family-owned concern founded by Johan Vrielink. Flevobike started to produce and sell recumbent bikes in 1986.
91 Interview with Johan Vrielink on October 20, 2004.
92 Interview with Allert Jacob on January 28, 2004.
93 Ibid.
94 Interview with Ymte Sijbrandij on October 20, 2004.
95 Interview with Allert Jacob on January 28, 2004.
96 Interview with Johan Vrielink on October 20, 2004.
97 Interview with Allert Jacob on January 28, 2004.
98 Ibid.
99 Ibid.
100 Alleweder newsletter January 1997 n.1, to be found on the Velomobiel's website.
101 Interview on January 28, 2004.
102 Interview with Johan Vrielink on October 20, 2004.
103 Interview with Allert Jacob on January 28, 2004.
104 Available at www.velomobiel.nl last accessed October 13, 2004.
105 Ibid.
106 Ibid.
107 Interview with Allert Jacob on January 28, 2004.
108 Ibid.
109 A list of all Velomobiel's customers and the series numbers of the products purchased can be found on www.velomobiel.nl/nl/velomobielrijders.htm.
110 On www.velomobiel.nl, last accessed October 13, 2004.
111 interview with Ymte Sijbrandij on January 28, 2004.
112 On www.velomobiel.nl, last accessed October 13, 2004.
113 Also based on an energy efficiency test reported in the Dutch newspaper *NRC Handelsblad* on October 8, 2001.
114 IHPVA stands for International Human-Powered Vehicle Association.
115 Interview with Ymte Sijbrandij on January 28, 2004.
116 The definition of success is related to the survival of the product in the market and not to financial performances.
117 The luggage unit in the Mitka vehicle was conceptualized (Heijnen, 2001) but not developed.

118 Yet, by following such rules, firms would never invest in radical projects and would only focus on creating incremental innovations. In competitive markets, such a "vicious cycle" could cause firms to fail because they were too cautious and relied too much on scientific assessment systems.

119 A figure on the Velomobiel's expenditure rate is unavailable but a rough estimation can be done using the hourly compensation cost for production workers in manufacturing, which is equal to €22 (Bureau of Labor Statistics, 2004). Assuming that the Velomobiel designer and producer worked for one year (40 hours per week) only on the Quest, the labor cost would amount to €45,760 plus the costs of vehicle production.

120 Researchers and economists are starting to abandon their assumption that humans behave rationally (the *homo economicus*), and instead are increasingly borrowing insights from psychologists to try to explain types of behavior that seem to defy rationality. Over the past years, studies addressing behavior have demonstrated that cognitive biases and mental shortcuts can lead managers into costly errors of judgment, simplifying or, worse, oversimplifying decisions under uncertainty (e.g. Kahneman & Tversky, 1979).

121 It also has a negative connotation in different languages.

References

Abernathy, W. J., & Clark, K. B. 1985. Innovation: Mapping the winds of destruction. *Research Policy*, 14: 3–22.

Abernathy, W. J., & Utterback, J. M. 1978. Patterns of industrial innovation. *Technology Review*, 80(7): 40–47.

Abrahamson, E. 1991. Managerial fads and fashions: The diffusion and rejection of innovations. *Academy of Management Journal*, 16(3): 586–612.

Ács, Z. J., & Audretsch, D. B. 1990. *Innovation and small firms*. Cambridge, MA: MIT Press.

Ács, Z. J., & Audretsch, D. B. 1991. *Innovation and technological change: An international comparison*. Hamel Hempstead: Harvester Wheatsheaf.

Afuah, A. N., & Bahram, N. 1995. The hypercube of innovation. *Research Policy*, 24(1): 51–76.

Ahuja, G. 2000. Collaboration networks, structural holes, and innovation: A longitudinal study. *Administrative Science Quarterly*, 45(3): 425–455.

Aldrich, H., & Auster, E. R. 1986. Even dwarfs started small: Liabilities of age and size and their strategic implications. *Research in Organizational Behavior*, 8: 165–198.

Aldrich, H. E., & Fiol, C. M. 1994. Fools rush in? The institutional context of industry creation. *Academy of Management Review*, 19(4): 645–670.

Aldrich, H. E., & Martinez, M. A. 2001. Many are called, but few are chosen: An evolutionary perspective for the study of entrepreneurship. *Entrepreneurship: Theory and Practice*, 25(4): 41–56.

Ali, A. 1994. Pioneering versus incremental innovation – Review and research propositions. *Journal of Product Innovation Management*, 11(1): 46–61.

Ali, A., Krapfel, R., & Labahn, D. 1995. Product innovativeness and entry strategy – Impact on cycle time and break-even time. *Journal of Product Innovation Management*, 12(1): 54–69.

Alvarez, S. A., & Barney, J. B. 2001. How entrepreneurial firms can benefit from alliances with large partners. *Academy of Management Executive*, 15(1): 139–148.

Amit, R., Muller, E., & Cockburn, I. 1995. Opportunity cost and entrepreneurial activity. *Journal of Business Venturing*, 10: 95–106.

Andersson, L. M., & Bateman, T. S. 2000. Individual environmental initiative: Championing natural environmental issues in US business organizations. *Academy of Management Journal*, 43(4): 548–570.

Angel, D. 2002. Interfirm collaboration and technology development partnership within US manufacturing industries. *Regional Studies*, 36(4): 333–344.

Aragon-Correa, J. A. 1998. Strategic proactivity and firm approach to the natural environment. *Academy of Management Journal*, 41(5): 556–567.

Aragon-Correa, J. A., & Sharma, S. 2003. A contingent resource-based view of proactive corporate environmental strategy. *Academy of Management Review*, 28(1): 71–88.

Arrow, K. J. 2000. Innovation in large and small firms. In R. Swedberg (Ed.), *Entrepreneurship*: 229–243. Oxford: Oxford Management Reader.

Ashford, N. A. 2000. An innovative-based strategy for a sustainable development. In J. Hemmelskamp, K. Rennings, & F. Leone (Eds.), *Innovation-oriented environmental regulation theoretical approaches and empirical analysis*. New York/Berlin: Physica-Verlag.

Ashford, N. A. 2002. Government and environmental innovation in Europe and North America. *American Behavioral Scientist*, 45(9): 1417–1434.

Audretsch, D. B. 1995. *Innovation and industry evolution*. Cambridge, MA: MIT Press.

Bacharach, S. B. 1989. Organizational theories – Some criteria for evaluation. *Academy of Management Review*, 14(4): 496–515.

Baker, T., Miner, A. S., & Eesley, D. T. 2003. Improvising firms: Bricolage, account giving and improvisational competencies in the founding process. *Research Policy*, 32(2): 255–276.

Baker, T., & Nelson, R. E. 2005. Creating something from nothing: Resource construction through entrepreneurial bricolage. *Administrative Science Quarterly*, 50(3): 329–366.

Bakker, R., Hoge, B., & Laan van der, F. 2004. De ideale velomobiel, *Ligfiets&*, 20: 12–17.

Balachandra, R., & Friar, J. H. 1997. Factors for success in R&D projects and new product innovation: A contextual framework. *Ieee Transactions on Engineering Management*, 44(3): 276–287.

Balachandra, R., & Raelin, J. A. 1984. When to kill that R-and-D project. *Research Management*, 27(4): 30–33.

Balbontin, A., Yazdani, B., Cooper, R., & Souder, W. E. 1999. New product development success factors in American and British firms. *International Journal of Technology Management*, 17(3): 259–280.

Bamberg, S. 2003. How does environmental concern influence specific environmentally related behaviors? A new answer to an old question. *Journal of Environmental Psychology*, 23(1): 21–32.

Banerjee, S. B. 2001. Managerial perceptions of corporate environmentalism: Interpretations from industry and strategic implications for organizations. *Journal of Management Studies*, 38(4): 489–513.

Banerjee, S. B. 2002. Corporate environmentalism – The construct and its measurement. *Journal of Business Research*, 55(3): 177–191.

Banerjee, S. B., Iyer, E. S., & Kashyap, R. K. 2003. Corporate environmentalism: Antecedents and influence of industry type. *Journal of Marketing*, 67(2): 106–122.

Bansal, P. 2003. From issues to actions: The importance of individual concerns and organizational values in responding to natural environmental issues. *Organization Science*, 14(5): 510–527.

Bansal, P., & Roth, K. 2000. Why companies go green: A model of ecological responsiveness. *Academy of Management Journal*, 43(4): 717–736.

Barczak, G. 1995. New product strategy, structure, process, and performance in the telecommunications industry. *Journal of Product Innovation Management*, 12(3): 224–234.

Baron, R. A. 1998. Cognitive mechanisms in entrepreneurship: Why and when entrepreneurs think differently than other people. *Journal of Business Venturing*, 13(4): 275–294.

Barton, S. L., Duchon, D., & Dunegan, K. J. 1989. An empirical test of Staw and Ross's prescription for the management of escalation of commitment behavior in organizations. *Decision Sciences*, 20: 532–544.

Baum, J. A. C., Calabrese, T., & Silverman, B. S. 2000. Don't go it alone: Alliance network composition and startups' performance in Canadian biotechnology. *Strategic Management Journal*, 21: 267–294.

Baumann, H., Boons, F., & Bragd, A. 2002. Mapping the green product development field: Engineering, policy and business perspectives. *Journal of Cleaner Production*, 10: 409–425.

Baumgartner, S., Faber, M., & Proops, J. 2002. How environmental concern influences the investment decision: An application of capital theory. *Ecological Economics*, 40(1): 1–12.

Beck, K. 2000. *eXtreme programming eXplained – Embrace change*. New York: Addison-Wesley.

Beerepoot, M. J. 2004. *The investigation of design methods for the development of sustainable Product Service Systems*. Unpublished final thesis, Delft University of Technology, Delft.

Berchicci, L., & Bodewes, W. E. J. 2005. Bridging environmental issues with new product development. *Business Strategy and the Environment*, 14(5): 272–285.

Berchicci, L., & Brezet, H. 2003. *The role of entrepreneurship in sustainable mobility innovation*. Paper presented at the Towards Sustainable Product Design 8, Stockholm, October 27–28, 2003.

Berchicci, L., & King, A. 2007. Postcards from the edge: A review of the business and environment literature. *The Academy of Management Annals*, 1(1): 513–547.

Berto, F. J. 1999. *The birth of dirt: Origins of mountain biking*. San Francisco, CA: Cycling Resources.

Biemans, W. G. 1989. *Developing innovations within networks; with an application to the Dutch medical equipment industry*. Eindhoven: University of Eindhoven.

Bijker, W. E. 1995. *Of bicycles, bakelites, and bulbs: Toward a theory of sociotechnical change*. Cambridge, MA: MIT Press.

Bodewes, W. E. J. 2000. *Neither chaos nor rigidity: An empirical study of the role of partial formalization in organizational innovativeness*. Rotterdam: Erasmus University.

Boelens, M. 2002. *Gebruikers terminal voor op Texel*. Unpublished Master thesis, Delft University of Technology, Delft.

Boks, C. B. 2002. The relative importance of uncertainty factors in product end-of-life scenarios: A quantification of future developments in design, economy, technology and policy. Delft University of Technology, Delft.

Booz, A., Hamilton Inc. 1982. *New product management for the 1980s*. New York: Booz, Allen, and Hamilton Inc.

Boulding, W., Morgan, R., & Staelin, R. 1997. Pulling the plug to stop the new product drain. *Journal of Marketing Research*, 34(1): 164–176.

Bovag-RAI. 2003. *Mobiliteit in cijfers 2003*, Vol. 2004: Bunnik: Bovag-RAI.

Brezet, H., & Hemel, C. v. 1997. *Ecodesign: A promising approach to sustainable production and consumption*. Paris: UNEP.

Brezet, H., & Rocha, C. 2001a. Towards a model for product-oriented environmental management systems. In M. Charter, & U. Tischner (Eds.), *Sustainable solutions: Developing products and services for the future*. Sheffield: Greenleaf publishing.

Brezet, J. C., & Silvester, S. 2000. *How to design eco-efficient services*. Delft: Delft University of Technology (internal report).

Brezet, J. C., Vergragt, P., & Horst, T. v. d. 2001b. *Kathalys, vision on sustainable product innovation*. Amsterdam: BIS Publishers.

Brockner, J. 1992. The escalation of commitment to a failing course of action: Toward theoretical progress. *Academy of Management Review*, 17(1): 39–61.

Broeke van den, A. M., Korver, W., & Droppert-Zilver, M. 2000. *MITKA: Gebruiksonderzoek naar een nieuw vervoersmiddel voor de korte afstand. Resultaten van de werknemersenquete bij NIKE (Hilversum)*. Delft: TNO Inro.

Brown, H. S., Vergragt, P., Green, K., & Berchicci, L. 2003. Learning for sustainability transition through bounded socio-technical experiments in personal mobility. *Technology Analysis & Strategic Management*, 15(3): 291–315.

Brown, S. L., & Eisenhardt, K. M. 1995. Product development – Past research, present findings, and future-directions. *Academy of Management Review*, 20(2): 343–378.

Brown, S. L., & Eisenhardt, K. M. 1997. The art of continuous change: Linking complexity theory and time-paced evolution in relentlessly shifting organizations. *Administrative Science Quarterly*, 42(1): 1–34.

Bruijn, H. d., & Heuvelhof, E. t. 2000. *Networks and decision making*. Ultrecht: Lemma.

Brundtland, G. 1987. *Our common future of the world commission on environment and development*. Oxford: Oxford University Press.

Bruyat, C., & Julien, P. 2001. Defining the field of research in entrepreneurship. *Journal of Business Venturing*, 16(2): 165–180.

Buchanan, R. 1992. Wicked problem in design thinking. *Design Issues*, XIII(2): 5–21.

Buijs, J. 2003. Modelling product innovation processes, from linear logic to circular chaos. *Creativity and Innovation Management*, 12(2): 76–93.

Buijs, J., & Valkenburg, R. 1996. *Integrale produktontwikkeling*. Ultrecht: Lemma.

Burall, P., & Design Council. 1996. *Product development and the environment*. London: Gower.

Bureau of Labor Statistics. 2004. International comparisons of hourly compensation costs for production workers in manufacturing. Washington, D.C.: US Department of Labor.

Burt, R. S. 2000. The network structure of social capital. *Research in Organizational Behavior*, 22: 345–423.

Calantone, R. J., Vickery, S. K., & Droge, C. 1995. Business performance and strategic new product development activities – An empirical investigation. *Journal of Product Innovation Management*, 12(3): 214–223.

Callon, M., Laredo, P., & Rabeharisoa, V. 1992. The management and evaluation of technological programs and the dynamics of techno-economic networks: The case of the AFME. *Research Policy*, 21(3): 215–236.

Carroll, G. R., & Mosakowski, E. 1987. The career dynamics of self-employment. *Administrative Science Quarterly*, 32(4): 570–589.

Casson, M. 1982. *The entrepreneur: An economic theory*. Totowa, NJ: Barnes & Noble Books.

Chandy, R. K., & Tellis, G. J. 2000. The incumbent's curse? Incumbency, size, and radical product innovation. *Journal of Marketing*, 64(3): 1–17.

Charter, M., & Tischner, U. 2001. *Sustainable solutions: Developing products and services for the future*. Sheffield: Greenleaf Publishing.

Chen, C. L. 2001. Design for the environment: A quality-based model for green product development. *Management Science*, 47(2): 250–263.

Chen, M. J., & Hambrick, D. C. 1995. Speed, stealth, and selective attack – How small firms differ from large firms in competitive behavior. *Academy of Management Journal*, 38(2): 453–482.

Christensen, C. M. 1997. *The innovator's dilemma, when new technologies cause great firms to fail*. Cambridge, MA: Harvard Business School Press.

Christensen, C. M., & Bower, J. L. 1996. Customer power, strategic investment, and the failure of leading firms. *Strategic Management Journal*, 17(3): 197–218.

Christmann, P. 2000. Effects of "best practices" of environmental management on cost advantage: The role of complementary assets. *Academy of Management Journal*, 43(4): 663–680.

Ciborra, C. U. 1994. A platform of surprises – The organization of global technology strategy at Olivetti. *IFIP Transitions A-Computer Science and Technology*, 49: 97–111.

Cohen, W. M. 1995. Empirical studies of innovative activity. In P. Stoneman (Ed.), *Handbook of the economics of innovation and technological change*: 183–264. Oxford: Blackwell.

Cohen, W. M., & Levinthal, D. A. 1990. Absorptive-capacity – A new perspective on learning and innovation. *Administrative Science Quarterly*, 35(1): 128–152.

Coombs, R., Richards, A., Saviotti, P., & Walsh, V. (Eds.). 1996. *Technological collaboration*. Cheltenham: Edward Elgar Publishing Company.

Cooper, R. G. 1975. Why new industrial products fail. *Industrial Marketing Management*, 4: 313–326.

Cooper, R. G. 1979. Identifying industrial new product success: Project new prod. *Industrial Marketing Management*, 4: 128–135.

Cooper, R. G. 1985. Selecting winning new product projects: Using the NewProd system. *Journal of Product Innovation Management*, 2: 34–44.

Cooper, R. G. 1986. New product performance and product innovation strategies. *Research Management*, 29(May–June): 17–25.

Cooper, R. G. 1992. The NewProd system: The industry experience. *Journal of Product Innovation Management*, 9: 113–127.

Cooper, R. G., & Kleinschmidt, E. J. 1986. An investigation into the new product process: Steps, deficiencies, and impact. *Journal of Product Innovation Management*, 3: 71–85.

Cooper, R. G., & Kleinschmidt, E. J. 1987. New products: What separates winners from losers? *Journal of Product Innovation Management*, 4(3): 169–174.

Cooper, R. G., & Kleinschmidt, E. J. 1991. New product processes at leading industrial firms. *Industrial Marketing Management*, 20(2): 137–147.

Cooper, R. G., & Kleinschmidt, E. J. 1995a. Benchmarking the firms critical success factors in new product development. *Journal of Product Innovation Management*, 12(5): 374–391.

Cooper, R. G., & Kleinschmidt, E. J. 1995b. Performance typologies of new product projects. *Industrial Marketing Management*, 24(5): 439–456.

Cordano, M., & Frieze, I. H. 2000. Pollution reduction preferences of US environmental managers: Applying Ajzen's theory of planned behavior. *Academy of Management Journal*, 43(4): 627–641.

Cramer, J., & van Lochem, E. 2001. The practical use of the "eco-efficiency" concept in industry: The case of Akzo Nobel. *Journal of Sustainable Product Design*, 1(3): 171–180.

Crawford, C. M. 1977. Marketing research and the new product failure rate. *Journal of Marketing*, 41(2): 51–61.

Damanpour, F. 1992. Organizational size and innovation. *Organization Studies*, 13(3): 375–402.

Damanpour, F., & Gopalakrishnan, S. 1998. Theories of organizational structure and innovation adoption: The role of environmental change. *Journal of Engineering and Technology Management*, 15(1): 1–24.

Danneels, E., & Kleinschmidt, E. J. 2001. Product innovativeness from the firm's perspective: Its dimensions and their relation with project selection and performance. *Journal of Product Innovation Management*, 18(6): 357–373.

Das, T. K., & Teng, B. S. 2001. Trust, control, and risk in strategic alliances: An integrated framework. *Organization Studies*, 22(2): 251–283.

De Brentani, U. 2001. Innovative versus incremental new business services: Different keys for achieving success. *Journal of Product Innovation Management*, 18: 169–187.

de la Bruhéze, A. A., & Veraart, F. 1999. *Fietsverkeer in praktijk en beleid in de twintigste eeuw*. Den Haag, Netherlands: Ministerie van verkeer en waterstaat.

De Neufville, R., Connors, S. R., Field, F. R., Marks, D., Sadoway, D. T. R., & Tabors, R. D. 1996. The electric car unplugged. *Technology Review*, 99(January): 30–36.

Dean, T. J., Brown, R. L., & Bamford, C. E. 1998. Differences in large and small firm responses to environmental context: Strategic implications from a comparative analysis of business formations. *Strategic Management Journal*, 19(8): 709–728.

Dekker, R. 2002. *Basisstation voor Mitka voertuig*. Unpublished Master Thesis, Delft University of Technology, Delft.

Diekmann, A., & Preisendörfer, P. 1998. Environmental behaviour – Discrepancies between aspirations and reality. *Rationality and Society*, 10: 79–102.

DiMaggio, P. J., & Powell, W. W. 1983. The iron cage revisited – Institutional isomorphism and collective rationality in organizational fields. *American Sociological Association*, 48: 147–160.

Dougherty, D. 1990. understanding new markets for new products. *Strategic Management Journal*, 11(SI): 59–78.

Dougherty, D. 1992. Interpretive barriers to successful product innovation in large firms. *Organization Science*, 3(2): 179–202.

Downs, G. W., & Mohr, L. B. 1976. Conceptual issues in study of innovation. *Administrative Science Quarterly*, 21(4): 700–714.

Doz, Y. L. 1996. The evolution of cooperation in strategic alliances: Initial conditions or learning processes? *Strategic Management Journal*, 17(SI): 55–83.

Doz, Y. L., Olk, P. M., & Ring, P. S. 2000. Formation processes of R&D consortia: Which path to take? Where does it lead? *Strategic Management Journal*, 21(3): 239–266.

Drucker, P. F. 1954. *The Practice of Management*. New York: Harper and Row.

Drucker, P. F. 1985. *Innovation and entrepreneurship: Practice and principles* (1st ed.). New York: Harper & Row.

Drucker, P. F. 1998. The discipline of innovation. *Harvard Business Review*, 76(6): 149–158.

Drumwright, M. E. 1994. Socially responsible organizational buying: environmental concern as a noneconomic buying criterion. *Journal of Marketing*, 58(July): 1–19.

Dunlap, R. E., & Liere, K. D. V. 1978. The "new environmental paradigm": A proposed measuring instrument and preliminary results. *Journal of Environmental Education*, 9(10–19).

Dutton, G. 1998. The green bottom line. *Management Review*, 87(9): 59–63.

Dutton, J. E., Fahey, L., & Narayanan, V. K. 1983. Toward understanding strategic issue diagnosis. *Strategic Management Journal*, 4: 307–323.

Dyer, W. G., & Wilkins, A. L. 1991. Better stories, not better constructs, to generate better theory: A rejoinder to Eisenhardt. *Academy of Management Review*, 16(3): 613–619.

The Economist. 2004. Don't laugh at gilded butterflies.

Ehrenfeld, J., & Lenox, M. J. 1997. The development and implementation of DfE programmes. *Journal of Sustainable Product Design*, April: 17–27.

Eick, J. 1998. *The everyday velomobile: Who uses it and who could use it?* Paper presented in the proceedings of the Third European Seminar on Velomobile Design, Roskilde Technical School, Roskilde, Denmark.

Eisenhardt, K. M. 1989. Building theories from case study research. *Academy of Management Review*, 14(4): 532–550.

Eisenhardt, K. M. 1991. Better stories and better constructs: The case for rigor and comparative logic. *Academy of Management Review*, 16(3): 620–627.

Eland, P. 2002a. Quest, Mango, *Velo Vision*, 6.

Eland, P. 2002b. The Oliebollentoertocht, *Velo Vision*, 5: 20.

Eland, P. 2004. Energy Efficiency, *Velo Vision*, 14.

Elfring, T., & Hulsink, W. 2003. Networks in entrepreneurship: The case of high-technology firms. *Small Business Economics*, 21(4): 409–422.

Elzen, B., Geels, F., & Green, K. (Eds.). 2004. *System innovation and the transition to sustainability*. Cheltenham, UK: Edward Elgar Publishing.

Ernst, H. 2002. Success factors of new product development: A review of the empirical literature. *International Journal of Management Reviews*, 4(1): 1–40.

Ettlie, J. E., & Elsenbach, J. M. 2007. Modified stage-gate (R) regimes in new product development. *Journal of Product Innovation Management*, 24(1): 20–33.

Fiol, C. M. 1996. Squeezing harder doesn't always work: Continuing the search for consistency in innovation research. *Academy of Management Review*, 21(4): 1012–1021.

Fischer, M. M. 2001. Innovation, knowledge creation and systems of innovation. *Annals of Regional Science*, 35(2): 199–216.

Fiske, S. T., & Taylor, S. E. 1984. *Social cognition* (1st ed.). New York: Random House.

Flannery, B. L., & May, D. R. 2000. Environmental ethical decision making in the US metal-finishing industry. *Academy of Management Journal*, 43(4): 642–662.

Flipsen, S. F. J. 2000. Eindrapportage Mobiliteits-concept voor individueel Transport op de Korte Afstand (MITKA). Delft: TNO Industry report.

Foster, R. N. 1986. *Innovation: The attacker's advantage*. New York: Summit Books.

Franklin, C., & Baylis, T. 2003. *Why innovation fails: Hard-won lessons for business*. London: Spiro Press.

Freeman, C. 1982. *The economics of industrial innovation*. London: Pinter.

Freeman, C. 1991. Networks of innovators: A synthesis of research issues. *Research Policy*, 20(5): 499–514.

Freeman, J., Carroll, G. R., & Hannan, M. T. 1983. The liability of newness – Age Dependence in organizational death rates. *American Sociological Review*, 48(5): 692–710.

Fuller, D. A. 1999. *Sustainable marketing: Managerial-ecological issues*. Thousand Oaks, CA: Sage Publications.

Fussler, C., & James, P. 1996. *Driving eco innovation: A breakthrough discipline for innovation and sustainability*. London: Pitman Publishing.

Galbraith, J. 1973. *Designing complex organizations*. London: Addison-Wesley.

Garcia, R., & Calantone, R. 2002. A critical look at technological innovation typology and innovativeness terminology: A literature review. *Journal of Product Innovation Management*, 19(2): 110–132.

Garcia-Pont, C., & Nohria, N. 2002. Local versus global mimetism: The dynamics of alliance formation in the automobile industry. *Strategic Management Journal*, 23(4): 307–321.

Garud, R., & Karnoe, P. 2001. Path creation as a process of mindful deviation. In R. Garud, & P. Karnoe (Eds.), *Path dependence and creation*. Mahwah, NJ: Lawrence Erlbaum Associates.

Garud, R., & Karnoe, P. 2003. Bricolage versus breakthrough: Distributed and embedded agency in technology entrepreneurship. *Research Policy*, 32(2): 277–300.

Garud, R., & Rappa, M. 1994. A sociocognitive model of technology evolution – The case of cochlear implants. *Organization Science*, 5(3): 344–362.

Gatewood, E. J., Shaver, K. G., & Gartner, W. B. 1995. A longitudinal study of cognitive factors influencing start-up behaviors and success at venture creation. *Journal of Business Venturing*, 10(5): 371–391.

Germain, R. 1996. The role of context and structure in radical and incremental logistics innovation adoption. *Journal of Business Research*, 35(2): 117–127.

Ghemawat, P. 1991. *Commitment: The dynamic of strategy*. New York: Free Press.

Gibson, J. L., Ivancevich, J. M., Donnelly, J. H., & Konopaske, R. 2003. *Organizations: Behavior, structure, processes* (11th ed.) Boston, MA; London: McGraw-Hill, Irwin.

Gilbert, D. T., Mcnulty, S. E., Giuliano, T. A., & Benson, J. E. 1992. blurry words and fuzzy deeds – The attribution of obscure behavior. *Journal of Personality and Social Psychology*, 62(1): 18–25.

Gilley, K. M., Worrell, D. L., Davidson III, W. N., & El-Jelly, A. 2000. Corporate environmental initiatives and anticipated firm performance: The differential effects of process-driven versus product-driven greening initiatives. *Journal of Management*, 26(6): 1199–1216.

Gimeno, J., Folta, T. B., Cooper, A. C., & Woo, C. Y. 1997. Survival of the fittest? Entrepreneurial human capital and the persistence of underperforming firms. *Administrative Science Quarterly*, 42(4): 750–783.

Gladwin, T. N., Kennelly, J. J., & Krause, T. S. 1995. Shifting paradigms for sustainable development – Implications for management theory and research. *Academy of Management Review*, 20(4): 874–907.

Gloria, T., Saad, T., Breville, M., & O'Connell, M. 1995. Life-cycle assessment: A survey of current implementation. *Total Quality Environmental Management*, 4: 33–50.

Goedkoop, M. J., van Halen, C., te Riele, H., & Rommens, P. 1999. Product service systems, ecological and economic basics: Report of PiMC, Storm C.S. and Pré consultants, for the Dutch Ministries of Environmental and Economical Affairs.

Graedel, T. E., Allenby, B. R., & AT&T. 1995. *Industrial ecology*. Englewood Cliffs, NJ: Prentice-Hall.

Granovetter, M. 1985. Economic action and social structure: The problem of embeddedness. *American Journal of Sociology*, 91: 481–510.

Green, K., Hull, R., McMeekin, A., & Walsh, V. 1999. The construction of the techno-economic: networks vs paradigms. *Research Policy*, 28(7): 777–792.

Green, K., & Vergragt, P. 2002. Towards sustainable households: A methodology for developing sustainable technological and social innovations. *Futures*, 34(5): 381–400.

Green, S. G., Gavin, M. B., & Aiman-Smith, L. 1995. Assessing a multidimensional measure of radical technological innovation. *Ieee Transactions on Engineering Management*, 42: 203–214s.

Green, S. G., & Welsh, M. A. 2003. Advocacy, performance, and threshold influences on decisions to terminate new product development. *Academy of Management Journal*, 46(4): 419–434.

Greiner, L. E. 1970. Patterns of organizational change. In G. W. Dalton, P. R. Lawrence, & L. E. Greiner (Eds.), *Organizational change and development*: 213–229. Homewood, IL: Irwin-Dorsey Press.

Griffin, A. 1997a. PDMA research on new product development practices: Updating trends and benchmarking best practices. *Journal of Product Innovation Management*, 14(6): 429–458.

Griffin, A. 1997b. The effect of project and process characteristics on product development cycle time. *Journal of Marketing Research*, 34(1): 24–35.

Griffin, A., & Page, A. L. 1996. PDMA success measurement project: Recommended measures for product development success and failure. *Journal of Product Innovation Management*, 13(6): 478–496.

Gulati, R. 1999. Network location and learning: The influence of network resources and firm capabilities on alliance formation. *Strategic Management Journal*, 20(5): 397–420.

Gutowski, T., Murphy, C., Allen, D., Bauer, D., Bras, B., Piwonka, T., Sheng, P., Sutherland, J., Thurston, D., & Wolff, E. 2005. Environmentally benign manufacturing: Observations from Japan, Europe and the United States. *Journal of Cleaner Production*, 13(1): 1–17.

Hagedoorn, J., & Duysters, G. 2002. External sources of innovative capabilities: The preference for strategic alliances or mergers and acquisitions. *Journal of Management Studies*, 39(2): 167–188.

Hagedoorn, J., & Schakenraad, J. 1994. The effect of strategic technology alliances on company performance. *Strategic Management Journal*, 15(4): 291–309.

Hall, J., & Clark, W. W. 2003a. Special issue: Environmental innovation. *Journal of Cleaner Production*, 11(4): 343–346.

Hall, J., & Vredenburg, H. 2003b. The challenges of innovating for sustainable development. *MIT Sloan Management Review*, 45(1): 61–68.

Hambrick, D. C., & Macmillan, I. C. 1985. Efficiency of product R-and-D in business units – The role of strategic context. *Academy of Management Journal*, 28(3): 527–547.

Hamel, G. 2000. *Leading the revolution*. Boston, MA: Harvard Business School Press.

Handfield, R. B., Melnyk, S. A., Calantone, R. J., & Curkovic, S. 2001. Integrating environmental concerns into the design process: The gap between theory and practice. *Ieee Transactions on Engineering Management*, 48(2): 189–208.

Handfield, R. B., Walton, S. V., Seegers, L. K., & Melnyk, S. A. 1997. "Green" value chain practices in the furniture industry. *Journal of Operations Management*, 15(4): 293–315.

Hannan, M. T., & Freeman, J. 1984. Structural inertia and organizational change. *American Sociological Review*, 49(2): 149–164.

Harrisson, D., & Laberge, M. 2002. Innovation, identities and resistance: The social construction of an innovation network. *Journal of Management Studies*, 39(4): 497–521.

Hart, S. L. 1995. A natural-resource-based view of the firm. *Academy of Management Review*, 20(4): 986–1014.

Hart, S. L. 1997. Beyond greening: Strategies for a sustainable world. *Harvard Business Review*, 75(1): 66–&.

Hart, S. L., & Ahuja, G. 1996. Does it pay to be green? An empirical examination of the relationship between emission reduction and firm performance. *Business Strategy and the Environment*, 5(1): 30–37.

Hart, S. L., & Milstein, M. B. 1999. Global sustainability and the creative destruction of industries. *Sloan Management Review*, 41(1): 23–33.

Hart, S. L., & Milstein, M. B. 2003. Creating sustainable value. *Academy of Management Executive*, 17(2): 56–67.

Hawken, P., Lovins, A. B., & Lovins, L. H. 1999. *Natural capitalism: Creating the next industrial revolution* (1st ed.). Boston, MA: Little, Brown and Co.

Heijnen, M. 2001. *Mitka Texel*. Unpublished Master Thesis, Delft University of Technology, Delft.

Hekkert, P. 1997. *The VIP method, vision in product innovation*. Delft: Delft University of Technology, Faculty of Industrial Design Engineering.

Hellriegel, D., Slocum, J. W., & Woodman, R. W. 1992. *Organizational behavior* (6th ed.). St Paul, MN: West Pub. Co.

Hemel, C. G. v. 1998. *Ecodesign empirically explored design for environment in Dutch small and medium sized enterprises*. Doctoral Dissertation, Delft: Delft University of Technology.

Henderson, R. 1993. Underinvestment and incompetence as responses to radical innovation – Evidence from the photolithographic alignment equipment industry. *Rand Journal of Economics*, 24(2): 248–270.

Henderson, R., & Clark, K. B. 1990. Architectural Innovation: The reconfiguration of existing product technologies and the failure of established companies. *Administrative Science Quarterly*, 35: 9–20.

Hillman, A. J., & Keim, G. D. 2001. Shareholder value, stakeholder management, and social issues: What's the bottom line? *Strategic Management Journal*, 22(2): 125–139.

Hippel, E. V. 1977. Dominant role of user in semiconductor and electronic subassembly process innovation. *Ieee Transactions on Engineering Management*, 24(2): 60–71.

Hippel, E. v. 1988. *The sources of innovation*. Oxford: Oxford University Press.

Hitt, M. A., Duane, R., Ireland, S., & Camp, M. 2001. Strategic entrepreneurship: Entrepreneurial strategies for wealth creation. *Strategic Management Journal*, 22: 479–491.

Hoang, H., & Antoncic, B. 2003. Network-based research in entrepreneurship. A critical review. *Journal of Business Venturing*, 18: 165–187.

Hoffman, A. J. 2001. Linking organizational and field-level analyses – The diffusion of corporate environmental practice. *Organization & Environment*, 14(2): 133–156.

Hoogma, R. 2000. *Exploring technological niches*. Enschede: Twente University Press.

Hopkins, D. S., & Bailey, E. L. 1971. New product pressures. *Conference Board Research*: 16–24.

Horst, T. v. d., Luiten, H., Brezet, H., & Silvester, S. 2005. *Sustainable business development*. Delft: TNO-TUDelft report.

Huisman, J. 2003. *The QWERTY/EE concept quantifying recyclability and eco-efficiency for end-of-life treatment of consumer electronic products*. Ph.D. Thesis, Delft: Delft University of Technology.

Huisman, J., Boks, C. B., & Stevels, A. L. N. 2003. Quotes for environmentally weighted recyclability (QWERTY): Concept of describing product recyclability in terms of environmental value. *International Journal of Production Research*, 41(16): 3649.

Hultink, E. J., & Robben, H. S. J. 1995. Measuring new product success: The difference that time perspective makes. *Journal of Product Innovation Management*, 12(5): 392–405.

Hunt, C. B., & Auster, E. R. 1990. Proactive environmental-management – Avoiding the toxic trap. *Sloan Management Review*, 31(2): 7–18.

Hustad, T. P., & Mitchell, T. J. 1982. Creative market planning in a partisan environment. *Business Horizons*, 25(March–April): 58–65.

Ireland, R. D., Hitt, M. A., & Vaidyanath, D. 2002. Alliance management as a source of competitive advantage. *Journal of Management*, 28(3): 413–446.

Isaak, R. 2002. The making of the ecopreneur. *Greener Management International*, 38: 81–91.

Jansen, J. L. A., & Vergragt, P. J. 1992. Sustainable development: A challenge to technology. Proposal for the interdepartmental Research Programme Sustainable Technology Development, Leischendam.

Janszen, F. 2000. *The age of innovation making business creativity a competence, not a coincidence.* London: Prentice-Hall.

Johannessen, J.-A., Olsen, B., & Lumpkin, G. T. 2001. Innovation as newness: What is new, how new, and new to whom? *European Journal of Innovation Management*, 4(1): 20–31.

Johansson, G. 2002. Success factors for integration of ecodesign in product development. *Environmental Management and Health*, 13(1): 98–107.

Joore, P. 2000a. *Opzet interactif gebruikonderzoek en dienstpakket Mitka.* Delft: TNO Industry.

Joore, P. 2000b. *Projectplan MITKA.* Delft: TNO Industry.

Joore, P. 2001. *Eindrapportage MOVE Mobiliteitsconcept voor individueel Transport op de Korte Afstand – MITKA.* Delft: TNO Industry.

Kahneman, D., & Tversky, A. 1979. Prospect theory – Analysis of decision under risk. *Econometrica*, 47(2): 263–291.

Kale, P., Singh, H., & Perlmutter, H. 2000. Learning and protection of proprietary assets in strategic alliances: Building relational capital. *Strategic Management Journal*, 21(3): 217–237.

Karakaya, F., & Kobu, B. 1994. New product development process – An investigation of success and failure in high-technology and non-high-technology firms. *Journal of Business Venturing*, 9(1): 49–66.

Katz, J., & Gartner, W. B. 1988. Properties of emerging organizations. *Academy of Management Review*, 13(3): 429–441.

Keeney, R. L., & Raiffa, H. 1993. *Decisions with multiple objectives: Preferences and value tradeoffs.* Cambridge: Cambridge University Press.

Kemp, R., & Rotmans, J. 2004. Managing the transition to sustainable mobility. In B. Elzen, F. Geels, & K. Green (Eds.), *System innovation and the transition to sustainability.* Cheltenham, UK: Edward Elgar Publishing.

Khilstrom, R., & Laffont, J. 1979. A general equilibrium entrepreneurial theory of firm formation based on risk aversion. *Journal of Political Economy*, 87(4): 719–748.

Khurana, A., & Rosenthal, S. R. 1998. Towards holistic "front ends" in new product development. *Journal of Product Innovation Management*, 15(1): 57–74.

Kim, J., & Wilemon, D. 2002. Focusing the fuzzy front-end in new product development. *R & D Management*, 32(4): 269–279.

Kim, J., & Wilemon, D. 2003. Sources and assessment of complexity in NPD projects. *R & D Management*, 33(1): 15–30.

Kimberly, J. R. 1979. Issues in the creation of organizations – Initiation, innovation, and institutionalization. *Academy of Management Journal*, 22(3): 437–457.

King, A., & Lenox, M. 2002a. Exploring the locus of profitable pollution reduction. *Management Science*, 48(2): 289–299.

King, A. A., & Lenox, M. J. 2000. Industry self-regulation without sanctions: The chemical industry's Responsible Care Program. *Academy of Management Journal*, 43(4): 698–716.

King, A. A., & Lenox, M. J. 2001. Lean and green? An empirical examination of the relationship between lean production and environmental performance. *Production and Operations Management*, 10(3): 244–256.

King, A. A., & Tucci, C. L. 2002b. Incumbent entry into new market niches: The role of experience and managerial choice in the creation of dynamic capabilities. *Management Science*, 48(2): 171–186.

Kirzner, I. M. 1997. Entrepreneurial discovery and the competitive market process: An Austrian approach. *Journal of Economic Literature*, 35(1): 60–85.

Klassen, R. D., & Angell, L. C. 1998. An international comparison of environmental management in operations: The impact of manufacturing flexibility in the US and Germany. *Journal of Operations Management*, 16(2–3): 177–194.

Klassen, R. D., & McLaughlin, C. P. 1996. The impact of environmental management on firm performance. *Management Science*, 42(8): 1199–1214.

Kleiner, A. 1991. What does it mean to be green. *Harvard Business Review*, 69(4): 38–&.

Kleinschmidt, E. J., & Cooper, R. G. 1991. The impact of product innovativeness on performance. *Journal of Product Innovation Management*, 8(4): 240–251.

Kline, S. J., & Rosenberg, N. 1986. An overview of innovation. In R. Landau, & N. Rosenberg (Eds.), *The positive sum strategy*. Washington, D.C.: National Academy Press.

Krishnan, V., & Ulrich, K. T. 2001. Product development decisions: A review of the literature. *Management Science*, 47(1): 1–21.

Landau, R., & Rosenberg, N. 1986. *The positive sum strategy*. Washington, D.C.: National Academy Press.

Larson, A. 2000. Sustainable innovation through an entrepreneurship lens. *Business Strategy and the Environment*, 9(5): 304–317.

Lenox, M. J., & Ehrenfeld, J. 1997. Organizing for effective environmental design. *Business Strategy and the Environment*, 6: 187–196.

Lenox, M. J., Jordan, B., & Ehrenfeld, J. 1996. The diffusion of design for environment: A survey of current practice. *Proc. IEEE Conf. Electronics and Environment*: 25–30.

Leonard-Barton, D. 1990. A dual methodology for case studies: Synergistic Use of a longitudinal single site with replicated multiple sites. *Organization Science*, 1(3): 248–266.

Leonard-Barton, D. 1995. *Wellsprings of knowledge: Building and sustaining the sources of innovation*. Boston, MA: Harvard Business School Press.

Lévi-Strauss, C. 1966. *The savage mind (La pensée sauvage)*. London: Weidenfeld & Nicolson.

Liedtka, J. 1991. Organizational value contention and managerial mindsets. *Journal of Business Ethics*, 10: 543–557.

Light, D. 1979. Surface data and deep structure. *Administrative Science Quarterly*, 24(4): 551–559.

Link, P. L. 1987. Keys to new product success and failure. *Industrial Marketing Management*, 16: 109–118.

Luiten, H., Knot, M., & Horst, v. d. T. 2001a. *Sustainable product-service-systems: The Kathalys method*. Paper presented at the EcoDesign Conference, Tokyo.

Luiten, H., Knot, M., & Silvester, S. 2001b. *Consumer involvement in the development of sustainable product/service systems*. Paper presented at the Sustainable Services & Systems (3S) Conference: Transition towards sustainability? October 30, Amsterdam.

Maas, T. 1998. *Bewegend leven in 2005*. Unpublished Master Thesis, Delft University of Technology, Delft.

Mackenzie, D. 1997. *Green design: Design for the environment*. London: Laurence King.

Magretta, J., & Stone, N. D. 2002. *What management is: How it works and why it's everyone's business*. New York: Free Press.

Maidique, M. A., & Zirger, B. J. 1984. A study of success and failure in product innovation – The case of the United States electronics industry. *Ieee Transactions on Engineering Management*, 31(4): 192–203.

Manzini, E., & Vezzoli, C. 2003. A strategic design approach to develop sustainable product service systems: Examples taken from the "environmentally friendly innovation" Italian prize. *Journal of Cleaner Production*, 11(8): 851–857.

March, J. G. 1991. Exploration and exploitation in organizational learning. *Organization Science*, 2(1): 71–87.

Margolis, J. D., & Walsh, J. P. 2003. Misery loves companies: Rethinking social initiatives by business. *Administrative Science Quarterly*, 48(2): 268–305.

Markusson, N. 2001. Drivers of environmental innovation, Vol. VF 2001: 1. Stockholm: Vinnova.

McCarthy, I. P., Tsinopoulos, C., Allen, P., & Rose-Anderssen, C. 2006. New product development as a complex adaptive system of decisions. *Journal of Product Innovation Management*, 23(5): 437–456.

McDermott, C. M., & O'Connor, G. C. 2002. Managing radical innovation: An overview of emergent strategy issues. *Journal of Product Innovation Management*, 19(6): 424–438.

McWilliams, A., & Siegel, D. 2000. Corporate social responsibility and financial performance: Correlation or misspecification? *Strategic Management Journal*, 21(5): 603–609.

Meijkamp, R. G. 2000. Changing consumer behaviour through eco-efficient services: An empirical study on car sharing in the Netherlands, Dissertation. Delft University of Technology, Delft.

Menon, A., & Menon, A. 1997. Enviropreneurial marketing strategy: The emergence of corporate environmentalism as market strategy. *Journal of Marketing*, 61(1): 51–67.

Miles, M. B., & Huberman, A. M. 1994. *Qualitative data analysis: An expanded sourcebook* (2nd ed.). London: Sage.

Mintzberg, H., Raisinghani, D., & Theoret, A. 1976. Structure of unstructured decision-processes. *Administrative Science Quarterly*, 21(2): 246–275.

Moenaert, R. K., Demeyer, A., Souder, W. E., & Deschoolmeester, D. 1995. R-and-D marketing communication during the fuzzy front-end. *Ieee Transactions on Engineering Management*, 42(3): 243–258.

Mont, O. K. 2002. Clarifying the concept of product-service system. *Journal of Cleaner Production*, 10(3): 237–245.

Mont, O. K. 2004. Product-service system: Panacea or myth? Doctoral Dissertation. Lund University.

Montoya-Weiss, M. M., & Calantone, R. 1994. Determinants of new product performance: A review and meta-analysis. *Journal of Product Innovation Management*, 11(5): 397–417.

Murmann, P. A. 1994. Expected development time reductions in the German mechanical-engineering industry. *Journal of Product Innovation Management*, 11(3): 236–252.

National Industrial Conference Board. 1964. *Why new products fail*. New York: Conference Board Record.

Nayak, P. R., & Ketteringham, J. M. 1986. *Breakthroughs!* (1st ed.). New York: Rawson Associates.

Nelson, R. R. 1959. The simple economics of basic scientific research. *Journal of Political Economy*, June: 297–306.

Nerkar, A., & Shane, S. 2003. When do start-ups that exploit patented academic knowledge survive? *International Journal of Industrial Organization*, 21(9): 1391–1410.

Normann, R. 1971. Organizational innovativeness – Product variation and reorientation. *Administrative Science Quarterly*, 16(2): 203–215.

Novak, S., & Eppinger, S. D. 2001. Sourcing by design: Product complexity and the supply chain. *Management Science*, 47(1): 189–204.

Oaksford, M., Morris, F., Grainger, B., & Williams, J. M. G. 1996. Mood, reasoning, and central executive processes. *Journal of Experimental Psychology-Learning Memory and Cognition*, 22(2): 476–492.

O'Connor, G. C. 1998. Market learning and radical innovation: A cross-case comparison of eight radical innovation projects. *Journal of Product Innovation Management*, 15(2): 151–166.

Oliver, C. 1991. Strategic responses to institutional processes. *Academy of Management Review*, 16(1): 145–179.

Op Het Veld, R. 2005. Rijprestaties belangrijker dan milieu (in Dutch), *Het Financieele Dagblad*, January 10.

Oskam, I. 1999. Milieubeoordeling van een nieuw mobiliteitsconcept, TNO industry report.

Ostrom, E. 1990. *Governing the commons: The evolution of institutions for collective action*. Cambridge: Cambridge University Press.

Ottman, J. A. 1998. *Green marketing: Opportunities for innovation*. Lincolnwood, IU: NTC Business Books.

Pascual, O., Boks, C., & Stevels, A. 2003. *Electronics ecodesign research empirically studied*. Paper presented at the Ecodesign 2003 Proceedings, December 9–11, Tokyo, Japan.

Peters, T. J., & Waterman, R. H. 1982. *In search of excellence: Lessons from America's best-run companies*. New York: Harper & Row.

Pettigrew, A. 1990. Longitudinal field research on change: Theory and practice. *Organization Science*, 1(3): 267–292.

Pfeffer, J., & Salancik, G. R. 1978. *The external control of organizations: A resource dependence perspective*. New York: Harper & Row.

Pinto, M. B., & Pinto, J. K. 1990. Project team communication and cross-functional cooperation in new program development. *Journal of Product Innovation Management*, 7(3): 200–212.

Porter, M. E. 1980. *Competitive strategy: Techniques for analyzing industries and competitors*. New York: Free Press.

Porter, M. E. 1985. *Competitive advantage: Creating and sustaining superior performance*. New York: Free Press.

Porter, M. E., & Van der Linde, C. 1995. Green and competitive – Ending the stalemate. *Harvard Business Review*, 73(5): 120–134.

Powell, W. 1990. Neither market nor hierarchy: Network forms of organization. *Research in Organizational Behaviours*, 12: 295–336.

Prakash, A. 2002. Green marketing: Policy and managerial strategies. *Business Strategy and the Environment*, 11: 285–297.

Pujari, D., & Wright, G. 1996. Developing environmentally conscious product strategies: A qualitative study of selected companies in Germany and Britain. *Marketing Intelligence and Planning*, 14(19).

Pujari, D., Wright, G., & Peattie, K. 2003. Green and competitive – Influences on environmental new product development performance. *Journal of Business Research*, 56(8): 657–671.

RAND. 1997. *Technologieradar*. The Hague: RAND Europe for the Dutch Ministry of Economic Affairs.

Reinhardt, F. L. 2000. *Down to earth: Applying business principles to environmental management*. Boston, MA: Harvard Business School Press.

Reynolds, P. D., & White, S. B. 1997. *The entrepreneurial process: Economic growth, men, women, and minorities*. Westport, Conn.: Quorum Books.

Rice, M. P., O'Connor, G. C., Peters, L. S., & Morone, J. G. 1998. Managing discontinuous innovation. *Research-Technology Management*, 41(3): 52–58.

Rittel, H., & Weber, M. 1973. Dilemmas in a general theory of planning. *Policy Sciences*, 4: 155–169.

Rivkin, J. W. 2000. Imitation of complex strategies. *Management Science*, 46(6): 824–844.

Roberts, E. B. 1991. *Entrepreneurs in high technology: Lessons from MIT and beyond*. New York: Oxford University Press.

Rogers, E. M. 1995. *Diffusion of innovations* (4th ed.). New York: Free Press.

Roome, N. 1992. Developing environmental management strategies. *Business Strategy and the Environment*, 1(1): 11–24.

Roozenburg, N. F. M., & Eekels, J. 1995. *Product design fundamentals and methods*. Chichester, UK: Wiley.

Rosenberg, N. 1990. Why do firms do basic research with their own money? *Research Policy*, 19(2): 165–174.

Rothwell, R., Freeman, C., Horlsey, A., Jervis, V. T. P., Robertson, A. B., & Townsend, J. 1974. Sappho updated – Project Sappho Phase II. *Research Policy*, 3(3): 258–291.

Roy, R. 1994. The evolution of ecodesign. *Technovation*, 14(6): 363–380.

Roy, R. 2000. Sustainable product-service systems. *Futures*, 32(3–4): 289–299.

Rubin, J. Z., & Brickner, J. 1975. Factors affecting entrapment in waiting situations. *Journal of Personality and Social Psychology*, 31(6): 1054–1063.

Russo, M. V. 2003. The emergence of sustainable industries: Building on natural capital. *Strategic Management Journal*, 24: 317–331.

Russo, M. V., & Fouts, P. A. 1997. A resource-based perspective on corporate environmental performance and profitability. *Academy of Management Journal*, 40(3): 539–559.

Ryan, C. 2003. Digital eco-sense: Sustainability and ICT – A new terrain for innovation. Sydney: Lab 3000.

Schaltegger, S. 2002. A framework for ecopreneurship: Leading bioneers and environmental managers to ecopreneurship. *Greener Management International*, 38: 45–58.

Schaltegger, S., & Synnestvedt, T. 2002. The link between "green" and economic success: Environmental management as the crucial trigger between environmental and economic performance. *Journal of Environmental Management*, 65(4): 339–346.

Schick, H., Marxen, S., & Freimann, J. 2002. Sustainability issues for start-up entrepreneurs. *Greener Management International*, 38: 59–70.

Schmidt, J. B., & Calantone, R. J. 1998. Are really new product development projects harder to shut down? *Journal of Product Innovation Management*, 15(2): 111–123.

Schon, D. A. 1967. *Technology and change: The new Heraclitus*. New York: Delacorte Press.

Schoonhoven, C. B., Eisenhardt, K. M., & Lyman, K. 1990. Speeding products to market

– Waiting time to 1st product introduction in new firms. *Administrative Science Quarterly*, 35(1): 177–207.

Schrage, M. 2000. *Serious play: How the world's best companies simulate to innovate.* Boston, MA: Harvard Business School Press.

Schumpeter, J. A. 1934. *The theory of economic development.* Cambridge, MA: Harvard University Press.

Schumpeter, J. A. 1942. *Capitalism, socialism, and democracy.* New York, London: Harper & Brothers.

Senge, P. M., & Carstedt, G. 2001. Innovating our way to the next industrial revolution. *MIT Sloan Management Review*, 42(2): 24–38.

Shane, S. 2000. Prior knowledge and the discovery of entrepreneurial opportunities. *Organization Science*, 11(4): 448–469.

Shane, S. 2001. Technological opportunities and new firm creation. *Management Science*, 47(2): 205–220.

Shane, S., & Venkataraman, S. 2000. The promise of entrepreneurship as a field of research. *Academy of Management Review*, 25(1): 217–226.

Sharma, S. 2000. Managerial interpretations and organizational context as predictors of corporate choice of environmental strategy. *Academy of Management Journal*, 43(4): 681–697.

Sharma, S., & Vredenburg, H. 1998. Proactive corporate environmental strategy and the development of competitively valuable organizational capabilities. *Strategic Management Journal*, 19(8): 729–753.

Shrivastava, P. 1995a. Ecocentric management for a risk society. *Academy of Management Review*, 20(1): 118–137.

Shrivastava, P. 1995b. Environmental technologies and competitive advantage. *Strategic Management Journal*, 16: 183–200.

Shrivastava, P. 1995c. The Role of Corporations in achieving ecological sustainability. *Academy of Management Review*, 20(4): 936–960.

Sijbrandij, Y. 2002. A voyage into velomobilia. *Velo Vision*, 5.

Silvester, S., Knot, M., Berchicci, L., & Luiten, H. 2000. *Gebruikerswensen en doelgroepdifferentiatie.* Delft: TNO Industry.

Simon, F. L. 1992. Marketing green products in the triad. *Columbia Journal of World Business*, 27(Fall–Winter): 268–285.

Simon, H. A. 1977. *The new science of management decision* (rev. ed.). Englewood Cliffs, NJ: Prentice-Hall.

Slywotzky, M., & Wise, R. 2003. *How to grow when markets don't.* New York: Warmer Books.

Song, X. M., & Montoya-Weiss, M. M. 1998. Critical development activities for really new versus incremental products. *Journal of Product Innovation Management*, 15(2): 124–135.

Sorensen, J. B., & Stuart, T. E. 2000. Aging, obsolescence, and organizational innovation. *Administrative Science Quarterly*, 45(1): 81–112.

Souder, W. E. 1980. *Management decision methods for managers of engineering and research.* New York: Van Nostrand Reinhold.

Souder, W. E., & Moenaert, R. K. 1992. Integrating marketing and research-and-development project personnel within innovation projects – An information uncertainty model. *Journal of Management Studies*, 29(4): 485–512.

Starik, M., & Marcus, A. 2000. Introduction to the special research forum on the management of organizations in the natural environment: A field emerging from multiple paths, with many challenges ahead. *Academy of Management Journal*, 43(4): 539–546.

Starik, M., & Rands, G. 1995. Weaving an integrated web: Multilevel and multisystem perspectives of ecologically sustainable organizations. *Academy of Management Review*, 20(4): 908–935.

Starr, J. A., & Macmillan, I. C. 1990. Resource cooptation via social contracting – Resource acquisition strategies for new ventures. *Strategic Management Journal*, 11: 79–92.

Staudenmayer, N., Tripsas, M., & Tucci, C. L. 2005. Interfirm modularity and its implications for product development. *Journal of Product Innovation Management*, 22(4): 303–321.

Staw, B. M. 1981. The escalation of commitment to a course of action. *Academy of Management Review*, 6(4): 577–587.

Staw, B. M., & Ross, J. 1987. Understanding escalation situations: Antecedents, prototypes, and solutions. In B. M. Staw, & L. L. Cummings (Eds.), *Research in organizational behavior*, Vol. 9: 39–78. Greenwich, Conn.: JAI Press.

Steele, L. W. 1989. *Managing technology: The strategic view*: McGraw-Hill.

Steenbergen, G. 2002. *Mobiliteit innovaties*. Unpublished Master Thesis, Delft University of Technology, Delft.

Stevels, A. L. N. 2001a. Application of eco-design in the electronics industry. In M. S. Hundal (Ed.), *Mechanical life cycle handbook: Good environmental design and manufacturing*: 461–484. New York: Dekker.

Stevels, A. L. N. 2001b. Five ways to be green and profitable. *Journal of Sustainable Product Design*, 1(2): 81–89.

Stevenson, H. H., Roberts, M. J., & Grousbeck, H. I. 1989. *New business ventures and the entrepreneur*. Homewood, IL: Irwin.

Stinchcombe, A. 1965. Organizations and social structure. In E. J. G. March (Ed.), *Handbook of organizations*: 142–193. Chicago: Rand McNally.

Strauss, A., & Corbin, J. 1999. *Basics of qualitative research techniques and procedures for developing grounded theory* (2nd ed.). London: Sage.

Suchman, M. C. 1995. Managing legitimacy: Strategic and institutional approaches. *Academy of Management Review*, 20: 571–610.

Tatikonda, M. V., & Rosenthal, S. R. 2000. Technology novelty, project complexity, and product development project execution success: A deeper look at task uncertainty in product innovation. *Ieee Transactions on Engineering Management*, 47(1): 74–87.

Teece, D. J. 1996. Firm organization, industrial structure and technological innovation. *Journal of Economic Behaviour & Organization*, 31: 192–224.

Thamhain, H. J. 1990. Managing technologically innovative team efforts toward new product success. *Journal of Product Innovation Management*, 7(1): 5–18.

Tischner, U., & Tukker, A. 2002. *SusProNet Report: 129*. Eindhoven: TNO STB.

Tukker, A., Eder, P., Charter, M., Haag, E., Vercalsteren, A., & Wiedmann, T. 2001. Eco-design: The State of Implementation in Europe – Conclusions of a state of the art study for IPTS. *Journal of Sustainable Product Design*, 1(3): 147–161.

Tushman, M. L., & Anderson, P. 1986. Technological discontinuities and organizational environments. *Administrative Science Quarterly*, 31(3): 439–465.

Tushman, M. L., & O'Reilly, C. A. 1996. Ambidextrous organizations: Managing evolutionary and revolutionary change. *California Management Review*, 38(4): 8–&.

Urban, G. L., Weinberg, B. D., & Hauser, J. R. 1996. Premarket forecasting really new products. *Journal of Marketing*, 60(1): 47–60.

Utterback, J. M. 1994. Radical innovation and corporate regeneration. *Research-Technology Management*, 37(4): 10–10.

Utterback, J. M. 1996. *Mastering the dynamics of innovation*: Cambridge, MA: Harvard Business School Press.

Uzzi, B. 1997. Social structure and competition in interfirm networks: The paradox of embeddedness. *Administrative Science Quarterly*, 42(1): 35–67.

Van de Ven, A. H., Hudson, R., & Schroeder, D. M. 1984. Designing new business start-ups – Entrepreneurial, organizational, and ecological considerations. *Journal of Management*, 10(1): 87–107.

Van de Ven, A. H., Polley, D. E., Garud, R., & Venkataraman, S. 1999. *The innovation journey*. New York: Oxford University Press.

Van den Bosch, F. A. J., Volberda, H. W., & de Boer, M. 1999. Coevolution of firm absorptive capacity and knowledge environment: Organizational forms and combinative capabilities. *Organization Science*, 10(5): 551–568.

van den Hoed, R. 2004. *Driving fuel cell vehicles: How established industries react to radical technologies*. Delft: Delft University of Technology.

van der Laan, F. 2004. Velomobiles – The next generation, *Velo Vision*, 14.

Van Gemert, G. 2001. *Kritische succesfactoren van Bike-up en car-down vervoersmiddelen*. Unpublished AIDE master thesis, Delft University of Technology, Delft.

Van Mises, L. 2000. The entrepreneur and profit. In R. Swedberg (Ed.), *Entrepreneurship: The social science view*: 89–109. Oxford: Oxford University Press.

Verschuren, P., & Doorewaard, H. 1999. *Designing a research project*. Utrecht: Lemma.

Verworn, B., Herstatt, C., & Nagahira, A. 2008. The fuzzy front end of Japanese new product development projects: Impact on success and differences between incremental and radical projects. *R & D Management*, 38(1): 1–19.

Veryzer, R. W. 1998a. Discontinuous innovation and the new product development process. *Journal of Product Innovation Management*, 15(4): 304–321.

Veryzer, R. W. 1998b. Key factors affecting customer evaluation of discontinuous new products. *Journal of Product Innovation Management*, 15(2): 136–150.

Walle, V. d. F. 2004. *The velomobile as a vehicle for more sustainable transportation*. Unpublished Master Thesis, Royal Institute of Technology, Stockholm.

Walley, E. E., & Taylor, D. W. 2002. Opportunists, champions, mavericks…? A typology of green entrepreneurs. *Greener Management International*, 38: 31–43.

Walley, N., & Whitehead, B. 1994. It's not easy being green. *Harvard Business Review*, 72(3): 46–&.

WBCSD. 2001. *Mobility 2001*. World Business Council for Sustainable Development report, available at www.wbcsdmobility.org.

Weaver, P., Jansen, L., Grootveld, G. v., Spiegel, E. v., & Vergragt, P. 2000. *Sustainable technology development*. Sheffield: Greenleaf Publishing Limited.

Weick, K. E. 1979. *The social psychology of organizing*. New York: Random House.

Weigel, R. H. 1983. Environmental attitudes and the prediction of behavior. In N. R. Feimer and E. S. Geller (Eds.), *Environmental Psychology*: 257–287. New York: Praeger.

Weigel, R. H., & Weigel, J. 1978. Environmental concern – The development of a measure. *Environment and Behavior*, 10: 3–15.

Weiszäcker, E. v., Lovins, A. B., & Lovins, H. L. 1997. *Factor four: Doubling wealth – Halving resource use*. London: Earthscan.

Wernerfelt, B. 1984. A resource-based view of the firm. *Strategic Management Journal*, 5(2): 171–180.

Weterings, R. A. P. M., & Opschoor, J. B. 1992. *The environmental capacity as a challenge to technology development*. Rijswijk, the Netherlands: Advisory Council for Research on Nature & Environment (RMNO).

Wheelwright, S. C., & Clark, K. B. 1992. *Revolutionizing product development: Quantum leaps in speed, efficiency, and quality*. New York: Free Press.

Whetten, D. A. 1989. What constitutes a theoretical contribution. *Academy of Management Review*, 14(4): 490–495.

Wright, P., & Ferris, S. P. 1997. Agency conflict and corporate strategy: The effect of divestment on corporate value. *Strategic Management Journal*, 18(1): 77–83.

Yamamoto, R. 2003. *Position paper for New UNEP Eco-design Guidance Manual, Japanese contribution: 1–16*. Paris: UNEP.

Yin, R. K. 1994. *Case study research design and methods* (2nd ed.). London: Sage.

Zahra, S. A., & George, G. 2002. Absorptive capacity: A review, reconceptualization, and extension. *Academy of Management Review*, 27(2): 185–203.

Zaltman, G., Duncan, R., & Holbek, J. 1973. *Innovations and Organizations*. Chichester, UK: Wiley-Interscience.

Zardkoohi, A. 2004. Do real options lead to escalation of commitment? *Academy of Management Review*, 29(1): 111–119.

Index

Das, T. K. 55
decisions: and organizational settings *58*,
58–9; programmed/non-programmed
31–2; under risk and uncertainty 30–2;
see also choices made
Delft University of Technology (TUDelft)
95, 96–7
design choices in case studies 163–6
Design for the Environment 63–4
designers, recommendations to 190–1
determinants of success and failure 20–5,
21, 22, 23
Dougherty, D. 34
Downs, G. W. 15
Doz, Y. L. 54–5
Drucker, P. F. 47, 189

Easy Glider and Easy E-Glider 116–18, **118**
ecodesign 63–4
economics approach to networks 54
entrepreneurs: bricolage approach for
192–3; defined 46–7; experimentation
194; green 1; organization formation by
47–9; success/failure of enterprises
49–50; use of networks 49
environmental ambition 162–3; and
bricolage versus breakthrough 176,
178–9; defined 6; and management teams
170–4; Mango (case study) 156–7, 168;
Mitka (case study) 141–2, 168; and
product complexity 174–5; and project
teams 173–4; and research study 74–5
environmental issues: and businesses 4–5;
as motivation for NPD 5–6; nature of 4;
and product innovation process 4–5
environmental new product development
2–3, **3**; call for radical undertakings
69–70; recommendations to scholars of
188–9
environmental product development 2–3,
3; complexity of greening 67–8;
research on 65–6; use of DfE tools 68–9
Eppinger, S. D. 35
escalation of commitment 32–3, 147
established organizations: exploitation of
existing knowledge by 42; incentives for
innovation 44; and the innovation
process 56, *57*, 58–9; problems with
innovation 44–5; reasons for success in
innovation 45–6; rigidities in routines
44; technological myopia of 44–5
expenditure on projects 182–3
experimentation, use of by entrepreneurs
194; *see also* bricolage

exploitation: of knowledge in established
organizations 42–3; versus exploration
in businesses 28–9
exploration: of knowledge in established
organizations 43; versus exploitation in
businesses 28–9

Faber, M. 5
factor-thinking 64
failure/success: of new organizations 20–5;
in new product development 20–5, *21,
22, 23*; radical/ incremental innovation
30
familiarity concept, newness as 26–7, 30
Flannery, B. L. 5
Flevobike 126–7
flexibility in innovative activities 193
Franklin, C. 30
Freewiel Techniek 104
Friar, J. H. 25
Fuzzy Front End (FFE) 18

Garud, R. 36, 167–8, 176, 178
Gazelle 95, 116–18, 119–20, 183
Gimeno, J. 33
Gloria, T. 68
Granovetter, M. 53
Green, K. 13
Green, S. G. 33, 34
green entrepreneurs 1
green products: defining 67–8; success of
in the market 69
greening 4; of businesses 60–3;
complexity of 67–8
Greiner, L. E. 182
Grousbeck, H. I. 46–7

Handfield, R. B. 68
Henderson, R. 14, 43
human-powered vehicles: bicycle design in
the nineteenth and twentieth centuries
88–9; core activities of producers 89;
new forms of 89–91; safety bicycles
88–9; velomobiles 90–3, *92, 93; see
also* Alleweder; Mango (case study);
Mitka (case study); Quest; Velomobiel

incentives for innovation 44
incremental innovation: compared to
radical 14, *28*; to create radical products
194; degree of innovativeness 26–30;
and research study 73–4; and success 30
industry, greening of 61
information-processing theory 17

Managing and Marketing Radical Innovations
Marketing new technology

Birgitta Sandberg, Turku School of Economics, Finland

This book responds to a growing demand in the academic community for a focus on customer-related proactive behaviour in the study of radical innovation development, combining a thorough theoretical discussion with detailed international case studies considering the role of this proactivity in five firms engaged in the process.

Unlike other studies in this area, this book demonstrates that anticipation plays an important role at the idea generation stage and Sandberg introduces a new way of describing a firm's proactivity as a dynamic pattern. Furthermore, the deeper consideration of customer related proactivity contributes to the study of market orientation, which increasingly focuses on the proactive side.

Contents: 1. Introduction 2. Proactiveness in the Firm 3. Proactiveness Towards Customers 4. Developing Radical Innovations 5. Customer Related Proactiveness in the Case Innovations 6. A Modified Framework of Customer Related Proactiveness During the Development Process 7. Conclusions 8. Summary. Bibliography. Appendix 1: Glossary of Key Concepts as Defined in this Study. Appendix 2: List of Interviews, Discussions and Correspondence. Appendix 3: The Most Important Publications Utilized to Complement the Case Descriptions. Appendix 4: The Most Important Publications Utilized in the Case Selection

February 2008: 234x156: 288pp
Hb: 978-0-415-43307-5: **£75.00 $150.00**

Routledge Studies in Innovation, Organization and Technology

Routledge books are available from all good bookshops, or may be ordered by calling Taylor and Francis Direct Sales on +44(0)1235 400524 (credit card orders) or by visiting our website www.routledge.com/business

Mobility and Technology in the Workplace

Edited by **Donald Hislop,** Loughborough University, UK

The contemporary period has witnessed the rapid evolution in a wide range of mobile technology. This book charts the profound implications these technological changes have for workers and business organizations. From an organizational point of view they have the potential to transform the nature of organizations, through allowing workers to be increasingly mobile. From the perspective of workers these changes have the potential to impact on their work-related communications, how they manage the increasingly blurred public-private divide, and the nature of the home-work boundary.

Issues covered include:

- Travel and changing nature of spatial mobility patterns.
- Work-Space and Place and the 'leaking' out of organizations into more public domains.
- Mobile Work Practices including detailed and heterogeneous case studies.
- Home-work dynamics and the changing nature of the home-work boundary.
- Implications for Public Policy

Contents: 1. Introduction, Work Space/Place, Work-Related Travel, Mobile Work Practices, Home Work Dynamics, Public Policy

July 2008: 234x156: 256pp
Hb: 978-0-415-44346-3: **£75.00 $150.00**

Routledge Studies in Innovation, Organizations and Technology

Routledge books are available from all good bookshops, or may be ordered by calling Taylor and Francis Direct Sales on +44(0)1235 400524 (credit card orders) or by visiting our website www.routledge.com/business

Energizing Management Through Innovation and Entrepreneurship
European Research and Practice

Edited by **Milé Terziovski**

This book provides an in-depth understanding of key variables that play a significant role at the various stages of the innovation process, leading to successful commercialisation of products and services. Combining interdisciplinary studies in entrepreneurship and innovation, the book consists of contributions focusing on theory, research and practise in the field of innovation, management and entrepreneurship. The role of the entrepreneur is addressed as an innovator who recognises opportunities and convert these into marketable products and services through personal commitment, financial resources and management skills; taking appropriate level of risk.

Contents: 1. Entrepreneurship and Innovation Management 2. Developing a Model of Corporate Entrepreneurship 3. Entrepreneurial Strategy: Sequential Investment and Information Gathering 4. Entrepreneurship in the Public Sector 5. The Impact of Management Practices on Industry Level Competitiveness in Transition Economies 6. International Entrepreneurship in Established Firms: Does it Matter? 7. Human Resource Management and Knowledge Management as Antecedents of Innovation 8. Implications of Strategic Planning in SMEs for International Entrepreneurship Research and Practice 9. Performance and Entrepreneurial Orientation in Small Firms: The Moderating Effects of Strategy, Structure, Human Resource Policies and Information Systems 10. Which Roles in Innovation Processes?: A Matter of Perspective 11. Conclusion and Implications

September 2008: 234x156: 224pp
Hb: 978-0-415-43929-9: **£65.00 $130.00**

Routledge Studies in Innovation, Organizations and Technology

Routledge books are available from all good bookshops, or may be ordered by calling Taylor and Francis Direct Sales on +44(0)1235 400524 (credit card orders) or by visiting our website www.routledge.com/business

Organisational Capital
Modelling, measuring and contextualising

Edited by **Ahmed Bounfour**, Institut de Recherche en Gestion, University of Paris XII, France

There is much debate as to how companies carry out their activities in the context of new information and communication technologies influencing organizations to decentralize and develop new managerial practises including outsourcing and networking. Recent theories have emphasized the importance of organization as a key component for building corporate competitive advantage and scholars have looked at this from a range of perspectives including in relation to intangible assets, human capital, work training and the process dimension. Yet the concept of organisational capital as such – in spite of its indubitable relevance and attractiveness- is still to be clarified until now.

The book provides the first multifaceted and international effort from a broad perspective, aiming at clarifying the concept of organisational capital and determining its analytical and operational implications.

Contents: Introduction, Chapter 1: Organizational Capital: Concept, Measure, or Heuristic?, Chapter 2: The Power and Frailty of Organisational Capital, Chapter 3: An Intellectual Capital View of Business Model Innovation, Chapter 4: Knowledge, Recognition and "Communautalism", Chapter 5: Designing Sequences for Knowledge Exchange:The Hau-Ba Model, Chapter 6: Dynamic capabilities of communities, Chapter 7: The dynamics of self-renewal: A systems-thinking to understanding organizational challenges in dynamic environments, Chapter 8: Applying KVA Analysis, Risk Simulation and Strategic Real Options: The Shipyard Case, Chapter 9: When IT does matter: Setting up "value contracts" between stakeholders, Chapter 10: Mapping Value Creation of Organizational Capital, Chapter 11: Attention Management in Organizations: Four Levels of Support in Information Systems, Chapter 12: Leveraging Organizational Capital for Innovation: The Process of Marketing Knowledge Co-Creation, Chapter 13: Organisational Capital and Competence Building, Chapter 14: IT, Organisational Capital and The Reporting (Measurement) Issue

November 2008: 234x156: 336pp
Hb: 978-0-415-43771-4: **£85.00 $170.00**

Routledge Studies in Innovation, Organizations and Technology

Routledge books are available from all good bookshops, or may be ordered by calling Taylor and Francis Direct Sales on +44(0)1235 400524 (credit card orders) or by visiting our website www.routledge.com/business

2008 12 19